Modernizing Civil Services

NEW HORIZONS IN PUBLIC POLICY

Series Editor: Wayne Parsons
Professor of Public Policy, Queen Mary and Westfield College,
University of London, UK

This series aims to explore the major issues facing academics and
practitioners working in the field of public policy at the dawn of a new
millennium. It seeks to reflect on where public policy has been, in both
theoretical and practical terms, and to prompt debate on where it is going.
The series emphasizes the need to understand public policy in the context of
international developments and global change. New Horizons in Public
Policy publishes the latest research on the study of the policymaking process
and public management, and presents original and critical thinking on the
policy issues and problems facing modern and post-modern societies.
    Titles in the series include:

Modernizing Civil Services

Edited by

Tony Butcher

Senior Lecturer in Government, Department of Politics, Goldsmiths College, University of London, UK

Andrew Massey

Professor of Government and Associate Dean (Research), University of Portsmouth, UK

NEW HORIZONS IN PUBLIC POLICY

Edward Elgar
Cheltenham, UK • Northampton, MA, USA

Published by
Edward Elgar Publishing Limited
Glensanda House
Montpellier Parade
Cheltenham
Glos GL50 1UA
UK

Edward Elgar Publishing, Inc.
136 West Street
Suite 202
Northampton
Massachusetts 01060
USA

A catalogue record for this book
is available from the British Library

Library of Congress Cataloguing in Publication Data
Modernizing civil services / edited by Tony Butcher, Andrew Massey.
       p. cm. — (New horizons in public policy)
    Includes bibliographical references and index.
    1. Civil service reform. 2. Civil service reform—Cross-cultural studies. I.
Butcher, Tony, 1943– II. Massey, Andrew, 1958– III. Series.

    JF1601.M63 2004
    352.6'3—dc21

                                                                    2003054119

ISBN 1 84376 201 3

Typeset by Manton Typesetters, Louth, Lincolnshire, UK.
Printed and bound in Great Britain by MPG Books Ltd, Bodmin, Cornwall.

Contents

Figures

Tables

Contributors

Joel D. Aberbach is Professor of Political Science and Policy Studies and Director of the Center for American Politics and Public Policy at UCLA. His research focuses on executive and legislative politics in the United States and abroad. His books include *Keeping a Watchful Eye: The Politics of Congressional Oversight* (Brookings Institution 1990) and (with Bert A. Rockman) *In the Web of Politics: Three Decades of the US Federal Executive* (Brookings Institution Press 2000).

Peter Barberis is Professor of Politics at Manchester Metropolitan University. He is author of *The Elite of the Elite: Permanent Secretaries in the British Higher Civil Service* (1996) and, with Timothy May, of *Government Industry and Political Economy* (1993). In addition he has edited two volumes on the civil service, is the editor and co-author of *The Encyclopaedia of Twentieth Century British and Irish Political Organizations* and is currently writing a biography of Jo Grimond.

Tony Butcher is Senior Lecturer in Government in the Department of Politics, Goldsmiths College, University of London. He has written widely on the civil service and public sector reform. He is the author of *Delivering Welfare* (Open University Press, second edition, 2002), and the co-author (with Gavin Drewry) of *The Civil Service Today* (Blackwell, second edition, 1991).

Amanda Finlay (CBE), is Director, Public and Private Rights in the Lord Chancellor's Department, and has responsibility for meeting customers' needs in the family and administrative justice systems. She was previously responsible for the implementation of the Human Rights Act in LCD and was Secretary to Lord Woolf's Inquiry, 'Access to Justice'.

Oliver James is Lecturer in Politics, University of Exeter, UK and a researcher of public sector organization and regulation. His publications include *The Executive Agency Revolution in Whitehall* (Palgrave Macmillan, 2003) and *Regulation inside Government* (co-authored, Oxford University Press, 1999).

Iris Kirkpatrick is currently Research Manager with Forward Scotland – an organization working to promote and influence policy in the field of sustainable development. She writes in an independent capacity in her particular areas of interest: governance, sustainable development and regeneration.

Andrew Massey is Professor of Government and Associate Dean (Research) at the University of Portsmouth. He has researched and published widely on public administration and public policy issues on Britain, the US and EU.

Richard Parry is Senior Lecturer in the School of Social and Political Studies at the University of Edinburgh. He co-authored *The Treasury and Social Policy* with Nicholas Deakin (Macmillan 2000). His recent research and publications have been on the UK Treasury, and on the impact of devolution on the civil services of the UK.

Wayne Parsons is Professor of Public Policy and Head of the Department of Politics, Queen Mary College, University of London. He is currently visiting professor in the policy sciences at the University of Vienna. Amongst his publications are *The Political Economy of British Regional Policy*, *The Power of the Financial Press*, *Keynes and the Quest for a Moral Science*, and *Public Policy*. His research interests cover the politics of economic ideas and the theory and practice of public policy.

Robert Pyper is Professor of Government and Public Management and Director of the Centre for Public Policy and Management at Glasgow Caledonian University. Research interests include policy and management in the British civil service and issues of accountability in public administration and management. His articles have been published in a range of journals, and he is the author or co-author of numerous books on aspects of British government. He is also editor of the journal *Public Policy and Administration*.

R.A.W. Rhodes is Professor of Political Science and Head of Programme in the Research School of Social Sciences, Australian National University. He is the author or editor of 20 books including *Transforming British Government, Volume 1; Changing Institutions, Volume 2, Changing Roles and Relationships* (Macmillan, 2000); and (with Mark Bevir) *Interpreting British Governance* (Routledge, 2003). He has been editor of *Public Administration* since 1986. He is President of the Political Studies Association of the United Kingdom.

Patrick Weller is Professor of Politics and Public Policy and Deputy Director of the Key Centre for Ethics, Law Justice and Governance at Griffith University in Queensland, Australia. He has written extensively in the areas of cabinet government, ministerial-public service relations and public sector reform.

Preface and acknowledgements

This book was stimulated by the 31st Annual Conference of the Public Administration Committee of the Joint University Council held at the Civil Service College, Sunningdale Park, from 3–5 September 2001. In keeping with the venue, the theme of the Conference was *Modernizing Civil Services*, and the programme included a range of papers from both academics and practitioners, from Britain and overseas, exploring the processes and problems of modernizing civil services. The book incorporates revised versions of eight of the papers originally presented at the Conference, together with two chapters specially written for this book by the editors.

Earlier versions of many of the chapters in this book appeared in a special issue of *Public Policy and Administration*, and we would like to thank that journal's editor, Bobby Pyper, for his support for this project. Thanks are due to all the contributors for revising their original papers and for making this book possible. We would also like to acknowledge the generosity of the University of Portsmouth in providing funding for the preparation of the final manuscript. Last, but not least, we would like to thank Carolyn Carr, who collated the individual chapters and played an important role in the preparation of the final version of the book.

Tony Butcher, Goldsmiths College, University of London

Andrew Massey, University of Portsmouth

1. Modernizing civil services: an era of reform

Tony Butcher

INTRODUCTION

The commitment to modernizing the public service has been a constant theme of Western governments since the early 1980s. It has encompassed many approaches under a variety of labels, such as New Public Management, reinventing government and re-engineering. The reform of the public service in Western liberal democracies has taken a number of different forms, including privatization, marketization, managerialism, decentralization and agencification. Different countries have used such measures to differing degrees. As a result of such developments, the public services of many countries have been transformed, with civil services being singled out for particular attention. The longstanding assumptions that public services should be organized according to bureaucratic principles, and delivered through a career bureaucracy serving governments of any political persuasion, has been seriously challenged.

For some commentators, changes in the structures and processes of the public service in Western liberal democracies since the early 1980s constitute what has been described as a new 'global paradigm' in contemporary public management (Hood 1995). Others have argued, however, that this claim has been overstated, and that, in practice, public service reforms have been characterized by a lack of uniformity and coherence (see, for example, Hood 1995, p. 105). Thus, the extent and nature of civil service reform has varied from country to country, with one commentator locating countries along a continuum of change between the two poles of systemic transformation and incremental improvements. The United Kingdom, Australia, New Zealand and Sweden are positioned at the reformist end of this continuum, and the USA and Germany at the incrementalist end. Canada, France and the Netherlands are located in the middle of the continuum (Nunberg 1995, p. 4).

Whether or not contemporary public management can be labelled a paradigm, as Massey (1997, p. 7) points out, it 'retains a powerful influence' upon the workings of the state. The hierarchical, bureaucratic form of public administration that prevailed in Western liberal democracies for most of the twentieth century, has been changing to 'a flexible, market-based form of public management' (Hughes 1998, p. 1). The governments of such countries have attempted to 'reshape rigid, hierarchical nineteenth-century bureaucracies into more flexible, decentralized, client responsive organizations' (Nunberg 1995, p. 4). The 1980s were a watershed in the remodelling of the central government bureaucracies of many Western liberal democracies, with the modernization process continuing through the 1990s and into the twenty-first century. The result is that significant changes have taken place in the size, shape and working practices of civil services and in the role that they play in modern day government.

PRESSURES FOR MODERNIZATION

A number of factors have helped to push the issue of the modernization of the public service on to the political agendas of Western liberal democracies (see, for example, OECD 1990, pp. 9–10 and 14; OECD 1993, pp. 9–10).

One extremely significant factor has been the economic and financial pressures facing the governments of such countries in the last quarter of the twentieth century and the early years of the twenty-first century. Since the oil crisis of the early 1970s, most liberal democratic countries have operated under difficult economic circumstances. In the words of one commentator 'While the demand for government services continued to be high, the ability to pay for them was reduced' (Ingraham 1996, p. 250). Thus, public service reform has been partly driven by demands to control public expenditure and reduce budget deficits, with governments under pressure to obtain a greater return for the taxpayer's money. In the words of the gurus of the reinventing government movement in the USA, there has been a need to squeeze 'ever more bang out of every buck' (Osborne and Gaebler 1992, p. 15). Economic and financial pressures have led governments to question the benefits of traditional large-scale public bureaucracies and reinforced demands for greater efficiency and value for money in the operations of civil services. Governments have 'reassessed their bureaucracies and demanded changes' (Hughes 1998, p. 4).

A second factor underpinning the modernization agenda has been public pressure on governments to deliver services that are more responsive to consumers. There has been growing disillusionment with civil services and other public service delivery agencies, which have been seen as insufficiently responsive to the users of their services. Concern has been expressed about the implications for service users of what has been seen as the excessive complexity of bureaucratic structures and procedures (OECD 1990, p. 10). There has been a growing recognition that the consumers of public services should be at the heart of the arrangements for service delivery.

The importance of consumer responsiveness is an important element in the third important strand in the development of the modernization agenda – the influence of what has been described as 'business-type "managerialism"' (Hood 1994, p. 134). It has been increasingly accepted that the capacity of governments to realize their objectives can be 'enhanced by management structures and practices which debureaucratize organizational systems', and that the principles of good management should be imported from the private to the public sector (Aucoin 1990, p. 117). Whereas the traditional public administration perspective was based on the idea that public sector management was different from business management, there is now a view that public administration 'has everything to learn from the private sector' (Gunn 1988, p. 21). There is a belief that 'better management' can solve a range of economic and social problems faced by governments (Pollitt 1993, p. 1), and that management techniques from the private sector should be imported into the civil service and other parts of the public service.

Another pressure for the reform of the public service has been the growing awareness of the potential of information technology in helping to improve the efficiency and effectiveness of public service operations (see OECD 1990, p. 14). Technological developments have transformed the processes of public administration. Indeed, one observer has identified the development of 'automation' – particularly in the area of information technology – in the delivery of public services as one of the four administrative 'megatrends' linked with the emergence of the New Public Management (Hood 1990b, pp. 6–7; Hood 1991, p. 3). According to Hood (1990b, p. 6), by the early 1990s, the development of automation in information-processing had made 'much of 1948-style public administration as quaint ... as the valve radio and the magic lantern'. One notable feature of this development for the public sector has been the way that it has created the possibility for decentralizing civil service and other public service activities. There has been a widespread consensus amongst liberal democratic countries that information-age technologies can be harnessed to 're-engineer' government (Bellamy 1999, pp. 128–9). Thus, the Clinton administration recognized the potential role of information and communications technology in the 'reinvention' of the US federal government in the 1990s (Bellamy and Taylor 1998, p. 4). In the UK, the computerization of the central government departments responsible for the delivery of social security benefits and the operation of the National Insurance system, together with the Inland Revenue, have brought about significant changes in the workings and culture of the civil service. The Blair government's programme for the modernization of government is partly based upon the conviction that information and communications technology can be exploited to provide new ways of delivering public services and to 'join up' government (Bellamy 1999, p. 128).

Finally, another important factor in helping to explain the modernization agenda has been the desire to improve political control of central government bureaucracies. In a number of Western liberal democratic countries, the higher civil service has been seen as an obstacle to control by elected politicians. Political leaders in Anglo-American liberal democracies in the 1980s came to office 'convinced that the civil service had its own policy agenda' and was unable to provide sound and unbiased policy advice (Peters and Savoie 1994, pp. 419 and 420). Concerned that permanent officials had become too powerful in the formulation of public policy, the political leaders of many Western countries have attempted 'to reassert political control over the bureaucratic machine' (Pollitt and Bouckaert 2000, p. 155). Thus, in the UK, the Thatcher government, elected in 1979, was very suspicious of the alleged preference of senior civil servants for consensus and continuity. Mrs Thatcher was not attracted to the traditional civil service qualities of detachment, versatility, caution and the ability to see things in the round. As Massey (1993, p. 29) observes, the purpose of civil service reforms following the election of the Thatcher government was not only control over civil service numbers, but also control over the power of the civil service, its responsiveness to change and its influence over policy-making. The promotion of managerialism within central government was 'a concerted attempt to impose the suzerainty of elected politicians upon the permanent bureaucracy' – ministers would be able to enforce policy direction. In Australia, the Coombs Report on Australian government administration in the mid-1970s referred to the argument that the senior civil service had 'an exaggerated conception of its proper role in the processes of government' (Royal Commission on Australian Government Administration 1976, pp. 18–19). By the time of the election of the Labor government of Bob Hawke in 1983, there was a growing consensus that senior civil servants had 'become too much of a "law unto themselves"' and that there was a need to reassert ministerial control (Pollitt and Bouckaert 2000, p. 201). In Canada, the Progressive Conservative government of Brian Mulroney that came to power in 1984 was generally suspicious of the established civil service and the close relationship that it seemed to have enjoyed with long-standing Liberal governments (Pollitt and Bouchaert 2000, p. 209).

APPROACHES TO PUBLIC SERVICE REFORM

The reform of the public service by Western governments since the early 1980s has encompassed a number of approaches (see, for example, Halligan 2001; Pollitt and Bouckaert 2000; Rhodes 1998). These have included cutback management, privatization, the greater use of market-type mechanisms, a stress on corporate management, the decentralization of managerial authority, the devolution of power to sub-national bodies and the reassertion of political control over bureaucracies. In terms of their impact on civil services, most of these approaches represent one of two traditions. On the one hand, there is the management tradition, in which civil services are judged mainly in terms of managerial efficiency and effectiveness. On the other hand, there is the governance tradition, which sees civil services as creatures of the state and its political institutions (Ingraham 1996, p. 249).

One approach to the reform of the public service has been the attempt by many governments to reduce levels of civil service staffing and public spending – what has variously been referred to as cutback management and downsizing. Typical was the approach of Conservative governments in the UK in the 1980s and 1990s. Elected on a manifesto that promised to reduce public spending and government bureaucracy, the Thatcher government literally cut the civil service down to size. Between 1979 and 1997, under the Thatcher and Major governments, the size of the civil service fell by almost one-third, from about three-quarters of a million to fewer than half a million civil servants. In the USA, the Clinton administration's National Performance Review promised to reduce the federal government workforce by over a quarter of a million staff. As a result of privatization, contracting out, departmental restructuring and other factors, governments in New Zealand made significant reductions in civil service staffing, with the number of employees almost halved between 1983 and 1994 (Boston *et al.* 1996, pp. 55 and 58–9). A similar downsizing of civil service personnel has taken place in other countries, including Australia, Canada and the Netherlands, staffing reductions being achieved through such measures as recruitment freezes, the privatization of central government activities and so on.

Another approach to public service reform has been privatization, usually associated with the transfer of state-owned assets to the private sector. Probably the best known manifestation of this approach was the privatization programme launched by the Thatcher government in the UK in the 1980s, which resulted in the transfer of large parts of the public sector to the private sector. One important consequence of this programme was that the central government departments responsible for the sponsorship of the public utilities lost important functions, as well as staff. Some parts of the civil service, such as Her Majesty's Stationery Office, were also sold to the private sector. The UK's privatization programme has been copied by many other countries. Thus, New Zealand governments have sold many state-owned enterprises, and there has been a programme of major asset sales in Australia since the late 1980s. A radical privatization programme was launched in France in the late 1980s by the Chirac government. Although much less used in the Scandinavian countries, privatization programmes have also been launched in a number of other West European countries, including Italy.

In addition to the sale of state owned assets to the private sector, public service reform in many countries has also included the use of market-type mechanisms in the delivery of services, commonly referred to as marketization. Thus, many countries have introduced policies of contracting out certain public services. In New Zealand, wherever possible, publicly funded services, including the purchase of policy advice, have to be subject to competitive tendering (Boston *et al.*, 1996, p. 5). The Australia Public Service employs what is known as the 'Yellow Pages Test': if a supplier is listed in the telephone book, the role of the public sector in delivering a particular service should be questioned (Halligan 2000, p. 52). Following an initiative launched by the Major government in the early 1990s, the British civil service was required to market test central government services to examine whether certain activities could be provided more efficiently and effectively by the private sector. One important outcome of the market testing initiative was the contracting out of central government information technology services to private companies (Bellamy and Taylor 1998, p. 155). The use of the private sector in supplying services provided by the civil service has continued, relabelled as Better Quality Services, under the Blair government, and there has also been the development of public-private partnerships. As the *Modernizing Government* White Paper puts it, the Blair government is adopting a pragmatic approach that involves looking very closely, but not dogmatically, at what should be contracted to the private sector (Prime Minister 1999, p. 35).

In many Western liberal democratic countries, a central feature of public service reform has been the introduction of private sector management techniques into the public sector, what Rhodes (1998, p. 20) describes as corporate management. This approach stresses efficiency and value for money, hands-on management, the use of standards and performance measurement, and the customer orientation. Private sector management methods are now an integral part of the way civil services operate. Senior civil servants are expected to be managers. The move towards corporate management has also included a closer focus on results, as typified by the development of a performance-driven culture in the UK civil service, including the use of targets and performance indicators by executive agencies. Performance measurement systems are also important features of the public service in Australia and New Zealand. In many countries, the development of performance measurement has been accompanied by the use of performance-related pay regimes for civil servants. In Australia, incentives are 'a primary means to achieve individual and organizational performance' (Halligan 2000, p. 53). In New Zealand, performance agreements between departmental chief executives and ministers have been an accepted feature of the public service since the late 1980s.

Making the public service more performance-orientated has been closely linked with attempts to make it more responsive to service users – the customer orientation. Many Western liberal democracies have developed a customer-orientated approach to the delivery of public services. Since the early 1990s, there has been a growing consensus that public services should be more responsive to the users of their services, with an emphasis on the setting of clear service standards. This approach was symbolized in the UK by the Major government's 'Citizen's Charter' programme, which attempted to transform the culture of the civil service and other public sector organizations through a greater emphasis on consumer responsiveness. Underpinning the Charter programme was the attempt to empower users of public services by giving them more information, through the publication of targets and performance indicators, on how well central government's executive agencies and other bodies were performing in the delivery of public services. The Blair government re-launched the Charter programme under the label of 'Service First', with a greater focus on the needs of service users. Similar initiatives have been introduced in many other countries. In Australia, since 1997, all Commonwealth agencies dealing directly with members of the public are required to develop a Service Charter detailing the standards of service which can be expected and providing guidance on complaints mechanisms. The National Performance Review initiative in the USA stressed the importance of making federal government agencies improve customer service, and the Clinton administration required that all federal agencies introduce customer service plans, and develop service standards and customer surveys. A 'Public Service Charter' was adopted in France in 1992, with the aim of making public services more user-centred. Canada's 'Public Service 2000' initiative launched in 1989 emphasized the importance of improving services to the public.

Another central feature of public service reforms in many countries has been decentralization. One form of decentralization involves the delegation of managerial authority to lower levels of public service organizations in order to give officials greater freedom. Thus, the aim of the Financial Management Initiative introduced in the UK by the Thatcher government in the early 1980s was to promote a system in which civil service managers had well-defined responsibility for making the best use of their resources. The Australian Financial Management Improvement Programme was also introduced with the objective of improving financial management and enhancing cost consciousness within the civil service (Zifcak 1994). A very important manifestation of administrative decentralization in some liberal democratic countries has been the separation of central government policy-making from policy execution through the creation of semi-autonomous agencies – what is often described as agencification. A leading example is the Next Steps programme introduced in the UK by the Thatcher government in 1988. Influenced by the Swedish agency model, the development of Next Steps agencies, now

officially referred to as executive agencies, has had a major impact on the
structure, management and culture of the British civil service. There have
been similar developments in other countries. Canada introduced decentralized agencies with managerial freedoms, Special Operating Agencies, in
1989 to deliver public services. The Netherlands introduced more than 20
departmental agencies, with decentralized administrative authority in the 1990s.

Decentralization also encompasses devolution – the transfer of administrative and political authority to elected bodies at the sub-national level.
Devolution of powers to local authorities has been a particular feature of the
public sector reform programmes in Sweden and Finland (Pollitt and Bouckaert
2000, pp. 84–5). During the 1980s, all four Scandinavian countries introduced the 'free local government' experiments designed to give local authorities
more freedom to meet local needs (see Stewart and Stoker 1989). In France,
the 1980s saw a major initiative involving the decentralization of powers to
elected local and regional authorities (de Montricher 1995). In the early
1990s, the Dutch government devolved central government responsibilities to
local authorities, provinces and regional bodies (OECD 1992, p. 63), while
Belgium has had an extensive programme of decentralizing central government powers to sub-national authorities since the late 1980s (OECD 1993,
pp. 37 and 41).

Although, under the Conservative governments of the 1980s and 1990s,
the UK experienced an increasing centralization of power, an important part
of the Blair government's programme of constitutional reform has been the
devolution of powers to elected assemblies in Scotland and Wales. Although
the legislation establishing devolution in Scotland and Wales states, unlike
the model of the separate Northern Ireland Civil Service, that officials working for the two devolved administrations continue to remain part of the
unified Home Civil Service, devolution has very significant implications for
the British civil service. In addition to organizational and structural change,
devolution presents new accountability demands for those civil servants working for the Scottish Executive. There is also the critical issue of whether
devolution will eventually lead to the creation of separate civil services for
Scotland and Wales.

Another feature of public service reform, particularly in Westminster-style
systems, has been the attempts by elected politicians to reassert political
control over central government bureaucracies (Rhodes 1998, p. 22). In the
UK, Mrs Thatcher took a close interest in appointments to the very top grades
of the civil service, leading to concern that her preference for senior officials
committed to enthusiastically implementing government policies conflicted
with traditional civil service notions of neutrality and impartiality (Drewry
and Butcher 1991, pp. 169–70). Under the Thatcher and Major governments,
the higher civil service's traditional monopoly on policy advice was chal-

lenged by the development of the No.10 Policy Unit and the use of outside think tanks (Campbell and Wilson 1995, pp. 67–8). The reassertion of political control has continued under the Blair government, which has broadened the range of policy advice available to ministers through the appointment of over 70 special advisers, leading to anxieties about 'creeping politicization'.

In Australia, the Hawke government of the 1980s also emphasized the need to reassert ministerial control and to make the civil service more responsive to political direction. This required 'a redistribution of power between the bureaucracy and the politicians', involving the abolition of permanent appointments at the top of government departments, and the introduction of fixed term appointments. There was also a diversification of the sources of ministerial policy advice (Halligan 1997, p. 31; 2000, pp. 57–9). Whatever the government in power in Australia since the early 1980s, political control has been 'the order of the day' (Rhodes and Weller 2001b, p. 246). In another Westminster-style system, Canada, the Mulroney government of the 1980s and early 1990s established a politically appointed chief of staff in each ministry at the second highest civil service grade (Pollitt and Bouckaert 2000, p. 212; Peters and Savoie 1994, p. 421).

In addition to the various approaches discussed above, there has been an increasing recognition among Western governments that the reform of the public service requires a different relationship between central government and its operating agencies. Public service reforms such as decentralization and marketization have provided an opportunity for the centre to focus more on coordination and long-term planning, and to strengthen the 'coherence' of government action (OECD 1995, p. 73). One example of this approach has been Norway, where there has been an emphasis on more coordination and cooperation across public sector institutions and with the private sector (OECD 1993, p. 15). The need for more 'joined-up' government was explicitly recognized by the Labour government elected in the UK in 1997. One of the major themes of its White Paper *Modernizing Government* (Prime Minister, 1999) was a call to correct some of the illogicalities and inconsistencies that had developed over the years following Conservative government reforms. The use of measures such as decentralized management, agencification and marketization all tended to fragment the policy-making process and the coordination of service delivery. *Modernizing Government* sought to address this problem by ensuring that public services were 'joined-up' and designed to respond to the needs of their users. It was also argued that much more attention should be paid to the policy process: there was a promise that the Blair government would be forward-looking in the development of policies, rather than simply reacting to short-term pressures.

MODERNIZATION AND THE PUBLIC SERVICE ETHOS

In attempting to modernize the public service, the liberal democracies that make up the old Commonwealth, the USA and much of Europe have had to wrestle with the tensions that have been built into their public administration systems from the beginning of the modern era of government. Public officials evolved the concept of public duty, that is, the belief that, although they must serve the government of the day to the best of their ability, this was not an unswerving loyalty; quite the contrary. The concept of public duty means that the public official 'regards the interests of society as being above his or her personal interests and is a public servant purely out of a perceived duty to serve the public' (O'Toole 1997, p. 82). The modern civil service, therefore, has at its heart the contradiction of the need to respond to elected politicians in a democratic society and the need to behave responsibly on behalf of society as a whole.

The existence of a public service ethic, described as 'a core set of principles that prescribe the minimum standards and guide the behaviour of all those involved in public life', is a widely held belief in Western liberal democracies (Pratchett 2000, p. 111). The public service ethos in the British context has been defined as 'a long-established set of values and rules, mostly unwritten, that sets out the standards that public servants ought to uphold', involving a recognition of the distinctiveness of public service. Its 'traditional ingredients' are said to include impartiality, accountability, trust, equity, probity and service (Public Administration Select Committee 2002, paras 6 and 12).

A central concern in contemporary debates about civil services is the impact of public service reform on this traditional ethos. Observers have referred to the perceived decline of the public service ethos since the 1980s, with suggestions that its very existence is threatened by the business values and managerialism that have been imported into the public service as a result of the application of the New Public Management. According to one observer, these new values and practices 'have acted to undermine the ability of public servants to follow the values of fairness, justice, honesty and impartiality in the advice they offer to their political masters and integrity in their dealings with the public' (Carr 2000, p. 2). There has been particular concern about this issue in the UK, where critics have argued that the values of the public service ethos that traditionally characterized the civil service have been undermined by the various changes introduced since the early 1980s. As the House of Commons Public Administration Committee has observed, 'a gap seems to be opening up between [the] traditional theory and the modern reality of public service' (2002, para. 13). Similar concerns have been expressed in other countries. The Australian experience of public management reforms has been seen as a threat to the basis of ethical conduct in the management and delivery of public services (Painter 2000, p. 181). In New Zealand, public management reforms have created a system in which the loyalty of employees is to their employer department or agency rather than to the public service, a situation that can 'be detrimental to the Public Service as a whole' (OECD 2001, p. 5).

There are signs that governments have recognized that public service reforms pose new ethical challenges (OECD 1998; Nolan 2001, pp. 192–3). The Organisation for Economic Co-operation and Development (OECD), made up of the leading industrialized countries, has drawn up an 'ethics infrastructure' to try to promote ethical public behaviour in what is seen as 'the new, innovative, risk-taking' approach that has replaced 'the old rule book approach' of public administration. Key elements of the framework include codes of conduct, and statements of values, rules and obligations (McRae 1997). According to the OECD (2000), public service ethics are 'a keystone of good governance'.

OUTLINE OF THE REST OF THE VOLUME

Civil services in Western liberal democracies have undergone significant changes since the early 1980s. The rest of this volume explores a number of themes inherent in the process and problems of modernizing civil services in such countries. The next three chapters discuss the application of the modernization agenda in the old Commonwealth, the USA and Western Europe, including the institutions of the European Union. Rod Rhodes and Patrick Weller discuss the conclusions of a comparative study of public service reforms in six countries – Australia, New Zealand, France, Denmark, the Netherlands and the UK – focusing on how the New Public Management has affected the roles of the heads of government departments. Although common themes in all six countries include the search for the more efficient management of the public service and greater political control of the bureaucracy, Rhodes and Weller conclude that change has been uneven. Despite each of the countries experiencing pressures for reform, there have been significant differences in aims, measures and outcomes.

As we saw earlier in this chapter, the USA is located at the incremental end of the continuum of change describing developments in civil service management since the early 1980s. The application of the New Public Management to the US federal government is discussed by Joel Aberbach in Chapter 3. Although the US federal civil service was subject to successive reforms in the late 1970s and 1980s during the Carter and Reagan administrations, the most significant initiative has been the Gore Report of 1993 – the National

Performance Review. Commonly referred to as 'reinventing government', after the popular book of the same title (Osborne and Gaebler 1992), the National Performance Review was central to the Clinton administration's attempt to create a government that works better and costs less. The reform initiative has continued, albeit under a different label, under the administration of George W. Bush. Aberbach discusses the problems associated with the National Performance Review and the related Bush programme. He concludes that the National Performance Review has been a modest success at best. Although civil service reform in the USA has had a significant impact on political responsiveness, its impact in other areas has been more limited. The design features that make the US political system resemble a market, with its focus on political and institutional competition, make it difficult to apply many of the features of the New Public Management.

The limited impact of the New Public Management on the USA federal civil service is in contrast to its deeper impact on the civil services of other Western liberal democracies, including those of Western Europe. As Andrew Massey discusses in Chapter 4, changes in the institutional structures of central government bureaucracies of the member states of the European Union (EU), and the working practices and culture of their civil services, are linked to the process of Europeanization. One result of EU membership is that institutional structures in the national administrations of member states have been amended. Increased interaction among the civil servants of member states has also led to the adoption of 'best practice'. As Massey discusses, the flow of influences has not been all one-way. The ideas underpinning the New Public Management introduced in EU member states have had an impact on the structure and operations of the public administration of the EU – the Commission and its bureaucracy. The most recent attempt at reform, a fundamental reform of the EU's public administration, is Commissioner Kinnock's quest to ensure that the Commission's administration is well managed and of the highest quality.

Chapters 5 to 8 focus on developments in the British civil service. As we saw earlier in this chapter, a major manifestation of civil service reform in Britain was the Next Steps programme launched by the Thatcher government in 1988. Seen by some observers as the most radical reform of the British civil service since the pioneering Northcote-Trevelyan Report of the mid-nineteenth century, the Next Steps initiative involved the separation of the service delivery functions of government departments from the policy-making core in Whitehall. The development of Next Steps agencies, now officially referred to as executive agencies, has had a major impact on the structure, management and culture of the British civil service. By 2003, over three-quarters of the civil service worked in either executive agencies or bodies working on executive agency lines. Despite the significance of executive agencies in the process of civil service reform in Britain since the late 1980s, however, there has been surprisingly little assessment of their impact. Chapter 5 is an important contribution to filling this important gap, providing an evaluation of executive agencies through a general survey of their performance. Oliver James focuses on the three criteria of economy, efficiency and effectiveness, with special reference to what for many years was the largest of the executive agencies, the giant Benefits Agency (merged with the Employment Service in the Spring of 2002 to form Jobcentre Plus). James concludes that executive agency performance has only partially met the expectations of the Next Steps reformers.

The creation of executive agencies is one of the major developments in a series of attempts by successive governments since 1979 to improve efficiency and effectiveness in the British civil service. These initiatives raise a number of important questions, including such issues as accountability, fragmentation and the public service ethos. Important questions about the British civil service have also been raised by the Blair government's programme of constitutional reform, much of which encroaches on the working and practices of the civil service. One major challenge is the devolution of powers to elected assemblies in Scotland and Wales, a key question being whether the establishment of devolved government will result in further change in a civil service that has already been the subject of extensive structural and managerial change.

Chapters 6 and 7 examine some of the issues for the British civil service arising from the establishment of devolved government. In Chapter 6, Richard Parry discusses the balance between the decentralization of political authority through the devolution settlement and the Blair government's modernization programme as it affects the post-devolution civil service. As we saw earlier in this chapter, an important element of the devolution settlement was the specification that officials working for the devolved administrations would remain part of the Home Civil Service, a decision that was justified by the need for the interchange of personnel and the exchange of best practice. As Parry suggests, however, the concept of the Home Civil Service could become a problem in the event of a future devolved administration politically opposed to the UK Government becoming suspicious that civil service reform did not recognize the reality of devolution.

In the second chapter on the implications of devolution for the British civil service (Chapter 7), Iris Kirkpatrick and Robert Pyper examine civil service accountability in post-devolution Scotland. The documents framing the devolution settlement said little about the details of accountability, and post-devolution arrangements in Scotland have seen a rather traditional range of parliamentary mechanisms, notably Question Time and committees with powers of scrutiny and investigation. The chapter concludes that, compared with the relatively under-scrutinized civil service of the Scottish Office in the pre-devolution period, there has been a substantial increase in the volume of scrutiny of the civil service under the new regime. It remains to be seen, however, whether this increased quantity of accountability will result in an improvement in the quality of official accountability.

In addition to the impact of devolution, the workings of the British civil service have also been affected by another major constitutional development launched by the Blair government, the incorporation of the European Convention on Human Rights, which seeks to safeguard certain civil liberties against governmental interference, into UK law. The Human Rights Act 1998, which came into effect in 2000, enables UK citizens to appeal to the UK courts on the grounds of a breach of the Convention. The consequences for the British civil service are significant, as, under the 1998 Act, all public authorities exercising executive functions are required to act in a way that is compatible with the Convention. The development of a stronger 'rights culture' across the public sector raises important questions, including the need to promote cultural change within the civil service. The incorporation of the Convention into UK law will also require departments and their officials to engage in more consultation in the formulation of policy. Amanda Finlay, a serving senior civil servant, provides a case study, in Chapter 8, of the implementation of the Human Rights Act in the Lord Chancellor's Department. Written from the perspective of an official who has been closely involved in the implementation of this important initiative, the case study demonstrates the importance of departmental policies, practices and procedures being compatible with Convention rights.

Implementing constitutional reform in a way that preserves a unified civil service, together with the integration of human rights into the procedures of government departments and executive agencies, are extremely important challenges for the British civil service. Another key challenge for the British civil service, and the civil services of other Western liberal democracies, is improving the policy process. One of the key themes of the Blair government's *Modernizing Government* White Paper was to improve the policy process by developing a new approach based on certain key principles. These principles include designing policy around shared objectives and carefully designed results, rather than around organizational structures or existing functions, making sure that policies are inclusive, involving others in policy-making, improving the way risk is managed, becoming more forward-looking and outward-looking and learning from experience (Prime Minister 1999, pp. 16–7). An important follow-up to the White Paper was a Cabinet Office report on the modernization of policy-making. In Chapter 9, Wayne Parsons examines this report and considers its merits as a model of strategic policy-making. Parsons argues that the report is inadequate as a model of strategic policy-

making, neglecting politics and democracy as important dimensions. He further argues that the report also neglects the contribution that other schools of
strategic thought could make to the formulation of a strategic model that may
be more appropriate and relevant to policy-making in conditions of ignorance, unpredictability, uncertainty and complexity.

The chapters in this volume indicate that the civil services of Western
liberal democracies have been passing through an era in which significant
changes have taken place, and that many of the traditional assumptions
underpinning the role and operating practices of civil services have been
fundamentally questioned. As the chapters make clear, the continuing process
of modernizing civil services since the early 1980s raises a number of important issues.

The way that some of these issues apply in the case of the British civil
service are brought together in the final chapter of this volume. Describing
some of the trends that have characterized the modernization of the British
public service since the early 1980s, some of which have been discussed in
other chapters, Peter Barberis observes that the British public service tradition is much more difficult to uphold in the circumstances of the early
twenty-first century. For Barberis, what he describes as 'the age of modernity' makes more difficult the maintenance of a civil society in which 'virtue'
and 'trust' feed the public service ethos. Indeed, he argues, there is a greater
need for civil society, virtue and trust at exactly the same time as their stock
is receding.

The concerns that Barberis discusses in the context of Britain have been
mirrored in other countries. As we saw earlier in this chapter, developments
in Australia have highlighted the consequences of public sector contracting
out for ethical conduct in the management of public services (Painter 2000,
p. 181). Similar concerns have been expressed about the possible unintended
consequences of New Zealand's public sector reforms (Boston *et al.* 1996,
p. 360). There remains a basic tension between the commitment of Western
liberal democracies to modernizing the public service and the traditional
values of the public service ethos associated with the form of public administration that prevailed in those countries for most of the twentieth century.

2. Localism and exceptionalism: comparing public sector reforms in European and Westminster systems

R.A.W. Rhodes and Patrick Weller

'We have a tradition that is rooted in pragmatism and flexibility' (Sir Richard Wilson, British Cabinet Secretary, 1998).

INTRODUCTION

Heads of government departments used to be regarded with some awe. They were people of weight: experienced, wise, and powerful, if deliberately remote and at least partially anonymous. They worked in the shadows, advising, managing and influencing their countries' direction. They were the mandarins, recognized as the real rulers, the providers of continuity.

Their reputation is now far more mixed. In part because parliament and the media wanted more immediate answers, with secretaries explaining their actions. In part because fiction has endorsed the caricatures; Sir Humphrey Appleby, the mandarin of 'Yes Minister', may be an exaggeration, yet in the eyes of many, his manipulative behaviour confirmed their view about the behaviour of British permanent secretaries. Yet the fundamental reason for their declining reputation is that belief in the efficacy of state action has cracked. Ministers have often blamed officials for being unresponsive, and sought to bring them under control by various management techniques including reduced tenure. So, the departmental head entered uncharted waters where many of the old assumptions no longer held true and where their power, influence and status was questioned. Yet at the same time their importance is not in doubt.

The heads of public service departments come under different titles: permanent secretaries in Britain, departmental secretaries in Australia; chief executives in New Zealand, *departmentschef* in Denmark, *directeurs d'administration* in France, and *secretaris-generaal* in the Netherlands. Throughout the chapter we refer to them as departmental secretaries or, for variety, simply as, the secretaries.

Whatever the label, we are always talking about the top official. In each country the incumbents play a pivotal role in government, linking the political to the administrative system and holding the primary responsibility for managing the delivery of services to the community. They are required to meet potentially contradictory objectives: national circumstances may vary the emphasis, but in each case heads of department must: provide strategic, managerial and operational policy advice to ministers; remain aware of the broad political strategy of the cabinet; take managerial responsibility for the meeting of departmental objectives, often after restructuring and review; and act as the accountable manager, responsible to parliament.

In many countries, the 'New Public Management' (NPM) or 'managerialism' complicated these tasks. It created new demands: the objectives of government departments became more explicit; ministers became more interested in the details of administration; the purchasers and providers of government services were divided, at times in theory, sometimes in organizational practice; and departmental secretaries had to become managers. Commentators argued top appointments had been politicized, favouring the 'can-do' manager who delivered a minister's policy.

In this chapter, we summarize the conclusions of a six country comparative study that explored how NPM affected the roles of top officials. We focus on this elite for one simple reason; they play a key role in public sector reform. As OECD (2000) observes, leadership by agency heads or departmental secretaries is a key tool for promoting public sector reform and building support inside government and with the public. So, whether the object is to measure performance, to increase competitiveness or to improve quality, departmental secretaries must 'change the talk' and then 'walk the talk'.

One version of recent changes suggests that ministers wanted to stamp their authority on the civil service and provide decisive policy direction. Senior officials lost tenure. They are now on contracts and subject to performance measurement. They are marginalized because there is great competition for the ministers' ear. Dependence on ministerial approval for contract renewal undermined traditional public service values, threatening the ability of the civil service to provide frank and fearless advice.

An alternative view sees the changes in a positive light because they make officials more responsive to political direction. Ministers should have the last words in areas of disagreement because only the elected have the right to decide what is in the public or national interest. They should not be hindered by officials who obstruct changes because they believe they know best what is in the national interest and can afford to wait for the minister to go before re-opening the debate with the next incumbent. The changes reflect the victory of the elected over the appointed. The civil service is subordinate to the immediate political interests of the government. Secretaries are selected for their compatibility with the government's policy directions and ability to put that policy into practice.

The analysis in this chapter shows that both stories mask more than they reveal. Change is uneven. Not every country rushed to embrace NPM (for example France) and, of those that did, there are big differences in their aims, measures and outcomes (for example between New Zealand and everywhere else). Equally, as the importance of the party political allegiance of officials fades in the Netherlands, Australia and Britain agonize over the alleged spread of such appointments, although the trend is better described as person-alization. Every system has examples of top civil servants 'retiring' or leaving abruptly, unable to find the right rapport with their minister, but Australia and New Zealand apart, in the other systems official careers remain protected. If there is one generalization covering all six countries, it can be summarized as 'Antipodean exceptionalism'. The New Public Management joins the kanga-roo, the duck-billed platypus, the Tasmanian tiger and the kiwi as another example of uniqueness in the southern hemisphere.

The structure of this chapter is simple. First, we describe changes to their policy, management and diplomatic roles. Second, we offer an explanation of these variations. It is common in the social sciences to engage with the literature and we were tempted! However, we resist the lure of erudition and instead defend the argument that the key to any such explanation lies in the analysis of governmental traditions. Just as the departmental secretaries interpreted the demands made on them and adjusted the balance of their various roles, so governments responded differently to the so-called imperatives of globalization. There was no necessary link between inflation, economic liberalism, the ideas of the NPM and public sector reform. Every country experienced the 'common' pressures but interpreted them and responded differently, if they responded at all. We argue that such ideas and pressures were interpreted through the prism of governmental traditions. We need no elaborate theory, or extensive literature review, to show this point. The simple and long-standing distinctions between Anglo-Saxon, Jacobin, *Rechstaatt*, and Scandinavian governmental traditions will answer our needs.

THE CHANGING ROLES OF DEPARTMENTAL SECRETARIES

Australia and New Zealand apart, there were only modest changes in the characteristics of top officials (and for detailed statistical data see Rhodes and Weller 2001a). Departmental secretaries in 2000 bear a marked similarity to their forerunners in 1970, and indeed before that. For France there is little change. For Britain, Denmark and the Netherlands there is a modest trend towards younger appointments. For Australia and New Zealand there is a marked increase in such appointments. Presumably, thrusting can-do managers need to be young! In the Antipodes, departmental secretaries are not only appointed younger but they also stay for shorter periods and leave younger. Outside Britain, the idea that the post of departmental secretary is now the final stage of a person's career is no longer tenable (and of course it never was in France). All have a degree or equivalent. Departmental secretaries are better educated today, in that they are now more likely to have both an undergraduate and a postgraduate degree. They are still predominantly appointed from within the career civil service, not outside. Do we need to add they are still white, male and middle aged?

If the statistical data reveals little change, the interviews with sitting departmental secretaries reveal much more. They see significant differences. We review the differences by looking at their changed political-policy advice, managerial and diplomatic roles. As ever, in such a broad sweep review, we confront the problem that whatever general statement we make, it will not be true in Zanzibar. One country is always the exception to the rule. We are pleased to announce that France will play the part of Zanzibar.

Political and Policy Advice

Has the appointment of department secretaries become politicized? Are people chosen because of their political allegiance rather than efficiency or expertise? Such questions are easily posed and there are easy answers. But it is hard to show a significant degree of politicization. If politicization means party political appointments, then there is little evidence to suggest it is true in any country except France and the Netherlands. In the Netherlands, although top civil servants have a known party allegiance, political representativeness has become much less significant with depillarization and party affiliation coming a long way second to expertise. In France, most appointments combine technical expertise with political experience but there are few overtly party political appointments. Departmental secretaries with equivalent party political affiliations or careers are almost unheard-of elsewhere. One New Zealand departmental secretary later became a party candidate and a former treasury secretary in Australia became a senator some years after retirement. But there was no regular movement from the civil service to parliament.

In every country, the final selection of a departmental secretary is political. Prime ministerial, ministerial and presidential approval may be required. But there is limited choice. The British prime minister must select from the list provided by the Cabinet Secretary. The New Zealand cabinet can go outside the official list, but it would be a public rebuke. Although it once rejected a nomination, it has never made its own selection. In Denmark, the minister will consult widely, but all appointees have come from within the service; they need to be technically expert and to know the system. In the Netherlands, the Council of Minister makes the choice but the minister's views are important, as are informal soundings of other departmental secretaries. In Australia, ministers have sometimes interviewed potential candidates, and strong ministers will get their choice, but the prime minister makes the final decision. In France, the minister decides, but is likely in important cases to consult with the prime minister and even, in cases of cohabitation, with the president. In all these countries the overwhelming majority of appointments are made from within the public sector. At so senior a level, few come direct from the private sector. So there is political involvement, but that does not make the appointments partisan.

If politicization is a means for a government to assert its authority over the public service, perhaps by the sacking of several departmental secretaries *pour encourager les autres*, then the best illustration is Australia after the 1996 election, when the Howard government sacked six departmental secretaries. But replacements were mainly from within the public service, except for two who had spent a large part of their career in the SES before temporarily joining the private sector.

For the other countries too we cannot make the case that party political beliefs motivated the appointments. Rather, people were selected because they fitted, in some way or other. Mrs Thatcher asked 'are they one of us?' But she did not mean, 'are they Conservatives?' She wanted a style of action; the can-do manager. In New Zealand, the State Services Commission proposes individuals who fit the needs of the government and sometimes of a particular minister. In Australia, ministers were consulted and often had views on what they wanted. If they could not get on with someone, they sought a change. There were enough people who had the relevant characteristics or skills to provide a field.

It is more productive to move beyond the idea of politicization to a different idea – personalization. Departmental secretaries are selected and kept in part because of their style and approach, in part because of their policy preferences, and in part because ministers are comfortable with them. Mutual toleration becomes less significant if they can be readily moved. In Denmark, if the minister and the departmental secretary cannot get on, the departmental secretary will be moved and found, for example, an alternative position often in the diplomatic service. Personal compatibility is necessary; the departmental secretaries must adjust to meet the demands of the ministers. If that means more political calculations, more meeting of interest groups, then that is part of the job.

The political-policy advice role has also seen an end to the civil service's monopoly of advice in many countries. Policy contestability is the order of the day. A monopoly over policy advice had once been one of the great sources of strength for departmental secretaries. They wielded influence because of their control of information and privileged access to the minister. That monopoly no longer exists. There were several causes of the change. Many interests in society are better informed and more demanding. Ministers are better educated. Pressure groups have the technology and information to offer alternative scenarios, different models of the economy and possible strategies. Ministers have an office full of staff who may be political and policy advisers with their own proposals for change. Advice is contested. Ideas are tested. Solutions are challenged.

The extent of change varies from country to country. Competition may be at its greatest in Australia, where some ministers felt they had little to learn from their official advisers. In New Zealand, the minister has the theoretical right to 'purchase' services, including policy advice from anywhere, even if the practice has yet to catch up with the theory. In Britain, departmental secretaries put together packages of advice from many sources; political advisers, think-tanks, consultants, academics, even the civil service. However, the civil service has backed away from any expanded idea of an advisory role on party political affairs.

In France, in theory at least, political and administrative advice are separate. *Directeur de cabinet* manages the political and *directeur d'administration centrale* manages administration but, in practice, both have to manage the politics-administration boundary. Role specialization does not resolve the conflict, just institutionalizes it. Denmark has integrated the two roles and expanded the political role to meet ministerial demands in ways that previously would have been seen as incursions into the party political arena. So, if the times demand that the departmental secretaries advise on party politics, where the ruling coalition's need 'to count to 90' in a parliament with 179 seats is paramount, then so be it. They will help with the soundings and the sums. Ministers look to their departmental secretaries for policy advice and present-day debate bemoans the lack of policy ideas from the political parties. The search for greater political control is common to all six countries and they have all sought a new balance between both political and policy advice and between their advisory and management roles.

Management

In every country, the search for a more economic, efficient and effective management of the public sector is a common theme. There have even been tentative steps in this direction by the French! The NPM changed the work of departmental secretaries. Departmental secretaries are now managers. This much seems obvious. Exactly what such phrases mean is less clear.

The seeming coherence of the NPM programme prompted the observation that reform was global. This view gained added credibility when the ideas became the conventional wisdom about how to run the modern state (World Bank 1992; OECD 1995). However, the new public sector management now covers all types of public sector reform; it excludes nothing. The case for the NPM as a global paradigm was overstated. Its ideas are internally contradictory, embracing for example prescriptions for top-down steering on the one hand and egalitarian empowerment on the other. Further, the likenesses between countries are superficial, masking significant underlying differences. Finally, the aims and results of NPM differ. Under Prime Minister Thatcher in the UK, the aim was to create the minimalist state. By contrast, in Denmark, reform was championed as a way to protect the state. The common language of management obscures national differences. Shared international pressures and common intellectual foundations do not necessarily produce standardized public sector outcomes. The six countries amply demonstrate the point.

The contrast between France and New Zealand is dramatic. More important, the wide-ranging programmes of reform are a feature of Westminster systems, not of continental parliamentary systems. The contents of the reform programmes differ markedly. Privatization is a distinctive characteristic of UK reforms but marginal in Australia where there was less to sell. There the drive for efficiency was more important. Denmark sampled a little of what the Ministry of Finance fancied.

The reform packages changed over the years. So, latterly, British reforms stressed responsiveness to the consumers of public services through such devices as the Citizen's Charter (now known as Service First) while Australia shifted to marketizing public services with the extensive use of contracts. So, to say the NPM affected departmental secretaries who now pay much greater attention to their managerial role begs several questions. Which 'bits' of the NPM programme were implemented in which country with what effects on departmental secretaries?

There are some common effects. Departmental secretaries must now account for how well their departments are doing. Client focus, greater emphasis on measuring outcomes, responsibility to meet targets and performance outcomes all need a degree of management attention. In most countries, many large enterprises have been hived-off as executive agencies, leaving the department as an advisory body, much smaller than before, but still needing to coordinate the different functions. Everywhere there are demands for more sensitive and effective management of resources. So departmental secretaries must ensure the department 'delivers'. This phrase does not mean operational management but organizing the department and managing its human resources. The focus is strategic management and the departmental secretary is more like a Chair of the Board – a facilitator and coordinator. Sir Richard Wilson's summary of management change in the UK has wide applicability. He said, 'Twenty years ago senior civil servants only had to take an interest in legislation, policy advice and bonding with ministers' but 'wave after wave of initiatives battered Permanent Secretaries until ... we found ways of ... bringing our management up to date' (1998).

There is little evidence that most ministers are concerned about managing their departments. They want policies delivered, ideas developed. The rest is left to their departmental secretaries. In Australia and New Zealand, ministers are involved in assessing their departmental secretaries. Such performance management may have problems; for example, the fit between performance and criteria, when both need to be interpreted flexibly. But if contracts, or term appointments, are introduced, then some means of assessing performance is essential. How else can we decide whether the contract or term should be renewed or allowed to lapse? That is one of the costs of such a system. Here, Antipodean exceptionalism is clearest because that original Westminster system, the UK, continues to sidestep the issue of assessing departmental secretaries' performance. Of the six countries, only Australia and New Zealand apply the precepts of the NPM to the role of departmental secretaries; 'everybody but us' is not just a feature of the British system. Of course, the French can simply observe that avoiding the NPM removes the need to agonize over performance indicators for departmental secretaries. Such observations tap a well of sympathy in these authorial breasts, but the Westminster systems have travelled too far to turn back now.

The changes pose other managerial dilemmas for departmental secretaries, notably around coordination, decentralization and control. We consider managing relationships with other organizations both in and outside the public sector under the heading of diplomacy.

Diplomacy

Managing external relations – whether with other government departments, states in a federal system, parliaments in a devolved system, local authorities, or public and voluntary sector organizations contracted to deliver services – has become an ever more prominent and demanding facet of a departmental secretary's job. In short, departmental secretaries must now manage networks.

Perhaps the most significant unintended consequence of public sector reform was the fragmentation of service delivery and the arrival, not of markets, but of networks (on Australia see Davis and Rhodes 2000; on

Denmark see Rhodes 1999; on the UK see Rhodes 1997; on the Netherlands see Kickert *et al.* 1997). Networks are a distinctive coordinating mechanism, separate from markets and hierarchies. They are an alternative to, not a hybrid of, markets and hierarchies. Of their characteristics, trust is central because it is the basis of network coordination in the same way that commands and price competition are the key mechanisms for bureaucracies and markets respectively.

> If it is price competition that is the central coordinating mechanism of the market and administrative orders that of hierarchy, then it is trust and cooperation that centrally articulates networks. (Frances *et al.* 1991, p. 15)

As a working axiom, networks are high on trust and contracts are low on trust. With the spread of networks there has been a recurrent tension between contracts on the one hand, with their stress on competition to get the best price, and networks on the other, with their stress on cooperative behaviour.

In Australia, Denmark, the Netherlands and the UK this trend is discussed under the label 'governance'. Departmental secretaries now have to manage packages of services, packages of organizations and, in federal or devolved systems in particular, packages of governments. The diplomatic skills – for managing networks, for 'sitting where the other person is sitting', and for eliciting cooperative behaviour through negotiation – are not new but they are now at a premium. In a federal system like Australia, fragmenting services by contracting out, compounded the complexity of its intergovernmental relations. In Britain, the departmental secretaries talk of the need for joined-up government and devolution to Scotland, Wales and Northern Ireland has created intergovernmental coordinating mechanisms common to federal systems. Similar concerns about improving coordination are equally obvious in the Netherlands.

There are two dilemmas for departmental secretaries in these governance pressures. First, they chase the holy grail of coordination. Public sector reform created a greater need for coordination while reducing governmental ability to coordinate. In the UK, Kavanagh and Seldon (2000) point out we have seen prime ministerial centralization in the guise of more resources for No. 10 and strong political and policy direction. The pendulum swings yet again as the centre promotes coordination and strategic oversight to combat Whitehall's departmentalism. They argue such 'power grabs' are 'a reaction to felt weakness, a frustration with the inability to pull effective levers'. In Denmark, the Economic Committee seeks to be the powerhouse of Danish government and the Dutch Committee of Departmental Secretaries (*het college van secretarissen-generaal*) recovers from its wartime record of collaboration to play a prominent role in present-day reform. However, despite strong pressures for more and pro-active coordination throughout Western Europe, coordination remains characterized by four features.

(i)   It is largely negative, based on persistent compartmentalization, mutual avoidance and friction-reduction between powerful bureaux or ministries, all of which which remain formidable inertial obstacles.

(ii) Even when cooperative, anchored at the lower levels of the state machine and organized by specific established networks, coordination is sustained by a culture of dialogue in vertical relations and of integration at the horizontal level.

(iii) It is rarely strategic, so almost all attempts to create pro-active strategic capacity for long-term planning ... have failed.

(iv) It is intermittent and selective in any one sector, improvised late in the policy process, politicized issue-oriented, and reactive (Wright and Hayward 2000, p. 33).

Second, if coordination is elusive, the costs of decentralization are both obvious and immediate – a loss of both central control and political accountability. The UK discovers what Australia knew for all the twentieth century, that combining functional decentralization with divided political authority means the centre confronts a patchwork quilt of elected and functional bodies with which it shares authority and therefore has to negotiate in intergovernmental forums. The Netherlands illustrates most clearly how combining a compartmentalized centre with fragmented implementation means that political accountability disappears in the interstices of the many organizational and system boundaries. The problem exists but remains unacknowledged by departmental secretaries and ministers alike in the UK.

The command operating codes found in unitary states must give way to diplomatic skills in intergovernmental bargaining. An instrumental approach to network management assumes the centre can devise and impose tools to foster integration in and between networks and realize central government's objectives. Such a code, no matter how well disguised, runs the ever-present risk of recalcitrance from key actors and a loss of flexibility in dealing with localized problems. Gentle pressure relentlessly applied is still a command operating code in a velvet glove. For the mandarin at the top of a pyramid, control deficits are an ever-present unintended consequence of fragmentation. Network structures are characterized by a decentralized negotiating style that trades off control for agreement. Management by negotiation means agreeing with the objectives of others, not just persuading them that the central view is correct or resorting to sanctions when they disagree. Departmental secretaries are re-applying old lessons, honing new skills, and managing the ever-changing balance between their political-policy advice, managerial and diplomatic roles.

CONSTRUCTING AN EXPLANATION

Of the several attempts to explain the variations in public sector reform in Western Europe, we want to develop Pollitt and Summa's suggestion that

> the most convincing explanations ... appear to rest ... upon the characteristics of the political and administrative systems already in place. ... [T]hese characteristics ... most significantly influenced what was possible in terms of the scope, process and speed of reform (1997, pp. 13–15. See also Pollitt and Bouckaert 2000).

We argue that governmental traditions are central to understanding recent changes.

A tradition is a set of beliefs absorbed during socialization. This heritage comes to each individual who, through his or her agency, then can modify and transform it even as they pass it on to others. This set of shared theories forms the background against which we construct the world. Traditions are contingent, constantly evolving, necessarily in a historical context and consist of theories and narratives. Narratives are the form theories take in the human sciences; narratives are to the human sciences what theories are to the natural sciences (see Bevir 1999; Bevir and Rhodes 2002). There is a sense, therefore, in which there is no NPM or public sector reform because all complex political objects are constructed in part by our prior theories of the world and the traditions of which they are part. How we understand reform depends, therefore, on the theories that we use. Reform is a narrative interpreted through traditions.

A governmental tradition is a set of inherited beliefs about the institutions and history of government (cf. Davis 1998: p. 158; Perez-Diaz 1993, p. 7). Commonly, a distinction is drawn between the Anglo-Saxon (no state) tradition; the Germanic *rechtsstaat* tradition; the French (Napoleonic) tradition; and the Scandinavian tradition, which mixes the Anglo-Saxon and Germanic. Thus, in the Germanic tradition, state and civil society are part of one organic whole; the state is a transcendent entity. The Anglo-Saxon pluralist tradition draws a more distinct boundary between state and civil society with contract rather than natural law as the basis to the state. Civil servants have no constitutional position. The Napoleonic tradition sees the French state as the one and indivisible republic, exercising strong central authority to contain the hostile relations between state and civil society. The Scandinavian tradition is also 'organicist', influenced by the ideas of the *rechtsstaat* tradition, but differs from the Germanic tradition in being a decentralized unitary state with a strong participation ethic (we paraphrase Loughlin and Peters 1997, pp. 46–55).

So each of the six countries interprets the public sector differently and, as a result, the reforms have different aims, measures and outcomes and different consequences for the departmental secretaries. For this analysis of departmental secretaries, we explore beliefs about central constitutional structures and about political-bureaucratic relations (adapted from Christensen 1995; see also Rhodes 1999). There is always the danger of reifying traditions when comparing them. For any country there will be multiple traditions and the key question is who articulates which tradition. We draw starker, simpler contrasts. We may oversimplify but this broad-brush comparison demonstrates the value of analysing traditions, does not preclude a later unpacking of the traditions of each country and suggests several ways of developing such an analysis. So we provide a country-by-country summary of those key beliefs about the constitution, the bureaucracy and civil society directly relevant to the changing roles of departmental secretaries.

Australia

The Australian administrative tradition is characterized by state intervention, innovation, and a non-partisan career public service. Thus, colonial statism evolved into the supportive state that is traditionally seen as part of the Westminster model family (see Davis 1998). A strong core executive, supported by an entrenched party system, runs a coherent and centralized but federal state. Through collective decision-making in cabinet, the executive can impose consistent policies and procedures across government. To sustain its interventionist role, the Commonwealth created a bureaucracy characterized by entrance examinations, elaborate rules for most public work, a strict hierarchy of offices, central agencies responsible for personnel, finance and policy, probity, administration through precedent and a marriage bar on employing women. The working environment was formal and tightly controlled. Two other characteristics of the Australian governmental tradition were also entrenched for most of the twentieth century; federalism and a network of public enterprises (see Keating and Wanna 2000; Wettenhall 1990). So, rule-bound bureaucracy, fragmentation and diversity are long-standing features of the Australian public sector.

If the story closed here, the Australian administrative tradition would be one of extraordinary consistency. It is a tradition that evokes nostalgia among both public service unions and those commentators such as Pusey (1991), who credit the Commonwealth administration with founding a 'nation building state'. Yet this world has gone to be replaced, first, by an era of corporate management concerned with greater efficiency through modern budget controls and, second, by the contracting-out of services once performed in the public service and greater responsiveness to clients. Australia's cultural revolution embraced the 'managerialist' movement.

This revolution was spurred on by Australia's declining economic fortunes under the impact of globalization. State institutions mediated these changes.

In the Australian case, the government 'retreat' did not take the form of less government but of government in a different form. It withdrew from traditional economic and social regulation and focused instead on improved efficiency and effectiveness for utilities and government-controlled commercial activities. The origins of the Australian state lie in innovative and diverse forms of state intervention. New forms of service delivery added further layers of complexity, but they went with the grain. So the state continued to support those in need but used the tax and transfer systems to target that support. Globalization and economic performance may be a spur to action but governments interpret their effects differently and can call on a varied repertoire of responses. There was no necessary change to the fundamental objectives of public policy. And as a member of the Westminster family, the executive faced few if any constraints in reforming its bureaucracy.

So, political control of the bureaucracy was the order of the day, irrespective of the party in power. Permanence and distance gave way to contracts, a degree of personalization and greater responsiveness to the elected government. The statesmen in disguise of the golden years were now more explicitly servants of power and willingly so, as officials initiated many of the initiatives. They were also embedded in networks. The essential diplomatic skills for managing networks are a long-standing feature of the Australian public sector. For example, Caiden (1990, p. 30) identifies putting oneself in the other person's shoes as a long-standing value and belief of Commonwealth officials. These skills are ever-present in the federal-provincial diplomacy of Australian intergovernmental relations (see Keating and Wanna 2000). So, there is nothing new under the sun but the skills now have to be exercised in new arenas of inter-organizational service delivery systems. As in Britain, the balance between political-policy advice, management and diplomacy has shifted markedly away from the traditional advice function. But antipodean exceptionalism meant the pace and extent of change was greater than in Europe.

Britain

Against a backcloth of fiscal pressure, the British government pushed through public sector reform shaped by a governmental tradition characterized by strong executive leadership, no constitutional limits to executive authority, civil service subordination to ministers and disciplined two-party politics which ensured parliament passed legislation. Administrative reform is always political and all British governments since 1979 have sought to cut government spending and to exert effective control over the administrative machine. The Conservative government aimed to reduce public spending by redrawing the boundaries of the state and evolved a clear set of political ideas to justify and 'sell' its various reform packages to the electorate. It attacked big government, local government and waste, used markets to create more individual choice and campaigned for the consumer. Privatization and marketization pushed back the boundaries of the state and gave the government more control (over financial totals) over less (service delivery). There was a protracted drive to introduce corporate management, to marketize public services and to reinforce political control. Marketizing had unintended consequences; it fragmented government, multiplied networks, and constrained central steering (Rhodes 1997, Chapter 5).

New Labour is both pragmatic in continuing the Conservative's reforms and innovative as they confront the unintended consequences of reform. With its policy of 'joined-up government', New Labour seeks to strengthen horizontal coordination (across government departments) and vertical coordination (of local government and other bodies delivering services). The implications of these shifts for the higher civil servants are clear. Their tasks remain a mix of policy, management and diplomacy, but the balance shifted from policy to management and the arrival of joined-up government signals a further shift from the 'managerially-oriented can-doer' to the 'boundary-spanning diplomat'. However, Antipodean excess was not for Britain. Contracts and performance measurement may lurk in the wings but they are not yet with us. Flexible pragmatism, ever a feature of the British civil service, modulated the effects of reform on permanent secretaries. 'Everybody but us' may understate the extent of the change but it captures the measured pace.

Denmark

The Danish government's response to fiscal stress was a 'revolution in slow motion' (Olsen 1983, p. 188). The aim was to preserve a popular welfare state by selected reforms aimed at getting better value for money. Public sector reform is difficult to distinguish from any other policy area; it was characterized by a negotiated consensus and a pragmatism that avoided clear winners and losers. The choice of means was a technical matter, not ideological, and driven by the higher civil service, not ministers. So, privatization and marketization were but two options among many, to be used when there was agreement they were the best way forward. The government sought greater control though corporate management reforms and the use of 'flexible' contracts but ministers remain sovereign in their own empires. They can dictate the pace of reform and frustrate central agencies. The reform orthodoxy of the Ministry of Finance claims the reforms improved efficiency because, for example, agencies have clearer goals, but the outcomes are uncertain, ambiguous and negotiated. Many changes continue 'the Danish tradition of foggy corporate governance in a different disguise' (Jensen 1998, p. 65). The consequence of such corporate governance for departmental secretaries has been their ever greater involvement not only in policy making but also in the politics of policy making. Integrated advice by the Island culture sustains a tradition of negotiated political and policy consensus in which public sector reform is but one more policy to be discussed in the endless game of building support.

France

In France, the key characteristics of its governmental traditions are a twin-headed executive with a strong head of state and an active head of government; and a powerful and centralized set of state institutions. Departmental secretaries in France also have a long and well-established tradition. The public sphere is said to be the incarnation of the national interest. The role of the state in general, and its high officials in particular, is to guard against the essentially self-interested and potentially divisive behaviour of the private sphere. There has been a long-standing belief in the benefits of state intervention among members of the political elite. The result is that over the years the French state developed as a centralized and strongly directive (or *dirigiste*) force (and for a review of the different academic interpretations of the French state, see Elgie and Griggs 2000, Chapter 1). Moreover, it has also led to a system of administrative training schools (the *grandes écoles*) designed to create a class of elite public sector officials whose prime function is to serve the state rationally and disinterestedly. They are imbued with the ethos of the state and they do not take their administrative and social responsibilities lightly. It is scarcely surprising that the nostrums of the private sector recycled by the NPM failed to strike a responsive chord. The powerful officials of a strong state were unmoved and the moving finger of the NPM writ and then moved on with nary a mark to show for its pains. We stop before we belabour the obvious to death.

The Netherlands

Although recent changes in the political-administrative system affected the position of the permanent secretary, the innovations are not radical. Historically, they worked in a pillarized political system. Because no single party could ever achieve a parliamentary majority, political elites had to cooperate to avoid democratic instability. So, Dutch bureaucracy was characterized by policy compartments with close links to societal actors and pressure groups. There was neither a professional training institute for civil servants, nor specific post-entry training. Civil servants were not centrally recruited: each department had its own recruitment programme and entry criteria. These 'policy compartments' largely determined policy. So, there was little room for cross-departmental, governmental coordination. The positions of the permanent secretaries and the council of permanent secretaries were weak. They acted as adviser to the minister, coordinator of the internal organization and of policy-formulation, but only if the director-generals did not carry out these tasks. Only permanent secretaries who could do all three functions were respected as influential.

After 1960, secularization, the demise of ideology and individualization resulted in de-pillarization. The policy compartments were opened as policy making fragmented. However, coordinating policy making remains the central problem of Dutch public administration. The 1980s and NPM, in such guises as privatization, marketization and agencification, temporarily reinforced the influence of the departmental secretaries because neo-liberal politicians saw them as allies in the reconstruction of the welfare state. In this new *Zeitgeist*, departmental secretaries are seen as public managers. Their job is to get results, while maintaining internal and external coalitions. More recently, however, the reforms have reinforced the primacy of the political, rather than promoting bureaucratic autonomy. Departmental secretaries must work in the 'ministerial shadow'. As elsewhere, reform strengthened political control. Despite fragmentation and in the face of management reform, the departmental secretaries remain key actors in their policy compartments and the challenge of coordinating the compartments remains the core issue for those wishing to assert greater political control. The tradition of bureaucratic autonomy may have been tempered but it remains a defining characteristic of the Dutch civil service and the bedrock of departmental secretaries' influence.

New Zealand

Traditionally, New Zealand had all those constitutional arrangements that the executive branches of government elsewhere can only dream of. It is a small unitary state with a single house of parliament and a tightly regimented party system. A party that won the election had few constraints on its power. It could restructure the form and procedures of the state, change the rules governing the economy and restructure the public service without facing any substantial hurdles. Its parliament, according to Geoffrey Palmer, who later became prime minister, had 'the fastest law in the west'.

Changes to the shape of the public sector were easy to introduce, therefore. A small, cohesive group of officials in the Treasury, united by theoretical insights derived from economics and a concern for the parlous state of an over-protected economy, combined with a powerful treasurer to drive through substantial change. With cabinet convinced, parliament subservient and the opposition in general agreement, the public sector in general and the terms and conditions of employment of departmental secretaries in particular, were whatever government determined. With no countervailing forces, it could go further, more easily, than governments elsewhere. Any restraints were self-imposed. So, the government is responsible for making appointments and assessing the public servants but the independent State Services Commission advises and assesses for ministers and, in practice, acts with some independence.

Future change may be less precipitous because the government introduced proportional representation. The need to build a coalition government may make change less easy and governments more cautious, although New Zealand remains a single chamber unitary state with the attendant capacity for innovation.

Antipodean Exceptionalism

What shines through most clearly in these brief comparisons is the contrast between European parliamentary systems and Westminster systems. Given that Denmark and the Netherlands are both decentralized unitary states, and that Britain has started down this road with its devolution reforms, then the contrast between unitary and federal states provides little leverage. But all the Westminster systems share a tradition of strong executive government that could force through reform in response to economic pressures. New Zealand's major reforms were enacted before the shift to proportional representation and coalition government. In Denmark and the Netherlands, despite ostensibly similar economic pressures, any such reform hinged on coalition government operating in a tradition of negotiated consensus. In France, the combination of departmental fragmentation at the centre, coupled with the *grands corps* tradition and its beliefs about a strong state, meant that public sector reform rested on the consent of those about to be reformed. It was not forthcoming. '*Plus ça change, plus c'est la même chose* is the ultimate cliché but, damn it, it just fits French bureaucracy. European traditions shaped reforms, often decisively. Not so in the Antipodes? How do we account for Antipodean exceptionalism?

First, local governmental traditions may be weak. The two countries inherited the Westminster system but almost immediately began to modify them to suit their circumstances. Reformers were more than willing to adopt a pragmatic attitude to their British inheritance, asking only what works. Australia has a cavalier attitude to its machinery of government, changing its structure at will in marked contrast, for example, to Britain, with ostensibly the same tradition but a marked inclination to preserve treasured institutions (Davis *et al*. 1999). In amending the conditions of employment of departmental secretaries both Australia and New Zealand followed a tradition of social and structural experimentation that can be traced back decades.

Second, the answer lies in the way elite actors in general, and departmental secretaries in particular, understood the problems they faced. Both ministers and departmental secretaries see their countries as acutely vulnerable to the pressures of globalization. To be competitive in the international economy, the state had to do less. There was no European Union framework of protectionism. The nation could no longer afford the supportive statism of yesteryear. Although ministers sought to exert greater control, it was not uniquely a party political driven reform. Their respective civil services led reform – the Treasury in New Zealand, Finance and PM&C in Australia. There was an agreed response to a shared definition of the economic dilemma facing Australia and New Zealand. It was not driven by the ideas of the NPM, although they had some influence on leaders of the reform. They raided the current *zeitgeist* for any ideas, especially economic ideas, which looked likely to help. This explains why the leading departmental secretaries were advocates of change. They believed the public services must become more responsive to citizens and accountable to ministers and these ideas had widespread support. The changes came from within as much as without. Where traditions count is in the speed of the reform. Westminster systems with executives subjected to few constraints can legislate almost at will.

CONCLUSION

Has there been a decline in institutional scepticism with departmental secretaries no longer giving frank and fearless advice? Are departmental secretaries too cowed to protect the general interest? Has politicization made it impossible for departmental secretaries to serve governments of different hues effectively? Has there been a loss of institutional memory? In this section we discuss these questions and reflect more broadly on the changing roles and influence of departmental secretaries.

On the first question, most of the arguments assume that, if ministers can dismiss their departmental secretary, then departmental secretaries will only tell the ministers what they want to hear. There is hearsay evidence supporting this argument; people tell of departmental secretaries who are uncertain of their position. No departmental secretary will admit to it – they would say that, wouldn't they? Most will argue it is in the minister's best interest to be told the truth about the likely consequences of decisions. Equally hard to answer is the question of what has changed. There may have been an improvement over the instances where the departmental secretaries ignored the political consequences of their advice for ministers in the knowledge that they were secure from any reprisal. There are many anecdotes to that effect. To the assertion that they are no longer frank and fearless, departmental secretaries will argue they are now responsive to their political masters. Some of the changes come from the politicians' desires for better control of the public service. Equally, some changes stem from within the civil service and the wish of public servants to reform their own environment so they can better serve the government. For all six countries, the argument that advice is now compromised is, at best, non-proven. There have always been tenured officials who prevaricated and procrastinated and contract appointees who acted in the great tradition and 'told it as it was'. There is no substitute for spine.

Public servants in most countries will deny they have a responsibility to protect the national interest that overrides their responsibility to serve the elected government. They will accept that they need to point out the long-term consequences of a policy proposal and to identify the potential problems. They are probably less likely than their predecessors to tell ministers they have the right answer and omit plausible options. But such effortless certainty was always restricted to one or two professional areas anyway (notably finance ministries in their various guises). They may now need to explain how a proposal can get through Parliament or to explain government policy to private and public meetings of interest groups. The boundaries have shifted. Codes and acts recognize the public duty to provide an efficient service. But whether there is a 'public duty' to serve anyone above the government remains controversial and hard to defend. Of course departmental secretaries have a technical competence they can bring to bear on most issues. They should explain why a line of action is the preferable. But they should go so far and no further. The argument that they have a larger duty is vitiated by the question: Who provides that authority? Not the public whose interests are to be defended. The brute simple fact of all parliamentary systems is that there is, and should be, elected democratic control over the policy framework of the public service.

A non-partisan public service is designed to serve governments of all political persuasions. Claims from the opposition often suggest the government has made bipartisanship impossible. Yet, when there are changes of government, the transition seems seamless. A few may lose their position, but in Britain, Denmark and the Netherlands most continue to serve. In France, there is an acceptance that some people will be shifted. A few officials in Australia may feel they do not want to serve a different government. But such people are still rare. Governments may be intent on reshaping the public service, but will acknowledge, in theory at least, that they have an obligation to pass on a working service to their successors.

Recent reforms may create problems for recruiting and promoting the best people for the public service. The Australian experience provides an example. Several departmental secretaries can argue that, as long as a government can shift them, not for any error but because they do not suit the style of the minister, people will not aspire so readily to the top positions. It is not that they are opposed to contracts. Many feel the rigid system of tenure gave too much authority to the departmental secretary who could sit out a minister when there were problems. But they believe that a contract should be genuine, that unless the departmental secretaries err badly there ought to be an expectation that they will serve for the prescribed term. They worry that the decline of a career service will mean the best leave early. Who will come from the private sector to a position that is in effect a tenant at will, who can be terminated by whim, often by a bad minister? If the older system gave too much authority to a departmental secretary who could not be removed, the danger is that the pendulum has given too much influence to the minister. There is a need for a better balance.

There is also a concern that rapid turnover and recruitment from outside the public sector will lead to a loss of institutional memory. Agencies must find people who understand public sector procedures. Gradually public servants build up this intellectual capital, and are not easily replaced. Those who leave can be hired back as contractors. But who will train the next generation of administrators? Contracting and downsizing fragment and scatter memory.

But these problems are far from universal. Again Antipodean exceptionalism confronts European traditionalism. Some countries have seen little change in their institutional position giving them a great capacity, as in Denmark and the Netherlands, to influence policy. The Antipodean contrast with the French system is stark. In France, a combination of technical expertise, professionalism and political motivation will decide who will be selected, and who will depart. But the system looks after its own. As members of a *grand corps* they are, in British parlance, 'one of us', to be looked after in a different post until fortunes change.

So, departmental secretaries are drawn from the public sector and, for several reasons including pay, accountability and knowledge of the system, the public sector will continue to be the main source of recruits for the top position. There is then a premium on keeping that pool of talent sufficiently large to meet the government's needs. There is a growing awareness that the public service not only needs to be reformed but also protected, even cherished. But for now, departmental secretaries continue to sit at the top of a hierarchy where the tasks of political-policy advice (to ministers), management (of their departments) and diplomacy (or managing external relations) come together. It is a singular combination. The balance between the tasks oscillates. But there they sit and any change in their influence is contingent. In all systems, when allied to a strong minister, they remain key actors.

Finally, it is important to correct any impression that top officials are the hapless victims of politically imposed changes. In Westminster systems departmental secretaries led the charge. In European systems they mediated, moderated and in France negated the impact of NPM. And in four of the six systems they were substantially exempt from the changes. The changes they initiated were changes for others. Middle-level managers and other employees might be subject to performance measurement and other types of evaluation and control but not so the top officials. The changes affect 'everybody but us'; a case of do as I say, not as I do. If leadership is the key to improving quality in the public sector, then top officials must do unto themselves as they do unto others if they are 'to walk the talk'.

ACKNOWLEDGEMENTS

This chapter is a revised version of a paper to the Public Administration Committee Annual Conference, 'Modernizing Civil Services', Civil Service College, Sunningdale, 3–5 September 2001. We would like to thank the UK Economic and Social Research Council's (ESRC) Whitehall Programme; the Institute of Political Science, University of Copenhagen and their Danish Research Council (DRC) funded project on 'Democracy and Institutional Change'; and the Centre for Australian Public Sector Management, Griffith University, Brisbane and their Australian Research Council (ARC) funded project on 'The Governance of Australia', for their support. The full report of the research can be found in Rhodes and Weller (2001a) and, as we draw on the individual country studies in that book, we must thank our collaborators Jonathan Boston (Wellington), Robert Elgie (Dublin), Lotte Jensen (Copenhagen) and Jouke de Vries (Leiden).

3. Protecting liberty and benefiting society: can market-based administrative reforms and market-based political institutions effectively co-exist in the US?

Joel D. Aberbach

THE US SYSTEM

The delegates to the American constitutional convention 'shared a hard-headed, unsentimental, skeptical view of the ability of human beings to withstand the temptations of power' (Dahl 1976, p. 73). They started with the assumption that people are self-interested; indeed they believed that the tendency to pursue one's own interests is 'sown in the nature of man' (Hamilton *et al.* 1937, p. 55). They also took it as evident that people had unequal faculties, leading naturally to an unequal distribution of property and other assets. The protection of these 'different and unequal faculties' (ibid. p. 55) was 'the first object of government,' (ibid. p. 55) but another goal was to 'break and control the violence of faction' (ibid. p. 53) (a faction was defined as 'a number of citizens, whether amounting to a majority or minority of the whole, who are united and activated by some common impulse of passion, or of interest, adverse to the rights of other citizens, or the permanent and aggregate interests of the community' (ibid. p. 54)). This second goal was to be achieved by controlling the effects of faction, since to do otherwise would deprive citizens of their liberty. A third goal was to establish and maintain a form of popular government that would achieve these ends.

The final design was a complex system of 'separated institutions sharing powers' (Neustadt 1990, p. 29) in which power would be partitioned so that no one person or institution would control and political leaders would be forced to bargain and compromise. One of the more interesting aspects of the founders' beliefs is that they did not exempt themselves – the elite – from the characterization of self-interest that dominated their analysis of human life. What they aimed for was a partition of power, a system designed 'by so contriving the interior structure of government that its several constituent parts may, by their mutual relations, be the means of keeping each other in their proper places' (Hamilton *et al.* 1937, p. 336). Ambition was to counter-act ambition. The 'interest of the man' was to be connected to 'the constitutional rights of the place' (ibid., p. 337).

The grand design of the system the framers devised was one in which every actor or institution would be checked by another. Power would be diffused. Individuals and institutions would be forced to accommodate one another, and the ambitions of political leaders would be harnessed for the public good. The resemblance to a well-functioning market economy is clear. Self-interested actors would compete, haggle, and produce outcomes result-ing in a political product that protected liberty and benefited the whole.

Where did administration fit into all this? There is little attention to this question in the US Constitution (Wilson 1975, p. 77). Simply put, the framers gave little thought to problems of administrative efficiency and accountability because, while they wanted a national government that would be more effec-tive than the one created by the Articles of Confederation, they did not envisage a large administrative state. Their government was going to coin money, collect some taxes (duties and excise taxes, but no income taxes), provide a uniform postal service, defend the country when necessary (mainly by mobilizing the state militias), conduct relations with foreigners, and the like, but it was not going to be overly intrusive in daily life and it certainly was not going to have a big bureaucracy, let alone a powerful executive branch.

Like the rest of us, the great often cannot see the future clearly, and eventually the government and with it the bureaucracy did grow. Because of the separation of powers system, and the fact that little attention was given to the administrative arm of the state, the bureaucracy that developed has been contested ground. It has multiple masters who vie for control. To quote Norton Long, 'the unanswered question of American government – who is boss? – constantly plagues administration' (Long 1949, p. 264).

The system that evolved has both a highly structured and rule-bound career service (one way of preventing any side from stacking the deck permanently in its favour) and a large number of temporary political appointees to run it (giving each presidential administration the opportunity to exert influence). Interest groups play a big role in the process, as the various actors in the system need allies in their struggle for influence. Alliances tend to form between administrators and members of Congress, particularly those in key committees, and are a source of great concern to presidents who wish to change policies or even influence policy administration. And both for ideo-logical reasons and because most domestic programmes were products of the Democrats, Republicans tend to be highly suspicious of government agencies and their personnel. All this in a context where 'since usually no one set of institutional actors has clear control and signals often conflict, it is difficult to hold the bureaucracy, or any other institution, reasonably to account' (Aberbach 1990, p. 4).

SEARCHING FOR A NEW PUBLIC MANAGEMENT: SOME DILEMMAS

Given the features of the American system, it is hardly surprising that there is a large US literature on bureaucratic problems and pathologies. American political scientists have long concerned themselves with problems such as iron triangles and the conditions under which they dominate policy, the failed attempts by the Progressives to separate politics and administration, the difficulties faced by elected officials in controlling the behaviour of bureaucrats, the tendency of political appointees to 'go native' once they take up their appointments in government agencies, and problems in securing efficiency in the public sector on a par with that supposedly found in the private sector. And American economists, particularly micro-economic theorists and the public choice political scientists inspired by them, have found the public sector a fertile subject for analysis. Ideas variously labelled agency theory, the new institutional economics, and transaction cost economics have taken root in the US. Clearly the fears of public choice theorists that the American bureaucracy is in league with special interests and with the particularistic interests advantaged by the committee system in Congress have a foundation in the facts. And equally clearly, as Colin Campbell notes in a recent article (Campbell 2001, pp. 253–82), much of the reform programme we commonly call New Public Management (NPM) reflects the thinking of US analysts and seems, on the surface, particularly well suited to reforming the US system.

Culturally, ideas rooted in notions about the dominance of self-interest and ways to use self-interest to control and channel behaviour (the basic notions of the new institutional economics and its brethren) ought to find a ready home in the US. As noted above, the theory behind the American political system has much in common with a market; selfish actors placed in competition with the hope that a general good will be the product of actors seeking to achieve their own interests. If that system produces pathologies, one can easily imagine that an appealing cure would call for a more rigorous application of a well-known medicine (the mechanisms of competition and private sector practices) that Americans believe have made the US a great economic success. My argument, however, is that the very features that make the US political system resemble a market also make it particularly difficult to apply many of the features of New Public Management.

In short, the US system focuses on political and institutional competition and the use of politics to maintain liberty. Institutions were designed to harness self-interest for the public good and to make sure that no faction dominated. Compromise and accommodation were the names of the game. Management was an after-thought, and not much of one at that. So administration is jerry-built on a purposefully convoluted political structure. It often does not work as well as one would like, is subject to capture by special interests, suffers from complex agency problems, and is highly contested politically. One might describe the American system as seeking a form of political rationality (policies acceptable to a majority that do not fundamentally damage the minority) at a cost in administrative rationality (initially not seen as a great cost because administration was, for the most part, ignored). The system stresses the politics of bargaining and complex solutions accommodating numerous institutional and economic interests over administration. If political and administrative goals or needs happen to clash, politics is more likely to triumph and to triumph more completely than in many other systems. New Public Management is about what Michael Barzelay has termed 'policy interventions within executive government' (2001, p. 156). Not only is executive government the most unclear part of US government, it is the part likely to fare worst when decisions are made because all those competing actors are likely to put their own needs, values or advantages first. This is not to say that NPM will be unappealing or fail to make inroads in the US, but simply that it will have a difficult time when market-based administrative reforms do not happen to mesh well with market-based political institutions and politics.

WHERE DO WE GO FROM HERE?

What I want to do now is: 1) give a brief introduction to NPM, especially as it has been attempted in the United States; 2) discuss issues in applying NPM in the US; and 3) raise some general issues about NPM, particularly about problems in applying private sector solutions to public management. The basic approach involves contrasting what NPM calls for with practices of the 'old' public administration or the private sector in order to illuminate conceptual and practical difficulties faced by NPM-inspired reforms.

NPM IN THE UNITED STATES

In his book on *The Global Management Revolution*, Donald Kettl says of the New Public Management that it 'stemmed from the basic economic argument that government suffered from the defects of monopoly, high transaction costs, and information problems that bred great inefficiencies. By substituting market competition – and market like incentives – the reformers believed that they could shrink government's size, reduce its costs, and improve its performance' (Kettl 2000a, p. 13–14). It would be an overstatement to say that NPM represents a coherent theory – it combines doctrines from the new institutional economics and managerialism – but it is about as theoretically based as any set of reforms one is likely to see in government, and it has transformed the academic study of administration and the actual conduct of administration in fundamental ways (Peters and Wright 1996, p. 628).

Allen Schick's influential report on the New Zealand reforms (the purest example of New Public Management) stresses that analysis of the deficiencies of New Zealand's government was deduced 'from the logic of institutional economics, not from the systematic study of public organizations' (Schick 1996, p. 18). Managerial concepts were important and account for ideas such as freeing managers to manage, but the contractualism and other 'most conspicuous' elements of the reforms stemmed from the microeconomics-based theory 'that government should be organized to minimize opportunism and transaction costs in relationships between self-interested parties' (Schick 1996, p. 23). (Actually, even the 'let managers manage' notions have roots in economic ideas, especially the notions about customer demand and preference (Aberbach and Rockman 2000a, p. 139–40).)

In any event, the New Zealand reforms were clearly marked by exceptional 'conceptual rigour and intellectual coherence' (Boston *et al.* 1996, p. 3). Indeed, Christopher Hood (1990a, p. 210) described the 1987 government document laying them out (the Treasury report titled *Government Management*) as the 'manifesto' of NPM. And Hood stresses that the document explicitly relates the elements of the actual reform programme to a set of 'cardinal principles' of administrative reform (ibid.).

Boston *et al.* (1996, p. 26), in their analysis of the 'New Zealand Model,' lay out a list of ten core NPM features that include notions such as the following:

- Public and private organizations can be managed on the same basis; with private sector management processes such as 'short-term labour contracts, the development of strategic plans', performance agreements, and performance-based compensation systems.
- Accountability should be for results and not process.
- Management control should be devolved, accompanied by 'improved reporting, monitoring and accountability mechanisms'.
- Most services now publicly funded should be either privatized or at least open to contest by private providers (contracting out).

- A preference for monetary incentives over non-monetary incentives.
- An emphasis on cost-cutting and cutback management.

We know that the American reformers were significantly inspired by the principles and actions of New Zealand and others because they told us so in the introduction to their own manifesto entitled *The Report of the National Performance Review*, often referred to simply as the Gore Report (1993, p. xxxviii). The report had the modest goal of 'creating a government that works better and costs less'. The nation could do no less, it told us, because the US must not be left behind in a situation where 'the needs of information-age societies were colliding with the limits of industrial-era government'. This was not a matter of choice, not a function of an optional change in ideology; it was an 'absolute necessity' (ibid.).

The American version of NPM was commonly called 'reinventing government' (or NPR for the National Performance Review) under the Clinton administration and has more or less continued (although without this label) in the Bush administration. Kettl's argument, in agreement with the report's language, is that 'the American reforms rank among the most sweeping' since they 'sought to transform the entire federal government in a very short time' (Kettl 2000a, p. 31), but he also notes that the actual product has 'been incremental rather than sweeping and comprehensive' (Kettl 2000a, p. 62).

NPR had three phases. NPR-1 stressed how government should work and developed four key 'principles' to organize its proposals. These were cutting red tape, putting customers first, empowering employees to get results, and cutting back to basics. Despite its emphasis on the 'how' of government, the last principle in this group (cutting back to basics) has clear and strong implications for the 'what' of government.

For the moment, though, the point to stress is that these principles have clear roots in the NPM movement. The first principle of NPR, cutting red tape, encompasses proposals for cutting regulations of all types, including internal regulations and regulations imposed on states and localities. Important proposals include minimizing restrictions on spending by agencies, decentralizing the personnel process by giving managers greater authority to hire, reward, and fire workers, and reforming procurement rules.

The second principle, putting customers first, inspired a series of proposals that involve not only the recipients of government benefits and services, but also the ways in which government organizations should be run. In the first instance, customers' views are to be solicited, in what might be termed the usual meaning of the admonition to put them first. The report, however, goes beyond that to endorse other market-oriented aspects of NPM. For example, where possible, agencies should be made to compete either with private providers or with each other if no private entity can perform a task. Where government monopolies are judged unavoidable, they should be run as much as possible like private sector companies. And where a current federal function can be shifted to markets – job training and workplace inspection are some examples cited – they should be.

A third principle, empowering employees to get results, is meant to 'create a culture of entrepreneurship' in the bureaucracy (Gore 1993, p. 66). Suggestions include giving lower-level employees more authority to make decisions and cutting the number of supervisory personnel. However, NPR also strongly endorses holding employees accountable for results, and therefore the NPR Report embraces the landmark Government Performance and Results Act (GPRA) passed in 1993. GPRA calls for strategic plans and annual performance plans with measurable goals. The NPR Report also refers approvingly to Britain's performance contracts and suggests that a similar system be adopted in the US.

The fourth principle endorsed by NPR-1 is cutting back to basics. Although, as noted above, this concerns the 'what' of government, an area that was meant to be the emphasis of NPR-2, the report stressed the importance of eliminating 'what we don't need' (Gore 1993, p. 145). This is an uncontroversial goal on the surface, but it does not take a deep knowledge of politics to guess that one person's unneeded programme is often another's high priority.

NPR-1 endorsed savings of $108 billion over five years, much of it from eliminating jobs in the bureaucracy. NPR-2, adopted in the wake of the Democrats' loss of Congress in 1994, advocated an additional set of savings of about $70 billion, mainly through programme changes, terminations, and privatization. This emphasis on cutting the bureaucracy and saving money (the 'costs less' part of the initiative), not surprisingly, became the main focus of public discussion about the reinvention initiative, with the 'works better' component a distant second in attention.

NPR-3 focused on improving a set of 'high impact agencies', those, in Donald Kettl's words, 'that dealt most directly with citizens and where failure ... could prove managerially and political damaging' (1998, p. 5). It also emphasized outcome measures, part of a trend widespread in other nations and called for in the GPRA, to move past outputs to the ultimate impact of government programmes. The problem, of course, is that the causes of outcomes are complicated enough so that few government programmes have control over them. The nation's health and safety and its economy, for example, are affected by numerous factors and it is often unclear how much impact federal programmes have had.

While Vice President Gore, the architect of the NPR in the Clinton administration, failed his 2000 bid for the presidency, his opponent, George W. Bush, basically continued many of the reinvention initiatives without using that designation. The FY 2002 budget document, for example, talks about re-examining the role of the federal government, and creating a government that is 'citizen-centered, not bureaucracy-centered,' 'results-oriented, not process-oriented,' and 'market-based' (OMB 2001, p. 1. See also Bush's memo to department heads dated 11 July 2001.) The administration's FY2003 budget proposal attempts to use performance analyses to guide funding choices, though it delicately admits that its attempts are 'far from perfect' (Peckenpaugh 2002a). The Bush administration has also been very active in trying to pro-mote competitions between private firms and federal workers for the jobs performed by workers that are listed as candidates for such competitions under the provisions of the Federal Activities Inventory Reform (FAIR) Act. During the campaign Bush promised to require competitions for up to half of the 850 000 jobs on the list, and the Director of the Office of Management and Budget has made proposals to begin implementing this promise (Friel 2001a; Agresta 2001). Obviously, NPR continues in spirit, if not in name.

How successful have NPR and the related Bush programmes been? Has American government been reinvented? That is not an easy question to answer, of course, but Donald Kettl, who has studied the reinvention effort more than most, gives it a grade of 'B'. That sounds pretty good, although one must remember the grade inflation that has taken hold in US universities. What is interesting are the components of the grade. Kettl (2000b) gives NPR high marks (As) for procurement reform and 'effort'. NPR gets low marks (Cs or worse) for identifying the objectives of government, performance improve-ments, political leadership, and, highly significantly in a separation of powers political system, relations with Congress (a subject I'll come back to later). In short, while it is fair to argue that government has been shaken-up (it is smaller, for example, although much of the downsizing was due to cuts in the Defense Department accompanying the end of the Cold War and now subject to change in the post-September 11 environment), it is much less than clear that it is better.

What is clear is the strong hold the rhetoric of the market now has on government reform efforts. But at the same time, there has been relatively little thought given to how the reform elements fit together. As Bert Rockman and I summarized the effort:

> NPR aims to cut programmes, save money, contract out government functions, privatize, rely on competition and markets, and adopt private sector techniques in a redesigned administrative system that emphasizes results. It also endorses bot-tom-up management and a focus on customer satisfaction. It says little about what should happen if the elements clash (Aberbach and Rockman 2000a, p. 142.)

In brief, a major strength of reinvention in the US has been in its rhetoric. It has appeal in a culture nurtured on markets and competition. The weakness of reinvention has been in its implementation and also, of course, in the questionable nature of some of its proposals, but at a broader level an important element of its weakness lies in problems fitting it with the American political system.

I now turn to a discussion of some of the problems of applying NPM in the context of American politics and institutional design. The emphasis is on the fit of NPM-inspired reforms to the situation in the US. Most of the discussion is organized around contrasts between what NPM calls for and the currently prevailing situation. The last two contrasts discussed involve more general issues, one concerning theory and the other the difference between the public and private sectors.

ISSUES IN APPLYING NPM IN THE US

Efficiency Versus Politics

To reiterate a point developed earlier, a fundamental difficulty facing US reformers operating in the orbit of NPM is that the United States government was not designed for administrative efficiency. NPM, on the other hand, though it is not wholly consistent, is focused on efficiency. The telling slogan of the National Performance Review was 'works better, costs less'. The goal was endorsed by just about everyone because it is the political equivalent of promising heaven on earth, but the problem in the real world is to bring all the relevant decision makers into line so that there is agreement about what the government should be doing in a given area, who should be doing it, how it should be done and at what cost. A major weakness of NPR was its failure to involve Congress in most of the reinvention exercise. One can understand why reformers who wished to produce a report quickly and make assertive statements would act in this way, but it made implementation exceedingly difficult. To take an example, 84 per cent of the savings developed by the designers of NPR-2 required legislative changes. That is because, as *In the Web of Politics* suggests, 'many of the "inefficiencies" in [American] administration are legislatively mandated, suggesting a political source for the problem rather than an administrative source' (Aberbach and Rockman 2000a, p. 142). These administrative 'inefficiencies' often protect particular interests or constituencies, and the US system is ill-designed to root them out.

Basics Versus Coalition Building

NPM, especially in its US version, puts a major emphasis on cutting government 'back to basics'. However, coalition building (and often social justice) requires that government (or its surrogates) do more than basics and often that they do it in a manner that is less than economically sound. Coalition building can be difficult in any political system, but it is especially difficult in a system such as that in the US, which puts such a high premium on coalition building and then puts such high barriers in front of the coalition builders. When one adds to the mix the likely controversy in defining what is basic and what is not, the US system is not well positioned to deal with decision making on 'basics' in an effective or consistent manner.

The American literature strongly emphasizes that US government programme goals are often unclear. John Kingdon, for example, argues that clarifying goals 'is often counterproductive because constructing a coalition involves persuading people to agree on a specific proposal when they might not agree on a set of goals to be achieved' (Kingdon 1984, p. 82). The result is programmes with unclear goals but well-placed support and all the difficulties this presents in implementing many aspects of NPM/NPR such as performance contracting and deciding what programmes the government does not need, that is, those that are not 'basic'.

Short-term Versus Long-term Time Horizons

At least in theory, and probably in practice, government decision-makers face a shorter-term time horizon than those in the private sector. Several years ago Graham Allison wrote a famous paper based on one of Wallace Sayre's 'laws,' namely that 'public and private management are fundamentally alike in all unimportant respects' (Allison 1999, p. 14). Allison's article draws on the reflections of high-level American executives who served in both sectors. The first contrast cited in the paper is time perspective:

> Government managers tend to have relatively short time horizons dictated by political necessities and the political calendar, while private managers appear to take a longer time perspective oriented toward market developments, technological innovation and investment, and organization building. (Allison 1999, p. 18)

One can certainly argue the case that modern private sector managers face greater pressures to show profits in the short term than those a few years ago, but there is little doubt that public sector executives and politicians in democratic systems are more consistently driven by the electoral calendar. And this calendar is quite short in the US where the House of Representatives is elected every two years. The contract system for public sector executives is a way to overcome this, but it clashes with the short-term pressures brought on by American's insistently frequent elections.

Customers Versus Interest Groups

NPR/NPM assumes that agencies can be reoriented to serve consumers, but the US system puts a premium on organized interests promoting themselves and defending their turf. Where those defined as the customers and the major organized groups are strongly overlapping sets, the case, for example, where policy whirlpools or iron triangles exist (Baumgartner and Jones 1993), or where the customers are close to a universe of the population or pay a fee for the services they receive, the Postal Service for example, there should be little controversy about the customer service movement. However, the more controversial the area, the more likely it is that there will be serious debate about providing services according to customer preferences and demands. Certainly in many areas where there are regulated interests or low status benefit recipients (such as welfare), many in society have a stake in the policy area and in the way it is administered. The interests of the regulated and the rest of the public may well clash or the funds redistributed from the better off to the poor may create serious conflicts about what should be provided. Whose interests should be served in such cases? Who, say in the case of food or broadcasting regulation, are the customers? The answers to these questions are not always clear, with politics the likely mechanism for determining the outcome.

On a related point, the language that Donald Kettl uses to describe the customer service movement is quite stark: 'The reforms have sought to transform the culture of public organizations, including encouraging employees to think about citizens as 'customers' to be served instead of 'clients' to be managed' (Kettl 1997, p. 452). Kettl's notion of bureaucrats managing clients certainly fits traditional American welfare bureaucracies quite well, but in many, perhaps most, other areas, it is the organized customers, that is, the interest groups, who have huge influence on management and who are served quite well. Few would oppose government agencies treating their clients with greater courtesy and respect, but many are uncomfortable with 'putting them first' because in many areas they already receive great deference.

Finally, there is some doubt about the NPR's market analogies about customer service. The assumption is that customer satisfaction is a primary goal in the private sector. Actually, the goal is profit. Satisfying customers is a means to that end, not the end in itself. Aside from the desire of private businesses to minimize competition so that they can maximize profits (at the expense of consumers), businesses must make a trade-off between what customers would like (outstanding service) and what they would like to pay (low prices). As a result, one must use customer satisfaction surveys of the type recommended by NPR very carefully.

Flexibility Versus Procedures

The National Performance Review and most NPM-inspired reform move-
ments put a major emphasis on 'cutting red tape'. The goal is greater flexibility
in administration so that the organization can be run more efficiently and
effectively. It is hard to argue with such lofty goals. However, one should
keep in mind the benefits as well as the costs of 'red tape'. As Herbert
Kaufman (1977) argues in his classic book on the subject, many of the
annoying procedures prevalent in bureaucratic organizations were created to
ensure due process, protect people from abuses, and make sure that affected
interests have a say in the policy process. Recent rules also promote openness
in decision-making. These are benefits that most in a democratic society
favour. One of the most challenging problems facing the movement to cut
regulations is the need to balance costs and benefits.

As Bert Rockman and I recently observed, 'administrative flexibility is
likely to be regarded as a virtue until some basic interest is damaged by it.
Then there will be a demand to have procedures put back into place to ensure
fairness, transparency, predictability, and related values' (Aberbach and
Rockman 2000a, p. 144). Peter Aucoin, whose work focuses on Westminster
parliamentary systems, notes that the crucial test of administrative deregulation in these systems will come 'when the inevitable administrative mistakes
and thus political embarrassments occur or when deviations from newly
accepted norms, such as employment equity, are discovered' (Aucoin 1990,
p. 132). This is even more likely in the US where members of Congress
regularly demand new rules and procedures when there are scandals and
abuses, and they are well positioned through the congressional committee
system to get them adopted. Indeed, Congress is the source of most of the
rules now in place that reformers would like to see cut.

Decentralization Versus Centralization

This is an oft-noted problem with the application of NPM (which has
attached itself to a pre-existing trend in this case). Reinvention seeks to set
loose the creative energies of employees, make them more responsive to
customers, and hold them accountable for results. These goals can clash. The
literature talks about the tension between the '*let* managers manage' and the
'*make* managers manage' elements of NPM. The let managers manage
approach starts from the assumption that managers know the right things to
do and that freeing them from unnecessary restrictions and supervision will
lead to the creative solution of problems. As Kettl notes, the customer service
movement is at the core of the let managers manage approach, focusing
managers on dealing with the '"works better" side of the "works better/costs

less" dilemma'. The make managers manage approach has goals set from the top, with managers given extensive freedom to do what they deem necessary to achieve the goals. The two, Kettl argues, 'drive in opposite directions' (Kettl 1997, p. 449). The American designers of NPR were unconcerned about any contradictions between them and borrowed liberally from each.

Private Service Versus Civil Service

Personnel policy is a key element in implementing New Public Management reforms. Government employees, NPM stresses, should be competent, innovative, and highly responsive to their environment (be it to top political leaders or customers, depending on the emphasis). Techniques employed include performance pay and bonuses, contracts with top executives and competition between government providers and private providers or within government itself between potential providers. Important assumptions are that monetary incentives are the way to motivate government employees to perform their jobs and that simulating the private sector to the extent possible is the way to produce results. In short, to make government work better, the more it looks like the private sector and has employee incentive structures like the private sector, the better it will be and the more likely that it will not be badly victimized by principal-agent problems.

US personnel policy reforms nearly a quarter century old put an emphasis on enhancing bureaucratic responsiveness. The somewhat unusual American public executive system, with large numbers of political appointees at the top (in office for limited terms) and career civil servants below them, means that many top executives were already effectively on short-term contracts (although without the prospect of financial bonuses) well before NPM. Ironically, because bureaucracy is such a contested area in American politics, the career civil service system, once established, was quite rigid, largely in reaction to the spoils system at the top. However, civil servants were also highly suspect politically, in part because many agencies are identified with programmes created by one of the parties (Democrats, for example, established and initially staffed most of the major social service agencies) and in part because civil servants have often made alliances with key members of congressional committees, something they do to protect themselves and their programmes in the complex political and institutional environment in Washington. As a result, presidential administrations (Republican administrations with particular intensity) have often regarded career civil servants with suspicion. This contributed to a set of reforms that reflect political concerns about bureaucratic responsiveness, reforms whose origins and purposes are probably more complex than those in many other nations affected by NPM.

The Civil Service Reform Act of 1978 created the Senior Executive Service (SES). SES replaced the previous rank-in-position system with a
rank-in-the-person system. The new service had the rhetorical ring of an elite
corps, but it also could be used politically because SES members could now
be moved from position to position without losing status. SES members were
to be eligible for a variety of bonuses and cash awards, features clearly
imitating private sector management practices emphasizing pay for performance, but also containing obvious possibilities for political manipulation.
Executives were to be evaluated using performance criteria, with those not
measuring up subject to removal. A few provisions were designed to promote
political responsiveness of an obviously partisan nature (administrations were
allowed to appoint up to 10 per cent of the SES executives government-wide
and up to 25 per cent in any agency), but most were at least ostensibly based
on notions about obtaining bureaucratic responsiveness familiar to readers of
literature related to the new institutional economics. In short, the new personnel system contained a mix of tools to promote responsiveness, a few directly
inspired by partisan considerations and most by an economic view of what it
takes to motivate civil servants to higher levels of performance. The latter
view certainly dominated the public rhetoric.

Several debates have raged about the public service in this environment.
One raises questions about quality, asserting that the calibre of civil servants
has declined, in large part because of public denigration by politicians and
the undermining effects of efforts like President Nixon's 'Responsiveness
Programme'. A second concerns the degree of political responsiveness of
career civil servants. The gradual ascendance of Republicans since the 1968
election has brought these issues to the forefront. Another issue concerns the
role of political appointees. Many see the elaborate (and growing) body of
political appointees as an impediment to effective management. Remuneration for public employees, a subject that goes to the heart of any system using
monetary incentives to induce responsiveness, has been debated in many
forms, with the bonus system under SES and pay for high level executives
receiving significant attention. Finally, contracting out, privatization, and
public-private competitions all have implications for the role of the civil
service.

Quality
Despite an often vicious campaign by politicians to denigrate the civil service
and a series of reports by prestigious public commissions and academics
warning of a 'quiet crisis' and worse at the top of the civil service (Volcker
Commission 1989), the available evidence is that public service has so far
held its own. Top civil servants in the US are highly educated, quite dedi-
cated, and maintain high morale in the face of heavy criticism and dire

predictions. In addition, certainly in educational attainments, they compare quite favourably to top private sector executives (Aberbach and Rockman 2000a, pp. 58–86). The current worry is that a large number of top public sector executives will soon retire and that the thinning out of the ranks beneath them as part of NPR's reduction of middle managers has left an inadequate pool for drawing replacements, and this may prove to be the case, but the data indicate that high quality people continue to find their way to the top of the career system, suggesting that public service at the federal level in the United States has an appeal despite its relatively low pay and its relative lack of prestige. And there are signs that the terrorist attack of 11 September 2001 may eventually increase the pool of those who want to work for the government, particularly the pool of young adults (Barr 2001, p. 2).

Political responsiveness

The Nixon administration was obsessed by fears of political unresponsiveness. This was particularly focused on career civil servants, but extended even to the administration's own political appointees. Nixon was convinced that the civil service was dominated by Democrats and made numerous efforts to diminish its influence on policy and change its composition.

While Nixon's administration succumbed to the Watergate scandal (and the subsequent congressional hearings that focused on the larger pattern of abuses in his administration), the next activist Republican president continued his quest to control the placement of bureaucrats and to isolate them as much as possible from important policy decisions. Reagan's administration had great success using the provisions of the Civil Service Reform Act of 1978 that allowed presidents to appoint some members of the SES and to move civil servants around agencies with greater ease. Data in our studies, for example, show how effective Reagan's people were in putting Republican careerists in top positions in the social service agencies, a major focus of their concern. In addition, our data show a rightward shift over time in the party affiliations and political ideologies of top civil servants (Aberbach and Rockman 2000a, pp. 101–19). The obvious conclusion is that, by any reasonable standard, the US bureaucracy appears to be a quite flexible and politically responsive institution. With determined use of the provisions of the Civil Service Reform Act, presidential administrations now have the tools, *if they choose to use them*, to at least limit bureaucratic influence and to shape parts of the bureaucracy to their liking. In short, the reforms enacted provided presidents with greater opportunities to shape a politically responsive executive branch.

Remuneration

While the clearly political elements of the reform have had relatively smooth sailing, the economic parts have faced rougher seas. The bonus system established by the reform act came under attack almost immediately. Congress reduced the number of those eligible to receive bonuses and then the Office of Management and Budget (OMB) used its rulemaking authority to further reduce the number eligible. The result was an unhappy set of top career civil servants, many of whom had consented to join the new SES lured by the promise that the bonus system would increase their compensation over the pay-compressed limits set by congressional salaries. Add to this the complaints by many career executives that the distribution of bonuses was unfair and manipulated for political purposes and one has a formula for great dissatisfaction (and probably a relatively ineffective and inefficient incentive system). The system was improved in the late 1980s by increasing the number of executives eligible for bonuses and later by increasing base pay starting in 1991 after a congressional pay raise, but it is clearly difficult to administer incentive pay schemes in an administrative climate as politically charged as the one in the United States (Aberbach and Rockman 2000b). And because of political limits placed on compensation, it has proven extraordinarily difficult to raise general levels of compensation to compete with the private sector, although there have been efforts to exempt some agencies and some job classifications (mainly technical ones) from the general limits imposed by the federal pay system.

Contracting out

The United States government has had a mixed history with contracting out. Department of Defense experiences with private contractors, for example, have been subject to repeated cost overruns and scandals involving excessive charges by the private sector. Still the notion of private sector efficiency remains strong and contracting has increased in scope, dominating spending in agencies like Defense, Energy, and NASA and in areas where agency competencies are weak like the development of information technology applications. The Federal Activities Inventory Reform Act of 1998 (the FAIR Act) required federal agencies to inventory all positions where employees perform commercial-like functions available from the private sector. The act did not require that the government go further than this, but the Bush administration announced plans to outsource or hold public-private competitions on 5 per cent of all government jobs considered 'commercial in nature' in fiscal 2002 and 10 per cent of them in fiscal 2003 (Friel 2001b). (About 850 000 federal jobs held by approximately half of the civilian federal workforce are on the list.)

These plans almost immediately ignited controversy, with Congress hearing testimony on something called the Truthfulness, Responsibility and

Accountability in Contracting (TRAC) Act that 'would freeze all current contracted activities to determine if they could be performed more cost effectively by the public sector' and ban targeted contracting-out of federal jobs (Peckenpaugh 2001). There is disagreement, as one might imagine, about how to compare costs and effectiveness across the sectors (the act's sponsor noted that a freeze on contracts was necessary to force agencies to improve contract oversight and track savings from contracting out). Particularly significant is the fact that Tom Davis, Republican chair of the House subcommittee with jurisdiction over this legislation (who is from a district in Virginia straddling the famous Washington beltway and home to numerous federal workers), was quoted as saying that he was 'alarmed' by the Bush administration's competition targets (ibid.). And, not surprisingly, Democrats have been especially active in challenging contracting methods and outsourcing. Their aim in advocating 'in-sourcing' is to make the public sector more competitive for jobs by 'subjecting equal numbers of contractor and government jobs to public-private competitions each year', a proposal strongly opposed by the Bush administration (Peckenpaugh 2002b). General contracting out is clearly going to be difficult to implement, particularly in light of the fact that the congressional committee system puts people whose constituencies are greatly affected by decisions in this area into key decision-making positions.

Overview
Despite great fears to the contrary, the civil service continues to hold its own in the US. Top civil servants, in fact, compare favourably to private sector executives in many ways, but their levels of compensation lag far behind. Civil service reform has impacted political responsiveness significantly. Its impact in other areas has been more modest. That is probably not too surprising in retrospect, given that the ambiguous position of the civil service in the US constitutional system highlights issues of political responsiveness. For similar reasons, nothing has been done to reduce the layers of political appointees at the top of the administrative hierarchy – in fact, their numbers have increased. The complex politics of the American public sector make even widely accepted notions like contracting out subjects for serious debate and open to political challenge. The use of bonuses and other monetary performance incentives has been implemented, but their effects are limited by severe constraints on the amounts that can be offered. The problems of making pay at the top of the public service match the pay of similar positions in the private sector are huge and probably not solvable. And the use of modest monetary incentives in such a situation is not likely to have the impacts on behaviour hoped for by NPM theorists. It may be better to re-emphasize the notion that public service is a different calling than private

service, with rewards that transcend the monetary. The next section discusses some recent evidence to support this notion.

Incentives Versus Reciprocity

NPM draws many of its ideas on motivating managers to perform better from economists' notions about incentives, principal-agent theory, and the like. However, contemporary experimental research raises serious questions about how to motivate agents. Gary J. Miller and Andrew Whitford, for example, presented a paper based on experimental evidence that challenges the conclusions of principal-agent theory and its implications for public bureaucracy. They found, consistent with other experimental data on 'trust-based' contracting, that:

> reciprocity (even in situations where contracts cannot be monitored or enforced) can provide efficiency improvements in social exchange. In a setting of public bureaucracy, we may suppose that this possibility reintroduces a range of managerial considerations that are secondary or omitted altogether from principal-agent theory. Foremost might be the creation and communication of reciprocity norms, combined with the selection of public employees … willing and able to engage such norms in a productive way.
>
> Furthermore, the results suggest that leadership that emphasizes reciprocity with subordinates may well be more effective than a leadership style that starts from the assumption that financial incentives are the only means for motivating subordinates (Miller and Whitford 2001, pp. 32–3).

The paper argues that emphasizing 'the necessity of a high incentive bonus eliminates the sense of social obligation, and therefore crowds out the social motivation of reciprocity' (ibid., 28). And it suggests instead emphasizing traditional notions in the public bureaucracy literature such as cooperation in a hierarchy, loyalty, and professionalism and its obligations. As the noted American athlete and commentator, Yogi Berra, once remarked: 'It's *déjà vu*, all over again'.

Profits Versus Performance

In the private sector, the bottom line rules, as American dot-com firms have now discovered. Companies can calculate their profits according to a standard metric and by generally agreed upon standards and they can be compared to others. (Not all do so, of course, as the Enron/Arthur Andersen scandal in the US makes all too clear.) The public sector rarely has a clear bottom line and it is often quite difficult to compare public operations to competitors. One goal of NPM-related reforms has been to bridge this gap by simulating markets through such mechanisms as within- and between-sector competition and by holding public organizations accountable for results. The latter has been a major emphasis of NPR in the US through its embrace of the Government Performance and Results Act (GPRA) of 1993.

GPRA requires agencies to set goals, measure performance, and report on results. Agencies must produce strategic (five-year) plans, annual performance plans, and annual reports on programme performance. According to the act, performance goals must be expressed in 'objective, quantifiable, and measurable form', and 'establish performance outputs, service levels, and outcomes of each programme activity' (Government Performance and Results Act 1993). Agencies were instructed to consult with Congress and others as they go about implementing the act and can receive OMB exemptions from certain non-statutory rules and regulations if that will help improve programme results.

The act has been a success in many ways. Agencies have produced performance plans, and there has been a significant effort by the General Accounting Office to evaluate progress towards full implementation. The problems, however, tell us much about the endeavour, especially in light of the focus of this paper – the fit of NPM to US government.

A major GAO government-wide survey done in 2000 of managers at 28 agencies showed that only at a fourth of the agencies did 50 per cent or more of the managers say that they used performance information for setting priorities, allocating resources, setting job expectations and the like (General Accounting Office 2001, p. 3). And a recent poll indicates that these problems persist, despite the Bush administration's emphasis on results-oriented government (Ballard, 2002). Indeed, the administration's highly touted effort to link dollars to deeds shows many of the flaws one would expect from a politically charged process. For example, while President Bush promised in his campaign and in well-publicized post-campaign memos from OMB to implement what the administration labels 'the President's budget and performance integration management initiative' (Daniels 2002), the administration's FY 2003 budget was selective in its use of its own performance ratings. As Richard Stevenson notes of a particularly egregious, although politically and policy driven, example of this selectivity: 'Although the Pentagon was judged to have serious flaws in all five categories of the management scorecard featured in the budget, Mr Bush is calling for $48 billion in new spending on the military, the biggest increase since the Reagan administration' (Stevenson 2002, pp. 1–2).

Whatever problems the executive branch has had with measuring performance and then using the results, and the preceding paragraph suggest that the problems are considerable, Congress continues to budget on its own system, so the links of performance data to final budget decisions are, at minimum, unclear. Indeed, Congress has been very leery of using performance criteria on a systematic basis. As former Republican member of Congress Bill Frenzel observed in Stevenson's account of the Bush administration's efforts to link performance ratings to the budget: 'Congress usually sees this sort of thing [the White House/OMB scorecards on agency performance] as a way to distort its priorities, afraid that unfavourable standards will be set for departments that are favourites of certain members of Congress' (Stevenson 2002, p. 2).

Moreover, members of Congress have been critical of agencies for failing to solve problems of overlap and duplication through their strategic plans, but it is Congress that mandates most of the overlap and duplication through statute, so this is a particularly hypocritical criticism. Indeed, on a more general level, while GPRA tells the agencies to state their goals clearly, that is often quite difficult for legal or political reasons because of the way Congress has written the authorizing statutes (Aberbach and Rockman 2000a, p. 52).

Agencies have also had great difficulty obtaining reliable performance data. The General Accounting Office reports only limited confidence in the credibility of performance data in the majority of agency fiscal year 2000 performance plans it examined (GAO 1999, p. 27). Also, the federal government relies on states and localities to implement many of its programmes, and the data produced by these governments have severe weaknesses (GAO 2001, p. 10). Finally, while measuring outcomes is the aim of GPRA, the federal government often has a quite limited or indirect influence in determining whether a goal is achieved.

In sum, problems flowing from the separation of powers, the federal system, political priorities, non-credible performance data, and significant technical difficulties in linking government actions to outcomes have hampered the very promising efforts of the federal government to implement GPRA.

CONCLUDING COMMENTS

The American system of 'separated institutions sharing powers' was set up on the assumption that people, including governing elites, are self-interested. The basic idea was that a government structured to promote competition would lead to actors checking one another, diffused power, compromise, and political outcomes that protected liberty and benefited the society. A problem from the contemporary perspective is that little thought was given to administration, and the bureaucracy that eventually developed has been contested ground, with multiple masters vying for control and the bureaucracy itself often taking steps to shore up political support for its programmes.

Concern about bureaucratic control (or lack thereof) has contributed to a large literature about the subject in the US, including a strong voice for economic ideas such as agency theory and the new institutional economics. This literature in turn has been a major inspiration for the New Public Management. It endorses market competition and market-like incentives as a way to reduce government's size and costs and improve its performance. Given both the self-interest assumptions of American government and the hold that free market ideas have in American culture, one would think that the American version of NPM, called reinventing government or NPR, would be a major success. However, NPR has been a mixed success at best (with a leading scholar of reinvention giving it an A+ for effort, but tellingly only a C+ for performance improvements and a D for identifying the objectives of government and for relations with Congress (Kettl 2000a)). My argument is that this is not surprising, in part because the very features that make the US political system resemble a market make it difficult to apply many of the features of NPM (market-based administrative reforms do not always mesh well with market-based political institutions and politics) and in part because of problems with some of the NPM ideas themselves.

The rhetoric of the market has aided in acceptance of the concepts behind the reforms, but problems in applying NPM in the US are many and varied. Many flow from the fact that the US government was not designed for administrative efficiency and its complex political structures make it difficult to implement NPM reforms. These design features put an emphasis on coalition building, yielding programmes with unclear goals (as well as unusual problems in deciding what all political systems have difficulty deciding, namely what is a 'basic' programme). Others come from conceptual elements within NPM/NPR. For example, while NPR stresses emphasizing customers, 'putting them first', the US system gives organized groups a huge advantage. This is by and large not a problem when the general citizenry are the customers or when customers pay a fee for services received, but when there is doubt about who should be defined as customers or the interests of groups of customers clash, then it is likely that the best funded or best organized group (the two often overlap) will have its interests put 'first'.

In brief, despite the large American literature on bureaucratic problems and pathologies and the huge cultural appeal of market-like solutions to problems, the design features that make the US political system resemble a market and the unclear role of administrators in the system make it difficult to apply many features of NPM successfully. Most everything (including features central to NPM/NPR) is subject to bargaining, modification, and compromise as political and administrative leaders make their deals. This does not mean that little has happened, or that NPM/NPR lacks positive accomplishments, just that those hoping for a new, 'modern' US administration will likely be disappointed. Some of the best of NPM/NPR will remain – greater emphasis on service, sensible aspects of internal deregulation, and greater emphasis on results, to mention some examples – but other parts will almost surely fade or be seriously altered.

The odds are that in the coming years a different set of concerns about 'modernizing' the public sector will become increasingly prominent. If Miller and Whitford and others challenging central aspects of principal-agent theory are correct, many of the new emphases will look a lot like the old. Reformers will be concerned about encouraging professionalism in the public service, facilitating cooperation in a hierarchy, and building esprit in the public service. There was an American film a few years ago entitled 'Back to the Future'. That may be a good, if surely incomplete, predictor of what lies ahead. So do not throw away your old public administration texts; some chapters may yet come back into style.

ACKNOWLEDGEMENTS

The first version of this paper was presented at the 31st Annual Conference of the Public Administration Committee held at the Civil Service College, Sunningdale, England, 3–5 September 2001 and published in *Public Policy and Administration*. A revised, updated version was given at a conference in Australia organized by Professor Mark Considine. The conference was sponsored by the International Political Science Association's Research Committee on the Structure and Organization of Government and held at the Centre for Public Policy, University of Melbourne in June of 2002.

I gratefully acknowledge research support from the Academic Senate and the Center for American Politics and Public Policy at UCLA and thank participants at both the Sunningdale and Melbourne conferences for their helpful comments.

4. Modernization as Europeanization: the impact of the European Union on public administration

Andrew Massey

'Even a fully-fledged Celtic depressive like me has to acknowledge that the prospects are encouraging' (Commissioner Neil Kinnock, quoted in a speech at the RSA, London, 15 October 2001).

INTRODUCTION

The Labour Government elected to office in Britain in 1997 is committed to modernization. In the 1999 White Paper, *Modernizing Government* (Cmnd 4310), the Cabinet Office authors affirm a belief in the efficacy of government to deliver services to the nation in a coherent and efficient way. Government would be used to harness the wealth, power, experience and initiative of the private and public sectors to deliver beneficial reforms in health, education, and law and order and develop opportunities to improve the quality of the nation's collective experience (Massey, 2001, pp. 16–31). Linked to innovations in information technology and initiatives on constitutional reform, social improvement and private/public partnerships, what is promised amounts to a new social contract. Veteran observers may detect an echo here of Harold Wilson's 'White Heat of the Technological Revolution', an earlier species of Labour modernizer (Beer 1982). There is also a similarity to some of the rhetoric that followed the election of Mitterand to the French presidency in 1981 (Tiersky 2000), or Clinton to the White House a decade later (Skowronet 1997). With few exceptions, social democratic parties in government seek to portray themselves as 'modern', especially when implementing neo-liberal policies.

Labour's plans, however, like those of all contemporary European governments, are located within the context of the Europeanization of European governance. It is a process that impacts upon members of the European Union and those aspiring to join, as well as other states that may be said to be affected by what some analysts have argued amounts to a form of international socialization (Fennig 2000). An understanding of modernization, then, must take cognisance of developments in public administration and an understanding of the modernization of public sector institutions within contemporary Europe requires the concept and process of Europeanization be addressed. It is instructive here to take the long view.

In remarking on the changes to public administration within the context of the modern state since the Treaty of Westphalia (1648), Waldo is struck by the diversity and 'seeming contrariety' of structures, institutions and organizations. 'Thus it is appropriate to suggest' he opines:

> that countries still wishing to become modern may find the diversity instructive: there is no single model, no single route. Rather, much will depend upon circumstances: upon history ... economic factors, class structure, ethnic composition, religious beliefs, educational institutions and so forth (1999, p. x).

A lesson learned from the contributions in this book and other comparative volumes, is that there is no universal general theory that can be applied to the administrative sciences; the object of study is mostly confined to the nation state (Kickert and Stillman 1999, p. 4; Common 2001). But this is not the same as denying the validity of a general theory that can be applied to European integration, of which Europeanization is a constituent element. The study of Europeanization, although exploring the impact of intergovernmental and supra-national institutions, is likewise mostly located at the national and sub-national level in terms of its effects (and empirical analysis). But its dynamics are (variously) national, regional, transnational, supranational and global.

The ontology of Europeanization, or perhaps more accurately, Europeanized institutions, is part of a broader global process that has its roots in the Cold War and its present in the global economic liberalism that is outstripping the political capacity of states to adequately deal with its consequences. Only in Europe is this referred to as Europeanization and this reflects the European (but not British) perspective of the existence of public administration as emanating from reasons of state; it is a legalistic deductive approach (Stillman 1999, p. 258). Whereas the US (and traditional British) approach induces the state from public administration, it is a more institutional and institutionalist approach than the European one, which is based upon a corpus of administrative law (Stillman 1999, pp. 247–59; Massey 1993; Price 1983). In the US, for example, there are several dynamics contributing to changes in public administration. One of the longest standing and most emphatic of these is American populism and a demand for the democratization of public administration, a tradition less urgent in Europe, though not entirely absent (Aberbach and Rockman 2000). Yet despite the different

British and Continental European traditions, there is an increasing convergence in the policy making and institutional decision making structures and
procedures of their public administrations. If they are modernizing then they
are doing so in concert, if not quite in harmony.

Accordingly, this chapter will discuss the concept of Europeanization and
locate it within the broader context of analysis of the state and European
integration. There then follows a section that reviews change and modernization at EU level, linking this to changes at national level and sub-national
level, before concluding with some general observations.

THE STATE AND MODERNIZATION

The study of public administration is the study of the state. Public administration is the implementation of politics, what Price refers to as the 'seamy
side' of politics (1983). The concept of the state and its purpose has exercised
thinkers and practitioners since antiquity, and its nature continues to be
addressed by modern analysts (Dunsire 1973: Hood 1998, pp. 15–16). The
fundamental changes taking place in Europe and globally have re-awakened
interest in the subject. Some public administration perspectives have sought
enlightenment from group cultural theory, with Hood arguing that:

> variation in ideas about how to organize public services is a central and recurring
> theme in public management, and that such variation is unlikely to disappear, in
> spite of the engineering metaphors and the prophets foreseeing convergence on a
> new stable form of modernity (1998, p. 6).

Such anthropological and cultural explanations regarding the nature and
behaviour of officials and public administrations, while seeking to construct
grand theory, do not necessarily aid an understanding of what modernization
means to national public administrations within the context of Europeanization.
That noted, however, as a starting point, grid/group theory, with its perspective on the role of rules and group constraints on individual/institutional
action, contributes an interesting analysis on how and why Europeanization
occurs and develops that is in marked contrast to other explanations. It puts at
the heart of these debates issues such as the extent to which professional
public servants ought to be allowed to 'get on with the job' or should be
constrained by rules and regulations. This is combined with the debates over
a communitarian, a hierarchical, or a public service ethos as a structuring
principle for public administration, contrasted to a privatized with-profit
approach to the provision of basic services (Hood 1998, p. 8).

Globally there is clearly a range of cultural and organizational models in
existence and even when states claim to adopt patterns from elsewhere (policy

transfer) the local context means the reality of that adoption is often different from the original, an example being the implementation of new public management structures, practices and regulatory techniques in South East Asia (Common 2001). Furthermore, that which purports to be modern is often simply the reinvention of old remedies for problems faced by managers and administrators across the ages. Hood's warning to be aware of this is timely (1998, pp. 7–17). Egalitarian forms of public administration and service delivery, such as front-line employee 'empowerment' or grass-roots public service provision, are vulnerable to collapse if the people they contain do not share the common beliefs and values that structure work (Hood 1998, p. 10). Concepts such as performance related pay (abolished for school teachers in England in 1902), hot-desking (proposed by Jeremy Bentham two centuries ago) and contract versus professionalized (cameral) systems (discussed by Shen Pu-Hai in China, 330 BC) have all enjoyed a re-birth in various guises under new public management (Hood 1998, pp. 15–17). Indeed, current debates about the nature of the state, public administration and modernizing the public policy process would be familiar to America's Founding Fathers and most groups of informed observers at any time in the last 200 years (Massey 1993; Parsons 1995). This does not make them either right or wrong; it is simply to note that which is currently labelled 'modernization' often has far deeper roots than many of its advocates realize. It is local context that is the defining element of how successful modernization will be. Beneath the grand designs, however they may be defined and generated, lies meta-analysis that seeks to deal appropriately with contemporary events, albeit set within their historical and political context.

EUROPEANIZATION

The functionalists and neo-functionalists of the 1950s and 1960s performed a useful analytical role when their analysis was deployed to describe and make sense of the evolving structures in Western Europe, especially those of the young European Communities (Adshead 2002; Chryssochoou 1999, 2001). In other words, as a descriptive tool of analysis, indeed a stylized map of the political and administrative terrain, their approach assisted understanding of the political processes at work. When they sought to arrogate to their perspective a predictive and normative capability their lack of accuracy and empirical relevance led to the widespread rejection of their approach in the 1970s (Chryssochoou 2001, pp. 53–8). Although sometimes linked together, functionalism and neo-functionalism should be seen as separate perspectives. Neo-functionalism is sometimes wrongly associated with the gradualist approach to European unity adopted by Monnet and his successors, a kind of 'functionalist federalism' (Chryssochoou 2001, p. 53). Neo-functionalism adopts an abstract conception of politics and sees it as an inherently conflictual process in terms of allocating values in the community. There is throughout this approach an administrative flavour to the political process, institutions are established to advance the political goals of a federal, integrative and politically elitist process (Chryssochoou 2001, p. 53). Within this approach (and that of intergovernmentalism) may be found the infamous democratic deficit of the European Union, a deficit neo-functionalism not only does little to address, but would also actually perceive as a necessary price for European integration.

Indeed, the neo-functionalists advocated a deepening of the elite socialization, 'the process by which influential actors of policy- and decision-making from different national settings learn to work with each other within a larger management setting' (Chryssochoou 2001, p. 54). Such an approach engendered criticism from various observers for its 'supranationally biased image of Community arrangements and dynamics, [and] underestimating the role of "summit diplomacy" in putting together complex package deals'; it also generally overestimated the importance of the Commission and other supranational institutions and institutional actors (Chryssochoou 2001, p. 57). In this respect neo-functionalists often found themselves overtaken by events, such as de Gaulle's famous withdrawal of France from the institutions of the Community and the subsequent constitutional crisis in the 1960s. By the 1990s, theory building had advanced to take account of these realities and included the construction of 'confederal consociation', the belief that the EU is best understood as:

a compound polity whose distinct culturally defined and politically organized units are bound together in a consensually pre-arranged form of union for specific purposes, without either losing their national identity or resigning their individual sovereignty to a higher authority (Chryssochoou 1999, p. 25).

It is this intergovernmentalist approach, replete with several varieties, that has found most favour with analysts. It may be further refined to state:

the distribution of preferences and the conduct of bargaining among the governments of the member states broadly explain the nature, pace and scope of integration, and neither supranational organization nor transnational actors generate political processes or outcomes of seminal importance (Sandholtz and Stone Sweet 1998, p. 3).

Until the end of the 1990s there had been few attempts at constructing a more general theory of European integration to rival that of neo-functionalism.

The development of the concept of Europeanization has been largely in response to this, reflecting the sheer complexity of supranational governance in the EU. For example:

the nature and extent of supranational governance, varies along a number of dimensions. In some sectors, the competence to govern is held exclusively by the Community; in others, national institutions are the primary sites of policymaking; and in many domains, the transfer of power from the national to the supranational level has been only partial. Within the same policy sector, the answer to the question 'who governs?' has changed over time. And in those areas in which (EU) institutions have become sites of policy innovation and change, one finds variation in the relative capacity of the member state governments (Sandholtz and Stone Sweet 1998, p. 4).

At its grandest Europeanization resurrects some of the neo-functionalist dynamic for supranationalism through institutional integration (with EU law as represented through the Union's own court (and national courts' compliance) being a key element (Stone Sweet, 2000)). Europeanization, through European (supranational) integration:

> is the process by which the EC (EU) gradually but comprehensively replaces the nation-state in all of its functions ... (rejecting) ... the comparative statics of intergovernmentalists as a mode of analysis incapable of capturing crucial temporal elements of European integration. ... The expansion of transnational exchange, and the associated push to substitute supranational for national rules, generates pressure on the EC's organizations to act. ... (EU) organizations, such as the Commission and the Court, respond to this pressure by working to extend the domain of supranational rules, in order to achieve collective (transnational) gains (Sandholtz and Stone Sweet 1998, p. 4).

This may be observed in action across a range of high profile strategic policy areas, such as competition policy (Dunford, Louri and Rosenstock 2001), the common agricultural policy (Tarditi and Zanaias 2001) and structural policies (Mairate and Hall 2001). It is also apparent in more low-level areas such as the toy directive, the machine directive, and directives and rules on medical devices and construction products, which impose common European standards and regulations in these arcane fields (Egan 2001).

In response to these dynamics, those analysts developing theoretical and empirical work on Europeanization have evolved a range of definitions to take into account the supranational nature of the policy process and its impact on domestic structures. Buller and Gamble (2002) argue, however, that Europeanization is simply 'a situation where distinct modes of European governance have transformed aspects of domestic politics' (p. 17). This most closely reflects the reality of the policy process in the supranational polity or polities. The mode of governance used by these authors is the process, methods or style of governing which brings about conditions for ordered rule and collective action (p. 18). The utility of this definition is that it allows a clear linkage to Stone Sweet and Sandholtz's attempt to create a general theory (supranational governance) (1998). In doing this it takes account of the impact of institutional changes designed to accelerate the demise of national institutions at odds with the integration programme designed in the Treaties of Rome, Maastricht and Amsterdam. But it also defines Europeanization not as a process, but as a situation, 'where certain effects can be shown to have occurred' (Buller and Gamble 2002, p. 17). An implication of this is not that Europeanization is inevitable, but is contingent upon social, political and economic interactions, while giving 'analytical primacy to the impact of European developments at the domestic level' (Buller and Gamble 2002, p. 18). Thus, 'in its crudest sense, Europeanization [is used] to denote a condition of becoming "like Europe"' and the term implies change or trans-formation in domestic politics and institutions that may be 'through "positive", "negative", or "framing" integration' (Buller and Gamble 2002, p. 18).

It may be argued, then, that Europeanization, in both its supranational integration guise and that of a domestic transformative dynamic:

> provokes, or activates, the Community's (EU) decision-making bodies, including the Council of Ministers. Member-state governments often possess (but not always) the means to facilitate or to obstruct rule-making, and they use these powers frequently. Nevertheless, ... as transnational exchange rises in any specific domain (or cluster of related domains), so do the costs, for the governments, of maintaining disparate national rules. As these costs rise, so do the incentives for governments to adjust their policy positions in ways that favour the expansion of supranational governance. Once fixed in a given domain, European rules – such as relevant treaty provisions, secondary legislation, and the ECJ's case law – gener-ate a self-sustaining dynamic, that leads to the gradual deepening of integration in that sector and, not uncommonly, to spillovers into other sectors (Stone Sweet and Sandholtz 1998, p. 5).

There is a growing corpus of work that illustrates this point and includes, in addition to the aforementioned examples, monetary union (Cameron 1998, pp. 188–216), regional policy (Caporaso 1998, pp. 334–52), and the develop-ment of civil nuclear fusion technology (Massey 1999). In the latter case, the institutional structures of member states and the procedures governing re-search activity are wholly subsumed into the supranational project. The application of Stone Sweet and Sandholtz's supranational governance theory is clearly set within a global context; as noted in the introduction, it is change in the world economy that is driving much political change.

Indeed, the corpus of work on environmental law (Wildavsky 1995; Spragia 1998) and world trade and consumer legislation (Vogel 1997) illustrates similar incentives to supranational rules (and difficulties in obtaining them). But in the specifically European context, the domestic impact is institution-ally greater because of the existence of more (and more binding) treaty obligations and the corresponding incentives to conform and comply. 'In a fundamental sense, governments are reactive, constantly adjusting to the integration that is going on all around them' (Stone Sweet and Sandholtz 1998, p. 12). Europeanization is often a fundamental constituent of analyses that argue the power of national governments and the nation state are being hollowed out and transferred up to supranational institutions and down to the regions (Rhodes 1997; Rhodes, Carmichael, McMillan and Massey 2003). But there is no reason, as Stone Sweet and Sandholtz strongly imply (1998 pp. 5–12), why intergovernmental approaches are in conflict with this view of Europeanization. Indeed, intergovernmental approaches may be seen as a sub-set of the institutionalist approach adopted in supranationalism. This is because integration varies over time, place and policy area and may rely as much on intergovernmental diplomacy and multi-level governance, as on grand treaties, or policy-network led changes to the directives on medical appliances. In the process of modernizing and Europeanizing government, all approaches appear as likely or unlikely to succeed in different times and different contexts and all are as evasive of the control of individual national governments.

It is clear from these arguments that there are several dynamics that trigger Europeanization within individual public administrations. Lodge identifies four of these:

1. Coercive triggers. These include at least three subsets; requirements to comply with European legislation; rulings by the European Court of Justice; European Commission executive acts.
2. Mimetic triggers. There are two sub-sets within this group; increased interaction among civil servants leading to the adoption of 'best-practice'; national coordination networks through things like peer-group review for the implementation of EU employment policy and monetary policy, among other fields.
3. Professionalization as a trigger. The two sub-sets here include policy networks as part of the transnationalization of societal actors leading to the 'logic of exchange' in areas such as regulatory agencies for telecommunications; the emergence of policy communities, following on from the work of Sabatier (1988).
4. Domestic politics as a trigger. There are three sub-sets here, which include strategic competitive adjustment, whereby domestic institutions and regulations are adjusted to comply with European standards to ensure protection of domestic markets. Secondly there is the way Europeanization shapes domestic policy opportunities through legitimizing particular policy beliefs and options. Finally, domestic triggers are found in the lobbying of elite groups to force the adjustment of domestic laws, regulations and institutions to the European model in order to ensure access to resources and the global 'playing field'. (Lodge 2002, pp. 48–9)

A review of the implementation of regulatory reform in Britain, Germany Ireland and Sweden illustrates all these triggers in action and underlines the case made by Sandholtz and Stone Sweet (1998, p. 4) that what constitutes

integration or Europeanization activity differs according to a complex con-
stellation of factors (Lodge 2002, pp. 48–60). In Sweden's case, it was the
desire of that country's political and economic elite to join the EU that led to
major reforms of its public administration (Lodge 2002, pp. 58–60). In other
words it was change engendered by the domestic elite in anticipation of what
was required for entry that was the dynamic, a process being repeated by
each tranche of aspirant nations.

It may be argued that despite Chryssochoou's perspective of Europeanization
and integration being largely intergovernmental, as quoted above, and the
reservations expressed by Stone Sweet and Sandholtz (1998, p. 8), the practical
impact of Europeanization is a process of federalizing. In this respect analysts
also need to take cognisance of the temporal or time aspect of Europeanization,
in other words, address what the entity is becoming and how space for national
decision making is being compressed chronologically as well as institutionally
(Ekengren 2002). The EU is and remains an international organization. But the
impact of integration across so many policy areas and the concomitant
Europeanization of its constituent public administrations has led the constituent
domestic governments to engage in intergovernmental diplomacy of a kind that
is more akin to the federal politics played out in the US (Aberbach and Rockman
2000) and Canada. The problem with any federal system, however, is that it is a
compromise between the centralizers and the devolutionists, each official will
have an allegiance somewhere and it may not always be where governments
would wish. The devolution that has occurred in the UK, for example, has
created separate institutions for Wales, Scotland and Northern Ireland and it is
clear the allegiance of officials in those countries has markedly shifted away
from London (Rhodes, Carmichael, McMillan and Massey 2003). Indeed,
devolution combined with Europeanization has conspired to bypass the 'heart'
of national government in London for the devolved countries to an extent that
calls into question the continued ability of national government to perform its
traditional role. This is a pattern repeated elsewhere and represents modernization as Europeanization.

MODERNIZING THE EU'S PUBLIC ADMINISTRATION

Given that the EU is an international organization, and its constituent states
remain (legally) sovereign, within a supranationality of pooled sovereignty,
most modernization takes place within national public administrations. Even
if the EU were to be perceived as a federalizing entity, it would remain the
case that the foci of modernization would be the constituencies and that
ensures the continuation of 'difference' in public administration. A comparative study of the implementation of the EU's environment policy in Britain

and Germany illustrates this effect (Knill 2001) and several patterns of Europeanization can be seen. Knill identifies three major types within environmental policy:

> European policies might be very demanding and prescribe a concrete institutional model for domestic compliance; they might be confined to changing domestic opportunity structures; or, in their 'weakest' form, have no institutional impact at all, while being primarily directed at changing domestic beliefs and expectations (2001, p. 213).

This perspective accords with that of Lodge, identified above, and is borne out by the experience of Europeanization across a range of sectors, including the major regulatory reforms implemented by the Swedes before and after they joined the EU (Ekengren 2002; Lodge 2002).

Certainly institutions are changed through Europeanization, indeed some (such as Britain's Intervention Board, for CAP activities, an executive non-departmental public body) are created purely as a result of European policies (Massey 1995b). Domestic opportunity structures are an obvious area of change, but more fundamental is the way in which Europeanization changes domestic beliefs and expectations; indeed even the language and comprehension of governance, as well as the national policy-making timetable, are structured by the EU. For example, the EU's meetings and Directives structure domestic policy-making; the concept of European competence and the need for European education and socialization are all implicit in national public administrations (Ekengren 2002, pp. 3–60). The daily reality for the national policy-makers of member states is a European one (Greenwood, Pyper and Wilson 2002, pp. 186–92). Elected ministers spend a large proportion of their time shuttling to and from meetings in Brussels deliberating and negotiating with EU Commissioners and fellow ministers from other states; all national policy decisions are benchmarked against EU law and policy (Egan, 2001; Hall, Smith, and Tsoukalis 2001). All member governments and administrations are 'severely constrained by policy outputs from the EU system' (Greenwood, Pyper and Wilson 2002, p. 189). This constraint may be seen in a cornucopia of policy studies, such as those referred to in this chapter. Even when new institutions themselves are not created as a specific result of EU measures, the existing institutional actors have had their behaviour substantially modified by the EU reality. It is a continuing example of new wine in old bottles.

In the British case, it may be seen that government ministers, parliamentarians and civil servants are both proactive and reactive towards the EU. They try to ensure British interests are fully represented at Commission and Council level, while implementing EU law and directives at the national level (Greenwood, Pyper and Wilson 2002, p. 189). In order to do this, the institutional structures in Whitehall have been amended. Two key divisions within the Foreign and Commonwealth Office (FCO) deal with external and internal EU issues and report to a second-tier minister (Minister of State) known as the 'Minister for Europe' (Greenwood, Pyper and Wilson 2002, p. 190). All other departments of state also contain EU units that brief ministers and ensure domestic legislation and activity accords and complies with EU law; indeed, nearly every part of British public administration now has a European aspect to its work (Greenwood, Pyper and Wilson 2002, p. 190). There is an attempt to coordinate this in the European Secretariat section of the Cabinet Office and its Cabinet Committees, but even here their work often cuts across other committees, such as those on regulatory accountability or social and economic aspects of migration. In some areas, such as agricultural policy or trade policy, the UK has virtually no separate policy-making role; the UK Parliament simply ratifies EU law. As well as these formal institutional changes, there has emerged an informal yet 'powerful elite. This is comprised of Number 10, the FCO, the Cabinet Office and the UKREP (to the EU) [which] point to the existence of a European network with the task of managing EU policy formation' within the UK (Richards and Smith 2002, p. 154).

The institutional reality appears to be that the Europeanization of British administration has in some way been absorbed into the workings (or 'software') of the Whitehall machinery as a part of the modernization agenda. This:

> adjustment again emphasizes the way in which regional and international pressures are mediated by existing state institutions. The impact of the EU on the formal structure, organization, and rules of Whitehall has been surprisingly limited. There has been little reassessment of notions of ministerial responsibility, collective responsibility, or even parliamentary sovereignty in the light of EU membership. How, for instance, can collective responsibility be sustained when decisions are taken in areas that have little or no relationship with the Cabinet? (Richards and Smith 2002, p. 155).

The answer to this rhetorical question is that they cannot. Europeanization as part of the globalization of economic power, indeed, as a defence against aspects of this process, has run ahead of the institutionalization of democratic accountability, a point raised at the outset of this chapter.

This new institutional reality pervades the public administrations of member states. For example, the sub-national governments that exist, established within a variety of federal or unitary governmental structures and tasked with a plethora of different functions organized along a bewildering array of structures, now routinely lobby the EU directly, bypassing their national government (Rhodes, Carmichael, McMillan and Massey 2003; Ekengren 2002). Officials at all levels have their lives structured by this reality, in taking into account EU rules and practice. With regard to the environment, for example, everything from the environmental impact of a new power station to the application of building regulations in individual cases of privately owned dwellings are located within their EU context. From national treasuries to local town halls, officials are influenced, guided and constrained by the Europeanization of public administration in the way in which they carry out their duties. To neglect this reality is to risk the invocation of the judicial review of a decision and it is here through the juridicalization of public administration, government by judges, that the imposition of Europeanization is keenly felt (Stone Sweet, 2000). Officials modify their behaviour to avoid the risk of such judicial review, ensuring that even when the EU's laws and doctrine are not being explicitly applied, their application is nonetheless omnipresent.

The flow of influence is not all one way, however. The criticisms of the EU's own public administration, the Commission and its bureaucracy, have led to an attempt at sweeping reform of the supranational institutions. This began with the slow imposition of New Public Management techniques into the EU's institutions, sporadically applied across the old Directorates General. This process was given a new impetus with the crisis faced by the Commission in 1999. Despite the crisis engendered by the forced resignation of the European Commission in 1999 amid calls for reform and allegations of nepotism, inefficiency, bureaucratic sclerosis and corruption, the continuing process of modernization within the Commission itself was, as noted, already underway at the time the crisis erupted.

It is evident, however, that the cathartic effect of the crisis strengthened the hand of Commissioner Kinnock in his quest to reform the institutions and workings of the Commission. He argued:

> To me, administrative reform is not, therefore, simply a quest for professional excellence, or efficiency, or customer satisfaction, essential though those qualities are; it is also vital to strengthening public confidence in democracy as an answerable system for delivering many of the essentials of modern life, and for helping to advance social and economic progress and security (2001, p. 2).

The genesis for the EU's reform project reflects the fact that while the Union has altered over four decades, the:

> organization, structures and working methods of the Commission as the executive administration of that Union have never really been sufficiently adapted to the changes that have taken place. Europe evolved, the Commission as an organization didn't keep pace. In forty years, the Community grew from six to fifteen Member States: the Treaty was amended substantially, the Single Market was created; the Single Currency became a reality; Communism collapsed, and the new democracies needed help and then applied for membership. And the financial management obligations of the Commission increased exponentially (2001, p. 3).

The criticism of the Commission largely reflected the startling increase in its activities that integration and Europeanization engendered. For example between 1988 and 1999 the number of financial transactions 'managed by the Commission rose from just over 60 000 a year to 620 000 a year' and the overall EU budget grew from 44 billion Euros to 95 billion Euros (Kinnock 2001, p. 3). Yet there was no corresponding rise in staff numbers and the systems under which they operated remained unreformed. National public administrations had often undergone fundamental modernization, and the political leaders as well as officials lobbied for reform in Brussels.

Recognition grew of a need to ensure officials with fiscal responsibilities were held properly accountable and the establishment of clear lines of accountability, control and command needed defining. Observers remarked that the 'borderline between political and administrative responsibility was often blurred' (Kinnock 2001, p. 3) and this needed addressing, as did the requirement for general updating and upgrading (modernization) of the technical ability, procedures and structures of the Commission. As a consequence the Commission, led by Kinnock as the responsible Commissioner, designed an 'Action Plan' and gave it strategic designation to:

> ensure that the Commission is a well managed policy-producing and policy-applying administration of the highest quality, integrity and service, focused firmly on its core tasks and executing them efficiently and with independence, transparency, responsibility and accountability (Kinnock 2001, p. 5).

The Commissioners began the process by disclosing their own financial interests and adopting new standards and codes of behaviour for Commissioners, codes clearly influenced by those of Britain's Committee on Standards in Public Life.

This has been followed by a 'Code of Good Administrative Behaviour' which defines new standards of behaviour for all officials employed by the Commission. Technical and human resource deficiencies are addressed through new personnel policy proposals that reinforce the need to act accountably and responsibly, combined with new training programmes to fill the skills deficit in some areas. Kinnock has described the new emphasis on accountability and transparency as 'a regime in itself' (2001, p. 6). As part of this, the Commission again borrowed from the British reforms, specifically the prior options process previously used when each non-departmental public body and Next Steps Agency underwent its quinquennial review (Massey, 1995b). The Commission asked itself, 'Do we really need to do all that we are doing at present?' and 'Can we do what we must do, and do it properly, with the resources at our disposal?' (Kinnock 2001, p. 7). In order to address these questions a comprehensive review of tasks and resources was undertaken by a 'Peer Group' of five Commissioners who assessed all services on the basis of 'common, detailed, written questions to every department, followed by oral hearings with all DGs and Commissioners' (Kinnock 2001, p. 7). As a result, a short-term plan sought to reorder Commission priority activities and made a detailed submission to Parliament justifying budgetary support for the one third of the identified needs not met from internal reorganization and prioritization.

The Peer Group began the process continued by the Commission of matching tasks and resources, known as activity-based management, which when combined with new strategic planning activities has sought to implement modernization of the Commission. Strategic planning and activity-based management:

> will clearly provide the two major ingredients of more effective internal control and they will also bring a profound structural change in accountability because for the first time in Commission history, all individual members of staff will have specifically allocated responsibilities, a written outline of what results are expected of them, and the knowledge that their performance will be measured against these objectives (Kinnock 2001, pp. 8–9).

This process is accompanied by greater flexibility in management and the decentralization of many management control tasks to the Directors General (DG) of the different departments. Each DG will produce an annual activity report to describe the objectives for each activity of the department they head. The report must also account for results and will become a public document, available to the European Parliament and the general public. Secondly, each DG is to assume personal responsibility for the internal control and accountability of his or her department and must sign an annual declaration assuring the College of Commissioners of the sound management and proper control of their department's activities (Kinnock 2001, p. 9). As part of this strategy managers are to assume the autonomy and flexibility necessary to establish the management systems best suited to their activities.

Much of this approach has long been observed by students of public administration in many countries, most noticeably the UK and US with their decades long experiment in the implementation of New Public Management, ushering in the era of government in the age of governance (Richards and Smith 2002). The feedback from national public administrations into the Commission came in the form of a demand for radical reform to match the modernization undertaken piecemeal elsewhere. With the British experience being one of the most innovative and far-reaching, convincing lessons from the British model were imported into the Commission via Commissioner Kinnock and his colleagues. With more than 600 000 financial transactions a year taking place by the 1990s it was clear the Commission's centralized ex ante control system was inadequate and the reforms are replacing it with control over these individual transactions being decentralized to individual DGs who are personally accountable.

CONCLUSION

What is occurring is a fundamental reform of the Commission, indeed of the EU's public administration, in the pattern of modernization through New Public Management. But it is:

> hard to think of an operational and cultural change more radical than one which replaces a 40-year-old financial management system in which responsibility could always be passed on to a central authority with a system in which individual responsibility is explicit and subject to continual monitoring and assessment. In terms of accountability it is a step from Stygian darkness to sunburst (Kinnock 2001, p. 11).

The 'sunburst', however, is clearly one located within the context of a regulatory state and governance defined from the perspective of New Public Management, replete with new audit and regulatory organizations.

But, as in the UK, it is also a reform of the culture, an attempt to change the bureaucratic paradigm in that:

> a substantial purpose of reform must be to establish systems, standards and practices that ensure that the Commission (which has a primary role of anticipating and providing for change in the European Union and the wider world) becomes very good at adapting to change and being comfortable with change itself (Kinnock 2001, p. 14).

The actions contained within the reform plan have been steadily advanced since their announcement and have been accompanied by other reform attempts. Reforms designed to improve European governance were adopted in July 2001 (Commission of the European Communities (COM) 2001) 428, quoted in COM (2002), 278), and an Action Plan to improve and simplify the regulatory environment (COM (2002), 278) and the quality of EU legislation generally. It may be seen that the reform process initiated by EU integration, and accelerated by a plethora of other (global, fiscal and ideological dynamics) has turned in upon itself: the EU is now being modernized in the image of its constituent parts.

5. Executive agencies and 'modernizing government'

Oliver James

EXECUTIVE AGENCIES AND 'MODERNIZING GOVERNMENT' [1]

The current agenda of 'modernizing government' is broad in scope and is linked by a bland, even banal, theme of 'modernizing government to get better government – for a better Britain' (Prime Minister 1999). The need for renewal is suggested in an age when 'most of the old dogmas that haunted governments in the past have been swept away' at a time in which 'information technology is revolutionizing our lives' and in a society demanding 'inclusive' and 'responsive' government (Minister for the Cabinet Office 1999, p. 4 and p. 9). However, a number of more specific reforms are suggested including 'e-government', 'joined-up government' and 'partnership' working across the public and private sectors (Prime Minister 1999; Cabinet Office 2000; Performance and Innovation Unit 2000). The reforms are suggested to improve 'value for money' and to promote 'citizen-focused' public services, in contrast to narrow economy or shrinking the size of the state (Minister for the Cabinet Office 1999).

The achievement of modernizers' goals is likely to be substantially influenced by the consequences of a previous reform to create executive agencies. The reform was one of the most substantial structural reforms in the history of UK central government and there are now 126 agencies employing about 60 per cent of the civil service. The Next Steps report team, who proposed the creation of agencies in 1988, had similar goals to the current modernizers and saw agencies as a way of improving the economy, efficiency and effectiveness of government (Efficiency Unit 1988). The current modernization agenda does not suggest a wholesale movement away from the use of agencies so they are likely to remain an important influence on value for money and citizen-focused services.

Whilst agencies are likely to remain an important feature of central government, the current reformers' concern with joined-up government is in part based on a critique of agencies' effects on performance and suggests some changes to their operation. Joined-up government, in its broadest sense, suggests that outcomes, citizens and their representatives' value should be delivered in a way that is not dictated by organizational boundaries (Minister for the Cabinet Office 2000; Performance and Innovation Unit 2000). The *Modernizing Government* White Paper suggested that 'great gains in public sector management have come from definition of task and delegation of management and the Government is determined that these are not lost. However, this concentration on specific tasks has sometimes distracted attention from the wider general objectives of government and people. The Government wants to give more attention to the coherence of policy across institutional boundaries ... to operate in a joined up way' (Prime Minister 1999). More specifically, the joined-up government agenda for central government suggests that current departmental and agency arrangements tend to divide, 'vertically', policy-making in departments from implementation in agencies. Policy makers do not always consult the full range of people involved in delivering services, including local bodies and other delivery units. The central government system involves separate departmental and agency clusters for delivering services. There is insufficient horizontal joining-up between departments and agencies to deal with cross-cutting policy and delivery issues spilling across organizational boundaries (PIU 2000, paras 3.1 and 3.2). The performance problems from a lack of joined-up government include public sector externalities which 'arise where control and performance appraisal systems fail to reflect the wider effects of a public organization's activities on the goals of other organizations' (James 2000, p. 331). However, the joined-up government agenda has been advanced by reformers with little systematic assessment of the practice of agencies, raising the question of whether the critique rests on a firm base of evidence about performance.

Section one defines the executive agency model and explores its use in UK central government since 1988. Section two asks whether executive agencies have been achieving the goals of economy, efficiency and effectiveness that are valued both by the Next Steps reformers and the current modernizers. Section three explores the effect of agencies on systemic performance and whether the problems of joining-up government outweigh the benefits of the structures. Sections two and three draw on surveys of agency performance and a case study of the largest agency, the Benefits Agency.

SECTION ONE: THE EXECUTIVE AGENCY MODEL

The Next Steps reform evolved over time and the bodies created as agencies were far from the same. However, the 1988 Efficiency Unit Next Steps report, Prime Minister Thatcher's announcement of the acceptance of the report's conclusions and the early guidance from the Next Steps Project Team are taken as defining the core of the executive agency model. The Next Steps report recommended that 'agencies should be established to carry out the executive functions of government within a policy and resources framework set by a department' (Efficiency Unit 1988, p. 9). The report claimed that several features of the traditional system were inhibiting performance and asserted that the civil service was too big to be managed as a single entity. More flexibility was needed to allow managers to adjust their systems to suit the needs of the job at hand. At the same time, people in departments needed to be freed to concentrate on their core activity of policy advice, where ministers, parliament, the media and the public were demanding that more time be spent on these activities. The use of agencies with clearly defined aims and associated units of budget operating in a policy and resources framework was supposed to focus managers' attention on getting the job done efficiently and effectively, reducing costs where this did not compromise effectiveness (Efficiency Unit 1988, pp. 9–13). The idea of agencies was heavily influenced by an Anglo-American big business model of multi-divisional organization, in which specialist units are given freedom to manage within a framework of focused accountability for the performance of each unit (James, 2001b). Whilst the original report suggested that an agency 'may be part of government and the public service, or it may be more effective outside of government' (Efficiency Unit 1988, p. 9), it was quickly resolved to keep agencies within central government (Goldsworthy 1991).

On the basis of the descriptions of the reformers, the agency model has two main elements: first, an organizational unit with management freedoms, semi-detached from a department to enable it to focus on the task at hand but formally remaining part of the department; second, an accountability framework of policy aims and resources set by the department, with a chief executive responsible for overall performance of the agency. Not all agencies set up under the Next Steps reform were the same. For example, agencies in the Ministry of Defence were set in the management command framework of the department whereas the other agencies reported to ministers and, in this sense, their accountability arrangements differed. However, a key difference set out by the reformers in the 1988 report was that some agencies were to be involved in charging customers for services whilst others received a grant from their department to cover most of the cost of their activities (Efficiency Unit 1988, p. 28). The two main types, based on this difference, were trading and non-trading agencies.

The presence of a customer group for trading agencies offered a supplementary form of influence over the agency through customers paying for services or choosing alternative sources of supply (Prime Minister, Chancellor of the Exchequer and the Chancellor of the Duchy of Lancaster 1994,

p. 22). The government extended the 1973 Trading Fund Act by legislation in 1990 to give some agencies financial freedoms. Agency trading funds were given a net running-cost system of budget control, enabling them to expand activities if covered by additional revenue, subject to the achievement of certain financial controls, such as a percentage return on capital. The framework contrasted with non-trading agencies which had controls over their inputs and fewer commercial-style freedoms to expand their activities (Goldsworthy 1991, pp. 30–1).

In 1989 there were just ten agencies with 9000 staff but the number grew rapidly to 76 bodies with 210 000 staff by 1992. As shown in Table 5.1, the main burst of agency creation occurred in the period 1990 to 1996. By 1996 there were 133 agencies employing 313 000 staff, 63 per cent of all civil servants. In 2000, after a subsequent period of lower agency creation with some mergers and reorganizations, the total stood at 126 agencies with 279 000

Table 5.1   Growth in agencies 1988 to 2000: number of agencies and civil servants working in agencies

Year	Agencies Created	Total Number of Agencies	Civil Servants in Agencies	All Civil Servants	Agency Civil Servants as Percentage of All Civil Servants
1988	3	3	6 000	580 000	>1
1989	7	10	9 000	569 000	1
1990	25	35	114 000	562 000	20
1991	24	59	200 000	554 000	36
1992	17	76	210 000	565 000	37
1993	16	92	250 000	554 000	45
1994	14	102	268 000	540 000	50
1995	14	109	305 000	517 000	59
1996	30	133	313 000	495 000	63
1997	2	134	305 000	475 000	64
1998	4	138	299 000	463 000	65
1999	5	136	271 000	460 000	59
2000	2	126	279 000	475 000	59

Note: Figures for civil servants in agencies and total civil servants in Britain only (that is, excludes Northern Ireland Civil Service).

Source: Survey of agencies.

civil servants or 59 per cent of all civil servants. The agency reform transformed the structure of many departments (James 1995; Hogwood 1997).
There was additional growth in staff located in departments designated as
operating on agency lines. These included Customs and Excise from 1991,
Inland Revenue from 1992, the Crown Prosecution Service and Serious Fraud
Office from 1997. The agency reform in these departments was an internal
management reform within the organization, for example to create 24 executive units in Customs and Excise, rather than a full application of the executive
agency model as defined here, and is excluded from this analysis. A survey of
all agencies created in the reform from 1988 to 2000 reveals 156 non-trading
agencies and 17 trading agencies. In terms of staff numbers, the split was 80
per cent non-trading and 20 per cent trading type.

SECTION TWO: THE VALUE FOR MONEY OF AGENCIES

There are many potential criteria for evaluating the value for money and
performance of forms of public organization (Pollitt 1995). They can be
evaluated broadly in terms of effects against a set of general criteria or more
narrowly in terms of performance against their stated objectives. Agencies
are assessed here on the criteria put forward by the Next Steps reformers,
who suggested that they would be associated with improvements in economy,
efficiency and effectiveness of public services. These aims are broadly consistent with those of current modernizers who express a desire to improve
value for money and to achieve citizen-focused public services, providing
services that the users of public services and taxpayers want. However, there
have been few assessments of how agencies have performed in practice (for
exceptions see James 2003; Talbot, forthcoming). In a review of agency
working, Trosa noted 'without an objective measure of the [Next Steps]
changes, however, doubt about the effectiveness of the reform will inevitably
remain' (Trosa 1994, p. 68). Most academic work on agencies has focused on
the operation of procedures for agencies in general (Massey 1995a), or
accountability (Judge, Hogwood and McVicar 1997; Polidano 1999; Gains
2000) or accounting arrangements (Pendlebury, Jones, Yarbhari 1992). Government attention has moved on to the modernization agenda. An agency
policy review announced by the Cabinet Office in March 2001, which had
still not been published over a year after its inception, was a belated and
limited recognition of the importance of assessing agency performance
(*Hansard* 2001).

Economy

The authors of the 1988 Next Steps report observed that 'it is difficult to put a figure on the benefits which should become available from our recommendations but the potential is obvious. Five per cent of Civil Service running costs amounted to £630m in 1986–87, and experience elsewhere certainly indicates that when good management has the opportunity to perform well, percentage improvements larger than this are achieved' (Efficiency Unit 1988, p. 16). Changes in real-terms central government running-costs and total spending, the latter total including running costs, are summarized in Table 5.2. There was a real-terms rise in administrative expenditure of £1183 million, or 9 per cent, between 1988–89 and 1997–98, and, in this respect, the agency model was associated with a deterioration in economy. However, after the main burst of agency creation ended in 1996, there was a fall of £706 million or 4.8 per cent from 1995–96 to 1997–98. But the level at the end of the period was still higher than at the start of the reform. In aggregate spending terms, looking at not only running costs but also expenditure on programmes, the economy of central government did not improve after the start of the agency reform. In the ten years after the reform, expenditure in real terms rose from £164 700 million to £195 800 million, a rise of £31 100 million or 18.8 per cent. This is a greater increase than in the same length of time before 1988. In the ten years 1978–79 to 1988–89, central government spending under the planning total, which is broadly similar to the definitions used in later total cost figures shown in Table 5.2, rose in real terms by 13 per cent (Chancellor of the Exchequer 1987, p. 34).

In terms of staff inputs, the agency model was associated with improvements in economy. In crude aggregate terms, the total number of civil servants fell from 580 000 to 463 000 from 1988 to 1998, a fall of 117 000 or 20 per cent over the ten years, as shown in Table 5.1. However, there were similar proportionate falls in staffing in the same length of time prior to the reform. The 1988 Efficiency Unit Report commented that civil service staffing was reduced by 15 per cent between 1979 and 1984 and by 20 per cent between 1979 and 1987 (Efficiency Unit 1988, p. 23). But the continued reductions in the 1990s were perhaps more impressive because of the lower base, all time civil service numbers having peaked in 1976 at 763 000 (Cabinet Office 2000c p. 7).

Focusing on resources used directly by agencies shows the contribution of agencies to the changes in the overall figures for central government. A survey of 72 agencies over the latter part of the 1990s, during the mature phase of the reform initiative, reveals that real terms administrative or running costs were £9127 million in 1995–96 and £9079 million in 1997–98, a fall of £417.8 million, or 4.6 per cent.[2] In these terms, agencies were associ-

Table 5.2   Economy of UK central government 1988–98: administrative costs and total costs (constant 1996–97 prices, £m)

	1988–89	1989–90	1990–91	1991–92	1992–93	1993–94	1994–95	1995–96	1996–97	1997–98
Admin Costs	12 863	12 817	13 295	14 250	14 378	15 117	15 069	14 752	14 319	14 046
Total Costs	164 700	168 000	171 600	179 400	189 500	196 300	199 300	200 800	198 700	195 800

Note: Administration costs are for civil departments, MoD figures are excluded because they included armed forces personnel costs and were subject to several definitional changes during the period.

Source: Chancellor of the Exchequer (1994, pp. 41–2, 1998, p. 57 and p. 64) (adjusted to 1996–97 prices).

ated with an improvement in the economy of these activities by nearly as much as the 5 per cent suggested in the original Efficiency Unit Report. Both types of agency exhibited falls in aggregate administrative expenditure between 1995–96 and 1997–98. However, the falls were larger for the non-trading type, which fell by around 4.5 per cent, than for the trading type which fell by just 1 per cent. But both types of agency were associated with lower improvements in economy than central government as a whole.

The picture is more complex in changes at the level of individual agencies. The mean score for all agencies was a small running cost rise of 1.7 per cent. This increase reflected modest rises in several, mostly small, agencies and a few large increases, the largest being the Forensic Science Service which increased its budget by 75.5 per cent, mainly because of increases in work commissioned by police forces (Minister for the Cabinet Office 1999a, p. 176). However, the median change in budget was a fall of 4.4 per cent. The largest fall was in the Insolvency Service which fell by 25 per cent. Overall, 57 per cent of agencies exhibited budget falls and, in this sense, use of the agency model was associated with improvements in economy in the majority of cases. There was variation in change in economy between individual agencies of different types summarized in Figure 5.2. The mean score of non-trading type was a fall of 2.3 per cent and a median score of a fall of 5.3 per cent. In contrast, the trading type showed a mean increase of 4.8 per cent and a median increase of 8.2 per cent (James 2003).

In the case of the Benefits Agency, the largest agency and an example of a non-trading type, real-terms administrative expenditure fell by 4.4 per cent between 1995–96 and 1997–98 but was still 17 per cent higher in 1997–98 than in the first year of the agency in 1991–92. Staff figures were 5 per cent higher at the end of the period than at the start of the agency's life. Over the life of the agency, real-terms total spending rose 15 per cent, although it was falling at the end of the period. In terms of own running costs, this agency did not appear to perform well, although, as for agencies in general, economy improved towards the end of the period (James 2003).

Efficiency and Effectiveness

The authors of the Next Steps report stated that efficiency and effectiveness were key aims of the reform, commenting that 'there is an immense opportunity to go for substantial improvements in outputs, with better delivery of services and reduced delays as an alternative to savings' (Efficiency Unit 1988, p. 16). These comments reflected a concern with both outputs and outcomes, with outcomes being the final and wider benefits of agencies' activities for different groups and an aspiration to improve the ratio of inputs to outputs and outcomes. Whilst the contemporary concerns of policy makers are not identical, much of the agenda expresses similar aspirations (Prime Minister 1999; Cabinet Office 2000).

The approach taken here is to examine agencies' performance for their 'stakeholders', the people benefiting directly or indirectly from their activities. These groups were listed in annual reports and other documents, including the annual Next Steps reviews. Taking the 1998 review as an example, customer groups discussed include private clients including firms, charities, other organizations and individuals, taxpayers, elected representatives, other government bodies and ministers (Minister for the Cabinet Office 1999). Paying customers were a particularly important group for trading agencies but the primary customer group for all agencies was departmental ministers. An overall survey reveals the general performance in the 1990s on a few key dimensions, supplemented by a deeper analysis of the case of the Benefits Agency.

The main 'evidence' about performance was the general, positive, assertions about agencies' performance made in the annual reviews of agencies, published from 1990. The official in charge of the reform enthused in the first review that 'As this Review shows, Next Steps is working where it matters – out there on the ground. Agencies are improving the way they give value for money and deliver services to their customers. People are showing what they can do when they are enabled to give of their best rather than just told to do so' (Prime Minister and Minister for the Civil Service and the Minister of State, Privy Council Office 1990:7). Sir Robin Butler commented 'I think that those goals of quality of service are being very widely achieved ... One is seeing the results of that in the speed and accuracy of calculations of social security benefits' (Treasury and Civil Service Committee, 1993, p. 53). Similarly, the *Continuity and Change* White Paper in 1994 commented that 'the Next Steps initiative has fundamentally altered the way the Civil Service is managed' (Prime Minister *et al.*, 1994, p. 13). Where academic or government research has assessed performance in these latter terms, the work has focused on high profile cases of failure, including the Child Support Agency, Fire Service College and Passport Agency (Harlow 1999; National Audit Office 1999c, 1999d), rather than more systematic surveys (although exceptions include Trosa 1994; Massey 1995a; Talbot 1996). But building on the limited and fragmented existing material allows a composite picture of the performance of agencies to be constructed on a few key dimensions.

Ministers are key stakeholders for agencies in the UK system of representative government and ministerial satisfaction with agencies seems a reasonable starting point for assessing the extent to which they achieved value for money and citizen-focused public services. A survey of the performance of 72 agencies against ministerial targets in the period 1995–96 to 1997–98 gives an indication of satisfaction. The limitations of performance measures requires that this analysis is supplemented by analysing the responsible ministers' comments in the Next Steps annual reviews of agencies to pick up on levels of satisfaction not reflected in performance against targets. The agencies are classified in three bands according to levels of satisfaction in Table 5.3. First, satisfactory or above, indicating achievement of most or all targets and anything but severe adverse ministerial comment. Second, some cause for concern, reflecting achievement of about half of targets and anything but severe adverse ministerial comment. Third, serious cause for concern, based on severe non-achievement of targets and/or severe adverse ministerial comment. It was not possible clearly to separate ministerial comment beyond the dichotomy between severe adverse comment and any other comment. A large majority of agencies were in the first category. But nine agencies, or 12 per cent, exhibited cause for concern or serious cause for concern, with three agencies or 4 per cent, in the latter category. Unlike in the case of economy discussed above, cross-tabulation of these findings with

Table 5.3   *Agencies and levels (shown as a percentage) of ministerial satisfaction: number of agencies and examples*

	Number (levels of ministerial satisfaction)	Examples
Satisfactory or Above	63 (88 per cent)	Information Technology Services Agency, Benefits Agency
Cause for Concern	6 (8 per cent)	HM Prison Service, Training and Employment Agency, Valuation Office, Public Trust Office, Intervention Board, Northern Ireland Child Support Agency
Serious Cause for Concern	3 (4 per cent)	Child Support Agency, Fire Service College, Student Awards Agency for Scotland
Total	72 (100 per cent)	

Source: Analysis of data from annual reviews of agencies (Minister for the Cabinet Office 1999).

agency type does not reveal a pattern linking variation in performance with type of agency or use of the agency for different types of activity.

However, there are a number of problems with using the achievement of performance targets as an indication of satisfaction with overall performance. Targets were criticized for not being challenging enough and not all aspects of performance were treated with equal importance. A study undertaken by Talbot in the mid-1990s revealed that in total, for all targets for all agencies, 59 per cent related to outputs (for example units of different goods or services produced in a year), 17 per cent related to efficiency (often a measure of unit cost of output), 12 per cent referred to processes (for example achievement of an administrative task) 9 per cent related to inputs and less than 1 per cent were about outcomes (for example effects of an agency's activity on a policy aim) (Talbot 1996). Research looking at ten agencies of different sizes between 1990 and 1996 found that there was a 70 per cent turnover of targets over the period (Talbot 1996, pp. 49–51).

The limited measures of outcomes and stakeholder satisfaction is supplemented by more process-based measures to build an overall picture of performance. These include the benchmarking scores for agencies, which are a mixture of process and outputs and outcomes, and the results of financial audits of the bodies. The benchmark scores for agencies were collected for the 'Business Excellence Model' (BEM) run by the Civil Service College (Minister for the Cabinet Office 1999, p. 9). The BEM was developed as a framework for assessing the performance of organizations across a range of activities and developed by the European Foundation for Quality Management. Over 200 companies across Europe and many public bodies adopted the system. There were nine criteria for assessment, a mixture of an evaluation of procedures and outcomes. The model measures procedural performance against leadership, policy and strategy, people management, resources and processes. There were outcome-focused measures of people satisfaction, customer satisfaction, impact on society and business results. The BEM process produced a scored profile for organizations against each of the criteria. A pilot BEM scheme in 1996 involved 30 agencies, about a third of the total, including the Benefits Agency. However data on these bodies was held by the Civil Service College on a confidential basis. Individual agencies were sensitive about the use of the scores and they were not publicly available (Samuels 1997). But aggregate scores for agencies as a group were available. If private sector performance is seen as a benchmark of satisfactory performance then the BEM scores point to mixed results. Agencies lagged behind, especially on leadership, impact on society and people satisfaction which scored just over half the private sector score (Samuels 1997, p. 4). However, agencies scored higher than the private sector on customer satisfaction.

A further, process based, measure of whether spending was furthering the aims of the organization for stakeholders and efficiency, in terms of whether inputs were contributing to outputs, is provided by the National Audit Office's (NAO) work in financial regularity audit. The Comptroller and Auditor General, the head of the NAO, audited the revenue and expenditure of central government including all agencies and checked whether monies provided by parliament were used only for the purposes intended and with due regard for propriety in expenditure. The audits checked whether the financial statements of agencies were free from material misstatement, whether caused by fraud, error or some other irregularity. Where these problems were seen as significant or 'material' the account was qualified by the auditor, or, if the problem was less severe, the auditor produced a report referring to the problem on the account. The results for the audit of all executive agencies' accounts compared to all UK central government accounts from 1993–99 reveal that each year one or two agency accounts were qualified, with a further number having reports attached to the audit. On average, 6 per cent of agency accounts were either qualified or had a report attached to them. These levels are slightly lower than the 7 per cent average for all central government accounts. On this measure of performance, agencies appear broadly similar with other parts of central government (NAO 1996c, 1997, 1998d, 1999b, 2000b). However, because this information focuses on financial control it provides only a partial perspective.

A broader range of evidence about performance for stakeholders offers an insight into changes from before the start of agency working is available from the case study of the Benefits Agency using official documents, surveys and interviews with officials. The agency's mission was to 'support the Government in establishing a modern welfare state ... by helping to create and deliver an active and modern social security service. The service will encourage independence and pay the right money to the right person at the right time, all the time' (Benefits Agency 1999a, p. 5). Effectiveness is judged in terms of these aims for the range of stakeholders for which the agency produced benefits, principally ministers, acting as a proxy for a broad set of taxpayer and voter interests, and client groups.

In terms of ministerial satisfaction, the agency was in the satisfactory or above category as summarized in Table 5.3. Since its foundation in 1991 the Benefits Agency achieved over 70 per cent of the Secretary of State's targets in eight of the nine years (NAO 1998b, p. 1). The performance each year is summarized in Table 5.4 below. The agency had internal management targets to supplement the Secretary of State's targets and achieved over 80 per cent of these targets in eight out of nine years. For example, the agency achieved 94 of the 109 targets set in 1997–98 (NAO 1998b, p. 1). Ministers were generally upbeat about the agency, praising achievements. In 1998 the then

*Table 5.4   Benefits Agency: Secretary of State's targets: targets achieved/
targets set for financial years 1991–92 to 1998–99*

Targets Achieved/Set by Year							
1991–92	1992–93	1993–94	1994–95	1995–96	1996–97	1997–98	1998–99
16/20	18/23	19/26	16/22	19/22	16/22	8/15	5/7

Source: James (2003).

Secretary of State, Harriet Harman, praised the agency's 'efforts to maintain continuing high standards of customer service' (Chancellor of the Duchy of Lancaster 1998, p. 192).

The performance against targets and overall ministerial satisfaction do not reveal the full picture of performance for ministerial stakeholders. There was evidence of considerable ineffectiveness in delivery of payments by the agency. External reviews pointed to high levels of fraud and error in these payments. The Comptroller and Auditor General qualified his opinion on the account for the tenth successive year in 1997–98, because of fraud and errors in benefit delivery. In 1997–98 these problems accounted for expenditure of £1530 million on Income Support and income based Jobseeker's Allowance, £184 million on child benefit, fraudulent encashment of orderbooks and girocheques amounting to £19 million. In total these problems constituted 7 per cent of total spending on the account (Public Accounts Committee 2000, Secs. 1–3).

Comparing the satisfaction of customers before and after the creation of the agency reveals evidence of improved customer satisfaction. Senior officials argued that there was an improvement in the standards of service that claimants received and improvements to decoration of offices and the 'feel' of the service in the early days of agency working (Interview: Official, Benefits Agency; Interview: Senior Official, Benefits Agency). A comparison of the quality of customer service before and after agency creation illustrates this change. The pre-agency system suffered from poor quality service to claimants. An NAO report on the quality of services to the public at local benefit offices was published in 1988. The report highlighted serious dissatisfaction. A customer survey found that 25 per cent of claimants found the service poor with 75 per cent rating the standard fair or good (NAO 1988, p. 1). By the mid-1990s the situation had improved. A Benefits Agency survey of customer satisfaction ran in the period 1991–92 to 1996–97 and was published in each annual report. It found that between 83 to 86 per cent of customers regarded the service as satisfactory or better (Benefits Agency, 1999a). However, this measure of customer service gave a far from comprehensive assessment. Efforts to use surveys were abandoned in 1995–96 because of concerns about whether they really represented the experiences of customer groups (NAO 1998b, pp. 8–19).

An indication of the efficiency of the agency is given by comparing the outputs of the agency, discussed above, relative to the inputs. Whilst the agency experienced an overall increase in its own resources over the period the workload of the agency rose substantially. Total expenditure, including transfers, fluctuated with economic cycles, reflecting that total economy was in large part linked to demand from those claiming benefit according to the eligibility criteria of social security legislation. The agency had an internal measure of efficiency based on the change in the agency's work output per unit of staff. On this system, the agency improved efficiency by 12 per cent between the start of its life in 1991–92 and 1995–96. However the index did not cover much of the work done in the central benefit directorates and was withdrawn by the agency (NAO 1998b, p. 32). However a crude index of agency spending per unit of workload can be constructed based on Social Fund Crisis loans. This workload figure was continuously available throughout the period; most other benefits changed and reflected changes in wider workloads related to economic cycles. The index of real-term budget per case fell throughout the 1990s, except in 1998, and ended up in the late 1990s about 20 per cent lower than in the early 1990s. The increase in resources consumed by the agency did not keep pace with the workload increases, demonstrating improved efficiency.

SECTION THREE: AGENCY STRUCTURES AND JOINED-UP GOVERNMENT

The current 'modernizing government' agenda suggests a particular concern for the effect of agency structures on systemic performance. The case study of the Benefits Agency shows how the agency structures of organizational separation and the performance accountability regime affected the behaviour of those working in the organization, their ability to bring about desired goals and the consequences for performance. The joined-up government (JUG) performance problems are summarized in Figure 5.1. It is difficult to quantify the costs and benefits involved, but some consequences of the structures can be traced and the magnitude of their effects on outcomes for different stakeholders can be assessed.

Organizational Separation

The vertical separation of policy, primarily located in the Department of
Social Security, from implementation in the agency solidified a long-standing
divide between policy making and operational parts of the social security
system. Horizontal separation distinguished the agency from other bodies in
the Department for Social Security and the rest of government, although
some common grading systems were maintained and the previous systems
were far from unified. Some staff in the agency felt that the attention given to
the organization's mission coupled with more awareness of the costs focused
management attention on making better use of staff and equipment than
previously (Interview, Official, Benefits Agency; Interview, Senior Official,
Benefits Agency). Evidence from interviews is supplemented by evidence of
the significant cost savings made in some areas, for example by market
testing switchboard operator systems, negotiating with telephone service providers, controlling private use of telephones by staff and checking bills using
improved inventories (NAO 1996, pp. 5–6). Whilst telephones were just one
area of the agency's activities there is no reason to think that this area was
untypical.

Despite these improvements, the vertical separation of policy from administration did contribute to serious performance problems. Some senior officials
argued that agency working elevated the status of people working in service
delivery. Michael Bichard was the first head of the Benefits Agency. He
contended that the big agencies, including the Benefits Agency, had been able
to forge a partnership with their policy colleagues. The Framework Document of the agency, setting out its responsibilities, gave it the right to be
involved in policy, and staff were more involved in giving feedback to the
policy sections in the department than previously. The agency had a seat on
the Departmental Policy Board and was usually represented by the head of
the Benefit Management Branch. Bichard suggested that the policy sections
had, before the agency, developed policy too remotely from operations and
this had resulted in a benefits system that was vulnerable to error and abuse.
He suggested that frontline staff often had a better idea of the problems with
the system than policy people (Bichard 1999, pp. 7–8).

Bichard went on to qualify his praise, stating that the views of people
delivering services were still not taken sufficiently into account by those in
policy making organizations (Bichard 1999, pp. 7–8). Even if the problems
of feeding information from the delivery side to the policy side existed before
the agency, agency working did not appear to have improved the situation.
Instead, it instituted an organizational divide between the two, leading to
poor coordination between the agency and the HQ in the early 1990s (Interview with Senior Official, Benefits Agency; Interview with Senior Official,

Department of Social Security). The second Chief Executive, Peter Mathison, in response to criticism from the Social Security Committee about the level of performance, suggested the department should shoulder some of the responsibility, stating 'we have identified where there are weaknesses in the system which may essentially be down to some detail of the policy design and we have identified some also where there are weaknesses around some of the rules and regulations' (Public Accounts Committee 1999, Q165). Other staff in the agency complained that the benefit system was designed by the department without sufficient reference to how they had to be administered (Interview with Senior Official, Benefits Agency; Interview with Senior Official Benefits Agency). This view was repeated by staff in non-policy development sections of the Department of Social Security. An interviewee commented that the agency had not been able to overcome the long standing problem of 'Grade 5s in the Adelphi [the location of most DSS HQ policy development staff] spending their careers developing huge and complex rule-books without much thought for the people who have to implement them' (Interview Senior Official, Department of Social Security).

Neither the agency nor department could cite many cases where changes had been made in response to comments from the agency. An exceptional case was of alterations to legislation about mortgage compensation that allowed for payment of arrears. Agency staff reported that levels of arrears were difficult to assess, leading to inaccuracies. They convinced DSS staff that legislation needed to be changed to make the payment system easier to administer. Within 12 months accuracy had improved by 1 per cent, saving £13 million. But the agency noted that this case was unusual (Benefits Agency 1999b).

The vertical separation contributed to problems of communicating information between the department and the agency, contributing to ineffectiveness. The state earnings-related pension debacle involved a failure to make people claiming pensions aware of changes to policy on eligibility. Whilst the mistake was originally made in 1986, before the agency's creation, the organizational structure imposed by the agency seemed to have worsened the problem. The handling of state pensions required coordinating Benefits Agency staff in Leeds, Newcastle, local offices responsible for various parts of delivery and departmental headquarters in London responsible for supporting ministers in the development, maintenance and evaluation of pensions policy. Once the department was made aware of the error in 1995 the information was not passed to the Benefits Agency and incorporated in the information they gave to clients. Benefits Agency leaflets and staff continued to give wrong information until 1999. In the end, Age Concern, a charity representing users of the services, rather than the agency or DSS staff, brought the full implications of the error to the attention of ministers (NAO 2000a, p. 28).

The absence of end-to-end responsibility and good communication was a major factor in the failure according to NAO (2000a, p. 10). However, not all the poor communication was the result of the agency/department split; there was poor communication within the agency itself (NAO 2000a, p. 26).

The creation of the agency as a separate unit to focus on its own tasks exacerbated the long-standing fragmentation of the government system. An important area of co-working was between the Benefits Agency and the Employment Service in delivering Jobseeker's Allowance from 1996. This benefit was delivered from jobcentres run by the Employment Service who paid the benefit as an agent of the Benefits Agency although much of the administrative work behind payments remained with the agency. Organizational separation contributed to performance problems. There was a lack of sharing of information resulting in the same information being requested twice, draining resources and inconveniencing claimants (Benefit Fraud Inspectorate (BFI) 1999b, Appendix B). Comments by Patricia Hewitt, a member of the Social Security Committee, illustrated problems that arose for customer quality in having to deal with two organizations. She noted that jobcentres sent out letters to clients based on information provided by the Benefits Agency but could not respond to queries, instead having to refer clients to the Benefits Agency for details which caused delay and inconvenience (Social Security Committee 1998, Q163).

One reason for the problems was differences between conditions of service in the two agencies. Staff in the Benefits Agency worked behind screens to protect them from clients whereas the Employment Service had a more open work environment. Under the so-called 'Bichard Agreement', named after the first head of the Benefits Agency, staff in the Benefits Agency were given the right not to be transferred to different working conditions when undertaking Jobseeker's Allowance related work. This restriction limited flexibility in the use of staff, contributing to lack of effective communication (Social Security Committee 1998, Q176). One senior official commented 'both agencies would have preferred Jobseeker's Allowance to go to one or another, rather than having to share it' (Interview with Senior Official, Benefits Agency).

The 'logic' of the agency model was for separate organizational operations and separate accounting for performance for each agency. However, the joint working was smoothed by several structures which went against the grain of the agency model but facilitated more effective delivery. These systems included joint meetings to address problems at different management levels. The Benefits Agency Chief Executive, Peter Mathison and the Chief Executive of the Employment Service, Leigh Lewis, met with other members of their boards in a joint board on a quarterly basis and prepared action plans. There was a Joint Operations Team with members from both bodies to facilitate joint working and local level meetings (Social Security Committee

1998, Q163). The delivery was further smoothed by staff transfers between the organizations so that staff were doing very similar work as previously but in a different organization. Such transfers ran against the grain of the agency model which suggests different terms and conditions in different agencies focused on different organizational missions, making these sort of transfers more difficult to achieve (James 2003).

Accountability Systems Including Performance Targets

The second part of the agency model is the performance accountability regime consisting of accountability as a unit, with a designated chief executive and performance targets. The department kept some input controls over the agency and was largely successful in keeping the organization to the running cost budget allocated to it. The agency's budget was set by the Secretary of State and operated within a gross running cost system of control. If the agency felt that changes in workload affected its ability to carry out its tasks it had to seek approval to change its business plan and funding levels. The budgetary control mechanisms were not successful in improving economy as discussed earlier on. However, the level of payments to claimants was largely determined by demand for services because of changes in economic conditions. The administrative budget similarly was affected by changes in workloads. For these reasons, the budgetary control mechanism can be seen as reasonably effective, especially the reductions in running cost budget which were achieved towards the end of the period through agreement between ministers and departmental officials and senior agency staff. Agency staff commented on the toughness of the regime they faced in evidence to the Social Security Select Committee. The chief executive described the request for a 25 per cent reduction in costs in a four-year period as feeling like 'somebody had three cups and a pea under one of them' (Social Security Committee 1998, Q142).

Whilst administrative costs could be controlled, subject to the need to cover workload, the accountability regime had less desirable effects on efficiency and effectiveness. The performance target system was reflected in the internal management targets of the Agency which were tied in to the external reporting regimes. A proportion of the pay for people in the organization including the Chief Executive was linked to achieving targets (Interview: Senior Official, Benefits Agency). For example, in 1997–98 the agency's management team monitored performance against all the 124 Secretary of State's and related internal management targets. On occasion this led to misrepresentation of performance. The survey of customer satisfaction was in part dropped because of worries about whether it reflected performance or was an exercise in trying to produce a survey that met the target. The Chief

Executive, in evidence to the Social Security Committee, commented that 'I felt that maybe the national survey was designed to try to get a figure of 86 per cent [the target]' (Social Security Committee 1998, Q174).

The performance target system led managers to pay insufficient attention to the performance of activities that were not the main focus of targets. A major problem was the focus on clearance times hampering efforts to achieve accuracy, contributing to the poor performance in the latter area described in the previous section. An official commented 'We used to be under pressure to get all claims done within the clearance time [target] more than anything else' (Interview: Official, Benefits Agency). Concern with budgetary targets led to less emphasis on redress when an error was made. The Parliamentary Commissioner for Administration (PCA) noted that even when the agency had been clearly at fault, it took pressure from him to persuade the agency to give redress (Interview: Senior Official, Parliamentary Commissioner for Administration).

The focus on targets for benefits hindered attempts to redesign systems within the agency. Area managers were sometimes responsible for the achievement of 40 different targets (NAO 1998b, p. 38). The targets were separately related to different benefits, so that each benefit was still treated largely as a separate activity within the organization. However, clients were often eligible for several benefits. The problem was noted by junior staff working in the local offices who commented 'each of the systems we have is based on a different benefit rather than allowing us to deal with an individual claimant who might be looking at several relevant benefits' (Interview: Official, Benefits Agency). This pattern of working led to inefficiency and a poorer quality of service for claimants than if more flexible client focused systems were adopted, but these would not have been compatible with the external target system for the agency. More generally, the potential advantages from collaborating with voluntary groups and charities in disseminating information about benefits and developing innovative ways of dealing with clients were not facilitated by a regime which focused attention narrowly on hitting targets for specific aspects of specific benefits.

The difficulties of setting and using performance targets to control the agency led to concern from ministers and civil servants in the department about the divide emerging in the vertical relationship. The department became concerned about the extent to which the agency was acting autonomously and the department's inability to act as an 'intelligent customer' (Interview: Senior Official, Department of Social Security). The Agency was developing its own systems which the department came to view as giving it a separate capacity and putting its own 'spin' on performance (Interview: Senior Official, Benefits Agency). Departmental civil servants and ministers felt that the target regime could not really be used to drive up performance; there was a lack of faith in the regime (Interview: Senior Official, Department of Social Security). However, the blame for poor performance was assigned to the department as well as to the agency by outside bodies especially the parliamentary Public Accounts Committee (Interview: Senior Official, Benefits Agency). The Department was especially concerned about the high level of fraud and error on benefits expenditure (Interview: Senior Official, Benefits Agency).

The department was able to partially 'fine tune' the performance system to ameliorate these problems. The performance targets were changed to reduce their number and to achieve a better balance between speed of clearance and accuracy (Interview: Senior Official, Department of Social Security). The appointment of the second Chief Executive was used as a further means to exercise control over the agency. The first Chief Executive, Michael Bichard, had been seen by the department as trying to make the agency too independent. Consequently when his successor was chosen, one of the criteria used was that the appointee should be 'managerial' and follow the spirit of the framework and targets set down by the department (Interview: Senior Official, Benefits Agency).

The agency model did not turn out to be a piece of transferable technology that could survive the different policy priorities of a new government. The problems of controlling the agency became more acute after 1997 when Labour ministers were appointed. Their agenda involved a change in emphasis towards encouraging employability and a social security system more 'responsive to, and providing a more direct service for the public' (Chancellor of the Duchy of Lancaster 1997, p. 192). The agenda was even more difficult to achieve using a system that did not have end-to-end responsibility for the design and implementation of policy, because the policy being implemented was more ambitious. The system was also inappropriate for a client focus, because the targets were oriented towards performance in terms of separate benefits (Interview: Senior Official, Department of Social Security; Interview: Senior Official, Department of Social Security).

The performance target regime encouraged the agency to concentrate its efforts on its own activities, regardless of the public-sector externality effects on other bodies, exacerbating problems of horizontal working. The agency's own targets did not include its effects on local authorities' work, particularly the high level of fraud and error and incorrect information being passed to local authorities. The agency had considerable difficulties in satisfying the stakeholders who were other public bodies relying on the agency to perform their own tasks. The Benefits Agency administered two benefits, Income Support and Jobseeker's Allowance, which had implications for a third benefit, Housing Benefit, mainly administered by local authorities. This was a sizeable programme costing about £11 100 million per year in 1996–97 or 12

per cent of the total £90 000 million spend on social security (NAO 1999a).
The agency passed information to local authorities about claimants to assist
them in the administration of Housing Benefit. Because about 66 per cent of
people claiming Housing Benefit were also on Income Support or Jobseeker's
Allowance there was substantial joint working (NAO 1997, p. 18). If a claimant was awarded Income Support or Jobseeker's Allowance by the agency
then the local authority had to assume that they had no income or capital,
which affected the award of Housing Benefit (BFI 1999d, Sec 8.1). The
agency's problems with fraud and error on these benefits had a further externality effect in terms of fraud and error on Housing Benefit. In the mid 1990s,
about 74 per cent of fraudulent claims on Housing Benefit were also fraudulent claims for Income Support (NAO 1997, p. 21). Overall, about 7 per cent
of the Housing Benefit budget was paid out in fraud and error in the mid
1990s (NAO 1997, p. 1).

Whilst the Benefits Agency had service level agreements with local
authorities since 1992 setting out the agency's aims in cooperating with these
organizations, an NAO study found that a majority of local authorities felt
that these agreements were not working (NAO 1997). The Benefit Fraud
Inspectorate (BFI) found that in 57 per cent of their inspections, liaison
needed to be improved between the Benefits Agency and local authorities.
The required improvements included better exchange of information, more
cross agency working and better feedback on fraud cases (BFI 1999d, Sec 1).
Whilst local authorities were inefficient in their administration of benefits
because of problems in the authorities, the BFI found that the agency made a
substantial contribution to the difficulties (BFI 1999d).

The agency's incentives to achieve its own fraud targets placed the body in
competition with local authorities in trying to stamp out fraud and placed
emphasis on trying to raise levels of fraud detection rather than prevention.
The schemes used the principle of finders-keepers for bodies detecting fraud,
which discouraged information sharing. In some instances the agency did not
pass on cases of fraud it discovered to the local authorities because it wanted
to keep the savings to help achieve its own fraud targets (NAO 1997, pp. 62–
3). The Benefit Agency's 'Spotlight' anti-fraud initiatives did not involve
local authorities as much as they could have, in part because of a concern to
pursue its own targets (NAO 1997, p. 71). In some cases there was an atmos-
phere of mutual suspicion between the agency and local authorities, although
the relationship varied around the country (NAO 1997, p. 66).

The performance target system led to coordination problems with other
agencies. In some senses the joint delivery of Jobseeker's Allowance with the
Employment Service was a success, in that most of the targets relating to the
benefit were met. However, the agency was always under pressure to use
resources to promote the achievement of its own targets. The Jobseeker's

Allowance working arrangements in part reflected non-agency structures established between the Benefits Agency and the Employment Service, including joint management boards. More severe problems caused by targets were reflected in working with the Contributions Agency which was responsible for protecting the rights of contributors and interests of taxpayers through efficient payment and recording of National Insurance contributions.

The Contributions Agency used National Insurance numbers to identify contributors. Most of these numbers were created by the Contributions Agency but about 30 per cent were created by the Benefits Agency and then passed on using a special form, CA5400. The two agencies had a National Service Statement in place to cover areas where their work coincided. However, there were no high level Benefits Agency targets for this service. There was no target time for passing the forms from the agency to the Contributions Agency. The Benefits Agency undertook poor quality interviews as part of the application process and used inexperienced staff. These problems resulted in 34 000 CA5400s, about 15 per cent of the total, being returned by the Contributions Agency each year. The return of forms was inefficient for the Benefits Agency because it had to undertake the application process again, but even more of a problem for the Contributions Agency because the allocation of numbers was a key part of its business. Fifty-four per cent of forms took more than 16 days, resulting in out of date information being used to create National Insurance accounts, damaging the collection of contributions (BFI 1999c, Secs 3.11–13).

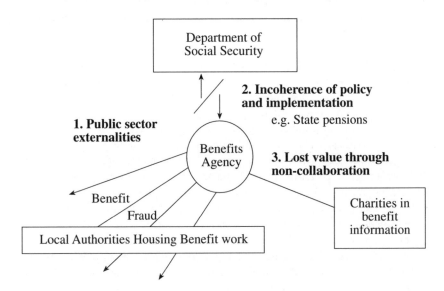

Figure 5.1   The Benefits Agency and joined-up government

CONCLUSION

The current modernizers of government have talked more in terms of improving value for money than just economy, so they might not be too concerned about the failure to achieve the improvements in economy that the Next Steps reformers expected. There were improvements in the administrative costs of non-trading agencies during the late 1990s and civil service staff fell by 20 per cent in the ten years after the reform. However, real-terms central government administrative expenditure rose by 9 per cent and real-terms total central government expenditure by 18.9 per cent over the decade following the launch of the agency reform. In the case of the Benefits Agency, a non-trading agency, real terms administrative expenditure fell by 4.4 per cent between 1995–96 and 1997–98 but was still 17 per cent higher in 1997–98 than in the first year of the agency in 1991–92. Staff figures were 5 per cent higher at the end of the period than at the start of the agency's life and real-terms total spending rose 15 per cent.

More limited conclusions can be drawn about efficiency and effectiveness. However agencies did appear to perform well in the opinion of key stakeholders. On the measure of ministerial satisfaction, 88 per cent of the 72 agencies surveyed in the mature phase of the reform were in the satisfactory or above category. On average over the period 1993 to 1999, only 6 per cent of agencies had problems with their accounts that were noted as significant by NAO. But the case of the Benefits Agency illustrates wider performance issues surrounding efficiency and effectiveness. Whilst the agency was able to improve customer service, there were serious shortcomings in effectiveness, particularly inaccuracy in the delivery of benefits amounting to, on average, 7 per cent of the payments budget which formed over 90 per cent of total spending. However, the agency was associated with better use of some resources. According to a crude measure of efficiency based on workload, the agency improved its own efficiency in the 1990s.

The need for more joined-up government appears clear-cut in the case of the Benefits Agency. The beneficial effect of agency structures in promoting a focus on the agency's task at hand was accompanied by a lack of attention to broader effects on performance of the social security system. The agency structures created horizontal and vertical fragmentation. There were substantial problems of vertical organizational separation between the sections of the Department of Social Security Headquarters, responsible for policy, and those in the agency responsible for implementation. Organizational separation exacerbated difficulties in horizontal working with other delivery bodies through different working conditions. In some areas this did not greatly compromise the delivery of services, such as Jobseeker's Allowance. But the success was in large part because of the use of joint boards, staff transferring

between the Benefits Agency and the Employment Service, and local working arrangements contrary to the main thrust of the agency model. The
performance system exacerbated problems of horizontal working by encouraging Benefits Agency staff to focus on their own work to the substantial
exclusion of considering the effects on other organizations' activities. These
problems were apparent in local authorities' administration of Housing Benefit,
where inaccurate information provided by the agency contributed to the
outcome of 7 per cent of expenditure being paid out inaccurately. In the light
of this performance, the new arrangements for social security run by the
Department for Work and Pensions, which replaced the Department for Social Security in June 2001, appears to be a reasonable response (Department
of Work and Pensions 2002, p. 18). The structures replace the Benefits Agency
and the Employment Service with a new working-age agency and a pensions
organization. The new working-age agency is intended to promote seamless
working between policy makers and those implementing policy, and to improve horizontal working in delivering of welfare payments (Benefits Agency
2001). The significance of the lack of joined-up working in other agencies
cannot directly be inferred from the Benefits Agency. The return of the Civil
Service College to the Cabinet Office in Autumn 1999, and the strengthening
of ministerial responsibility for the Prison Service after 1997 seem to reflect
issues of vertical fragmentation, whilst some agency mergers, particularly in
defence, reflect issues of horizontal fragmentation and loss of economies of
scale (James 2003). However, the joined-up government agenda is likely to
be less relevant to the extent that an agency's performance does not affect
other public sector bodies, as is more likely to be the case with trading
agencies that are not part of departments' mainstream activities.

NOTES

1. This chapter is a revised version of a paper presented to the Public Administration Commit-
    tee Annual Conference 2001 and published as 'Evaluating Executive Agencies in UK
    Government' *Public Policy and Administration*, 2001, **16** (3), 24–52 and includes material
    published in O. James (2003), *The Executive Agency Revolution in Whitehall*, Basingstoke:
    Palgrave Macmillan..
2. The year 1995–96 marks the point where two thirds of the agencies had been created and
    constitutes the start of the mature phase of the agency reform. The three-year period is long
    enough for trends to emerge but not too long to prevent the identification of a substantial
    set of stable agencies to track over time. Of the 102 agencies that existed at the start of
    1995, 30 were reorganized, privatized or abolished in the period to 1998, leaving 72 bodies
    for examination.

APPENDIX

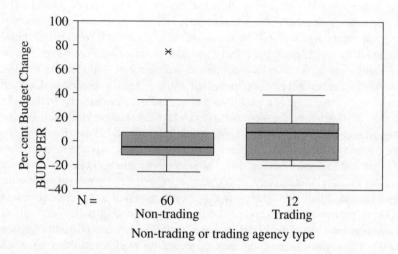

Note: The information necessary for this classification was gathered from the Next Steps annual reviews (Chancellor of the Duchy of Lancaster 1997; 1998; Minister for the Cabinet Office 1999a).

Figure 5.2   Survey of agencies: budget changes 1995–96 to 1997–98

6. Devolution, integration and modernization in the United Kingdom civil service

Richard Parry

INTRODUCTION

Two forces are at work in the UK constitutional project of the Blair government. The first theme is of a decentralization of political authority that admits the possibility of policy divergence from Westminster norms. This takes the form of three devolution settlements, happily conceded to be a 'variable geometry' that seeks to meet the political demands of each territory. Scotland and Wales both have coalition administrations of Labour and Liberal Democrat; the relation between executive and legislature in Scotland is similar to that at Westminster, but the National Assembly for Wales has a constitutional structure that blurs the distinction between the two. Northern Ireland uses proportional representation in the executive as well as the legislature, with strongly differentiated departments 'owned' by political parties which nominate ministers.

The second theme is of a centralized project of modernization that seeks to promote optimal international practice in public sector management (Newman 2001). This includes themes of efficiency, public participation and performance achievement that are held to be a normal part of a successful government and not a democratic option to be accepted or rejected. This started off under the rubric of 'Modernizing Government' through a White Paper of that title issued in March 1999. Subsequently this became the motif of all Labour's initiatives, and civil service reform became a programme of its own.

Modernization is promoted by a joint élite (in an analytical, not a pejorative, sense) of ministers, special advisers and permanent civil servants to whom it represents an attempt to get a grip on the British central bureaucracy. This élite is located in the Cabinet Office, the No. 10 Office and to some extent in the Treasury. It is personified by Tony Blair and his choice as Head of the Civil Service (1998–2002) Sir Richard Wilson. Authors such as Seldon and Kavanagh (1999, Chapter 10) have looked admiringly at the presidential-style machine Blair has put together; others such as Hennessy (2000, Chapter 18) have found themselves sceptical of the semi-Bonapartism of the 'Tony wants' school, as a damaging adaptation of the traditional Cabinet system.

Modernization is disseminated throughout Great Britain (but not in Northern Ireland) by dominant forces within the Labour Party. The party seeks a consistent message from all its cadres, whether in UK central government, local government, or the devolved administrations. Despite devolution, the party resists attempts to make modernization a contestable political choice. There are also extensive networks at official level, within both central government and the wider public sector; Labour's modernization documents show remarkably little respect for jurisdictional boundaries.

The two themes are not in complete tension; there is still much political and policy integration in devolved areas, and the Scottish and Welsh administrations have home-grown management planning based on their programmes for government. Nevertheless there is a duality of constitutional anchors offered to civil servants as part of the devolution settlement: it works solely to its own ministers, whether at UK or devolved levels; but its Welsh and Scottish members remain part of the Home Civil Service and so enjoy the protection of civil service codes.

The maintenance of the Home Civil Service was an important, though inadequately argued through, aspect of the devolution legislation. Civil Service unity is not quite such an axiomatic proposition as might be supposed. There has long been another UK public service – the Diplomatic Service – working to the same political mandate as the Home Civil Service, and a further one – the Northern Ireland Civil Service – which for most of its history has not. Closer examination reveals other civil services of the Crown, such as the Northern Ireland Court Service, responsible to the Lord Chancellor. There is regular interchange between these services. A further comparative factor is that the present UK model has no parallels in other intergovernmental systems, whether British-derived (Canada, Australia) or European federalist (Germany). In a comparative context it would be totally normal for a devolved political system to have its own public service with full responsibility for pay, conditions and appointments – and in most cases a greater permeation of partisan appointments into the upper echelons than would be found in the UK.

The practicalities of the issue mask deeper issues about the identity and self-awareness of officials who had been recruited to serve the British state. Modernization policies are a reminder of new Labour's policy reach into the devolved systems, and also a source of new thinking about policy leadership and delivery that can be exploited by innovative ministers and senior officials. The Permanent Secretaries of the Scottish Executive and National Assembly for Wales, Sir Muir Russell and Sir Jon Shortridge, are modernizers in their early fifties who have both shown an enthusiasm for making use of these opportunities and are familiar figures in the central corridors of Whitehall.

This chapter explores the balance between political deconcentration and integrative modernization as it faces civil servants in 2003, and assesses developing events in Edinburgh, Cardiff, Belfast and Whitehall. It draws upon interviews conducted in 2001–02 on 'The Home Civil Service as an Integrative Force in the Post-Devolution Polity' as part of the Economic and Social Research Council (ESRC) Devolution and Constitutional Change Programme. Methodologically, this research tried to use the techniques of élite interviewing to get a sense from senior civil servants of the way the devolved systems are developing. The common theme is of a considerable commitment to make devolution work (in Whitehall as well as the devolved nations) combined with some sense of disorientation as the anchors of civil service norms are loosened. Nearly all the main civil service actors, however committed to their nations, have spent decades in a Whitehall-orientated world of practices and procedures, and 18 recent years under Conservative administrations.

Despite a greater recent diversity of background and style, senior officials come to occupy the ready-to-wear suits waiting in civil service offices for those of the right skills and mentality. Moreover, the ready-to-wear expectation extends to ministers as well. If there is one cause of the frustrations and misunderstandings of the first two years of devolution, it is a lack of mutual comprehensibility of the worlds of the civil servants and the new ministers. The Westminster system is based upon an initiation into a powerful symbolic world of behaviour and practice. The backbench apprenticeship of UK ministers is paralleled by the building of a civil service career through a succession of postings and promotions.

Devolved systems have lacked these symbolic patterns. Most elected members have come from non-parliamentary backgrounds and expect to find continuities between their old and new work lives. The gender, age and professional distribution is different. The Home Civil Service represents the structures and culture of appropriate behaviour felt by the continuing officials and offered by them to the mostly new ministers. As Newman says, 'cultural analysis views public and social policy as fields which are socially constructed: that is, problems and solutions are formed within the framework of particular narratives, ideologies and assumptions. Successful narratives are those that come to be taken for granted or viewed as "common sense". "Common sense" does not arise naturally but is forged out of struggles to establish certain ideas as dominant' (Newman 2001, p. 7). Inheritors of these ideas become their custodians, with an often acute sense of duty to promote them in changing circumstances and pass them on to their successors. The devolution settlement promotes the Home Civil Service as such a successful narrative and encourages its leaders to carry it forward.

THE CIVIL SERVICE IN THE DEVOLUTION SETTLEMENT

The logic behind the retention of Scottish and Welsh devolved officials is ostensibly a pragmatic one based on the needs for interchange and best practice. As the Scottish devolution White Paper said:

> These arrangements will give the Scottish Executive the support of a tried and tested civil service machine, and access to a wide pool of talent and experience. They will also contribute to fostering good working relationships between the Scottish Executive and the UK Government (Scottish Office, 1997. Cmnd 3658, para. 10.12)

A fuller justification was given by Tony Blair in a speech to senior civil servants on 13 October 1998 (the so-called 'Islington agenda'):

> I attach great importance to preserving a unified Civil Service working for all three administrations in Edinburgh, Cardiff and Westminster. We do not want anybody who works in the Welsh Office or the Scottish Office to feel that they are being cut adrift from the Civil Service. I also attach great importance to establishing efficient machinery for close working between the UK Government and the devolved administrations.

Blair's 'cut adrift' phrase hinted at a key aspect of constitutional transformations: the securing of the allegiance of the permanent bureaucracy to the new structures of accountability. The Civil Service is listed alongside the Crown and the UK Parliament as one of the reserved matters under 'the Constitution of the United Kingdom'. A theme of the devolution transition planning was the note of reassurance given to officials from senior management that their traditional values and position in the Constitution would not be overturned.

The Home Civil Service also offers a ready-made tool-kit of rules and procedures. The civil service runs on codes and manuals like *Government Accounting*, now continually updated on the web via www.government-accounting.gov.uk. Traditionally, detailed control and oversight has been associated with the Treasury. But the Barnett formula has greatly reduced the detail of Treasury spending control over the Scottish and Welsh administrations, which have had to develop many of their own procedures for financial scrutiny within the Executives, linked to new structures of auditing and accountability with elected members. The web of relationships with Whitehall has now been tilted more to the personnel side. Here, the way that the Scottish and Welsh administrations are treated shows a greater similarity to the position of the former Scottish and Welsh Offices than is now the case on the financial side.

The operational framework comes from two documents issued as part of the Major government's civil service reforms of 1996 and revised in 1999 to take account of devolution (accessible via www.cabinet-office.gov.uk):

1. the *Civil Service Code* sets out the constitutional and ethical framework within which 'the Civil Service will conscientiously fulfil its obligations to, and impartially assist, advise and carry out the lawful policies of the duly constituted Administrations' (para. 9)
2. the *Civil Service Management Code* combines points of detail with pre-scribed practice for making the civil service one based, in the official phrase, 'on merit on the basis of fair and open competition'. This Code gives the Scottish and Welsh administrations a basis for their relations with ministers. Examination reveals that the special provisions in the Code for the devolved administrations are confined to the grading of posts and the position of special advisers (see Table 6.1). For grading, the change is potentially significant as it reflects the freedom of the administrations to choose their own balance between running costs and programme expenditure. For special advisers, it sets a restrictive frame-work based upon Whitehall practice.

The Codes, which are paralleled by local adaptations of the UK Ministerial Code, are much more influential than the Concordats agreed in 1999 between the devolved administrations and UK government departments. These were elaborate and quite legalistic documents listing areas of cooperation and setting out procedures for dispute resolution. They provide a hierarchy: an overarching Memorandum of Understanding, Concordats, and in some cases service level agreements. The quasi-diplomatic aspects of these documents have not been necessary and exchange of information has happened rou-tinely. In contrast, the civil service codes bite on the day-to-day life of officials and both express and operationalize the value system that they feel.

WHAT A UNIFIED CIVIL SERVICE MEANS

The Home Civil Service is stratified into three levels. At the bottom are the grades below the Senior Civil Service, where there is now complete delega-tion of pay and gradings. One of the previous unified grades (grade seven, formerly Principal) falls within this group. The Cabinet Office takes a hands-off and generally sympathetic approach but remains interested in general pay patterns in these grades. Devolved administration staff are in contact with the

*Table 6.1   Where devolved administrations are treated differently in the
              Civil Service Management Code*

UK departments	Scottish and Welsh administrations
Grading of posts (para 6.1.2)	
'appropriate to their business needs, are consistent with the Government's policies on the civil service and public sector pay, and observe public spending controls'	'appropriate to their business needs and are consistent with the Government's policies on the civil service and take account of the Government's policies on public sector pay'
Special advisers (Introduction, annex A, para 3)	
No maximum number	Maximum of 12 (Scotland)/6 (Wales)
Appointments cannot extend 'beyond the end of an Administration'	Appointment cannot extend 'beyond the end of the term of office as member of the Scottish Executive/ National Assembly for Wales First Secretary or Secretary of the person whom he is appointed to advise'
Up to three are not confined to only providing advice to ministers	(no such provision)

Note: Quotes taken from the Civil Service Management Code.

Performance and Reward Division of the Cabinet Office, and at the level of
Principal Establishment Officer there is a Personnel Directors Group that
meets regularly and exchanges information. When the Scottish Executive
negotiated a three-year pay deal and new appraisal system in 2000, it was run
past the Cabinet Office. In the absence of any stage of Treasury approval for
the pay strategy of the Executive, there was neither mechanism nor inclination for holding up what in pre-devolution days might well have been
scrutinized at length for its possible impact on the rest of the civil service.
The deal was regarded as innovative and was mentioned in the Civil Service
Reform Programme Annual Report 2000 (para. 3.2).

Attracting less interest than pay is recruitment – the business of advertising, selecting, making offers and ensuring that appointees actually take up
their job. Both Scotland and Wales have been under pressure to bring in more
staff to meet the policy-making demands of devolution, with Wales experiencing distinct difficulties in meeting its targets in 2000. Both the devolved

administrations have been actively pursuing new talent, but in different ways. The Scottish Executive ran open competitions for entry into the Senior Civil Service in 2000 and 2002. It has also made extensive use of interchange with Whitehall departments. The National Assembly has made more of external advertising of specific posts. Even though the great majority of civil servants in Scotland and Wales (and also some in Northern Ireland) work in non-devolved UK departments, there has been a subtle shift in attitudes from 'joining the civil service' to 'joining the devolved administration'.

The Senior Civil Service (SCS) is the corporately-organized group of the most senior Home Civil Service staff in departments and agencies, comprising grades with starting salaries of around £50 000 in 2003. Here, personnel management is centralized, with individual contracts and a pay and grading system separate from that of departments and using the Senior Salaries Review Body. But here also there are elements of delegation, because there are no centralized grades other than Permanent Secretary and departments have freedom to create new SCS posts provided that they have, in terms of the job evaluation system used, a Job Evaluation for Senior Posts (JESP) score of seven. The original SCS pay system consisted of nine overlapping pay bands linked to JESP scores but in practice the relativities between individuals and between posts seemed inconsistent. The system was modified in 2001 to something more like the old system of grade two, three and five (Deputy Secretary, Under Secretary and Assistant Secretary) with three non-overlapping pay bands and a lesser weight given to JESP scores.

Within the Senior Service, there is a top stratum of 150 posts (defined by a mixture of JESP scores and salary) falling within the ambit of the Senior Appointments Selection Committee (SASC, see Richards 1996). This is a civil service committee with the close involvement of the First Civil Service Commissioner (Baroness Prashar in 2003) and makes recommendations to the Prime Minister, who formally agrees to appointments even in the Scottish and Welsh administrations. SASC is a powerful mechanism for collective knowledge at the upper reaches of Whitehall. The scale is small enough for individuals' names to be known and to be considered in relation to a number of present and impending vacancies. SASC also decides on the mix of internal and external advertising for posts. Sir Muir Russell of the Scottish Executive was a member of the Committee.

The definition of which posts fall within which stratum could be of significance to the devolved administrations. We might hypothesise that they would keep posts out of the SASC grades to avoid Whitehall involvement in them; or alternatively promote jobs into them as a sign of status and pay for their occupants. At present Permanent Secretaries seem to be letting the chips fall according to the rules rather than favouring either strategy. There is an imbalance between administrations, with Wales having, in addition to the Permanent

Secretary, only two mainstream SASC posts (the former Deputy Secretaries, now called Senior Directors), in addition to the Clerk and the Counsel-General to the Assembly. Scotland has seven heads of department, including two created in 1998–99, and Northern Ireland has nine departmental Permanent Secretaries of similar rank in a separate system (and at a level below the Head of the Northern Ireland Civil Service and the single Scottish and Welsh Permanent Secretaries).

In terms of job evaluation, the head of department jobs in the devolved administrations might fall either side of the JESP 18 divide, and Northern Ireland and Scotland seem graded high relative to Wales. Part of the issue is that senior officials in both Scotland and Wales have been reluctant to move to a straightforward Northern Ireland model of one minister – one department – one head of department. To do so would be to jeopardize the joined-up aspect of the old Scottish and Welsh Offices and create issues of the span of control of the Permanent Secretary and of the pay and grading of the head of department job. The answer has been to leave things as they are. When, after a hiatus that must have included consideration of these issues, the vacant secretaryship of the Scottish Executive Development Department was filled in July 2001, the post continued to support two Cabinet ministers. It is typical of the balancing acts involved that the post was advertised externally but filled by an internal applicant (Nicola Munro), the long-overdue first woman head of a Scottish department.

MODERNIZING GOVERNMENT – THEMES AND MECHANISMS

The civil service provisions of devolution would be simpler if the devolved administrations simply had to observe rules on the management of the civil service. But as the concordat between the administrations and the Cabinet Office of October 1999 makes clear, the unity of the Home Civil Service also encompasses implementation of the *Modernizing Government* White Paper (Minister for the Cabinet Office 1999b) programme, including the delivery of better public service in the UK, information age government, best practice in public service delivery (efficiency, public appointments, agencies) and 'better regulation'; and also cross-cutting issues like anti-drugs policies, social inclusion and women's issues. The devolved administrations also have an intellectual buy-in to Whitehall thinking on policy-making and public management through the Performance and Innovation Unit, the Social Exclusion Unit and the Centre for Management and Policy Studies. These links could be seen as a use of civil service unity to influence the policy and managerial approaches of the devolved administrations in a way not made explicit in the legislation.

This extended concept of the united strategy of the civil service owes much to an accident of timing. The Major government had promoted public sector management initiatives like the Citizen's Charter which started the dubious habit of regarding all delivery agencies (and even privatized utilities in some cases) as part of a total UK public service effort. The Blair government took this further in *Modernizing Government* of March 1999 (Minister for the Cabinet Office 1999b), which spoke of 'designing policy and around shared goals and carefully defined results, not around organizational structures or existing functions' (Prime Minister 1999, Cmnd 4310, para. 2.6). The White Paper also committed the government to a doubling of the number of women and ethnic minorities in the Senior Civil Service by 2004/05 (para. 6.25), targets being pursued with vigour but in the case of women now accepted to be unrealistic. The pre-devolution Scottish and Welsh administrations were fully part of these policies, which have retained a progressive and non-contentious political impulsion among post-devolution ministers and officials. Had the Blair government's plans for public sector reform been delayed for a few months more the political stakes in Scotland and Wales would have been different.

The civil service at UK level responded with search for both 'quick wins' and a longer-term structure. During 1999 four Permanent Secretary sub-groups were set up to explore the themes of Vision and Values; Bringing In and Bringing On Talent; Performance Management, and Diversity. The project teams were also interdepartmental, and led by Sally Hinkley and John Barker of the Cabinet Office. Some Scottish and Welsh officials were on these sub-groups but their meetings straddled the devolution implementation period. The Bringing In and Bringing On Talent was the most detailed, with 'baskets' of proposals for wider recruitment and interchange. The Performance Management group, chaired by Sir Michael Bichard who was to retire early from the Department for Education and Employment in 2001, had what for a civil service document was uncharacteristically business-jargon rhetoric: 'the first step is to define and relentlessly communicate a compelling and stretching aspiration for the future' (Cabinet Office 1999a, p. 5)

In the autumn the Permanent Secretaries met, and in December 1999 Sir Richard Wilson presented his report to the Prime Minister on Civil Service reform. The themes had now been redefined to six: 'stronger *leadership* with a clear sense of purpose; better *business planning* from top to bottom; sharper *performance management*; a dramatic improvement in *diversity*; a Service *more open* to people and ideas, which brings on talent; and a better *deal for staff*' (Cabinet Office 1999c). Business planning is related to the UK government's objectives as set out in Public Service Agreements. 'Champions' were nominated to promote aspects of the programme, and these included Jon Shortridge on the appraisal and competence aspects of performance management. With Muir Russell on SASC, both the Scottish and Welsh chief officials were drawn into central civil service management even more than they might have been in pre-devolution days.

In meeting these objectives, the devolved administrations were treated alongside UK government departments in a circus of money and meetings. They were required to produced an Action Plan by February 2000 with bids for money from an 'Invest to Modernize' fund from which Scotland received £3.6 million and Wales £2.1 million. Scotland, but not Wales, sought money for early retirements at senior level, which facilitated three vacancies on the Management Group in 2000–01. In 2000–01 meetings under the title of 'Making It Different' were held throughout Britain in which senior officials mingled with junior staff.

The civil service is caught between the theme of 'driving through' change centrally, and respecting the themes of devolution and delegation in the constitutional project. As the Permanent Secretary Sub-groups recognized, the targets for diversity and opening-up might seem to imply a reversal of the delegations to departments made in 1996. But this is not particularly a devolution issue. Scotland and Wales have been accommodated, their special circumstances recognized and their joined-up administrations presented as good guys in the reform process. Both have their local versions of Modernizing Government – 'Twenty-first Century Government' in Scotland and 'Delivering Better Government' in Wales – and have been formulating business plans based upon their executive's programmes. Wales completed its business plan first and it was evaluated by officials from Scotland and Northern Ireland, demonstrating that a policy-related exercise specified within civil service reform could be carried through in a devolved administration. The art is to combine credit and money from Whitehall with sensitivity to local political circumstances, including a coalition government.

It is possible to conceive of three variants in the attitude of the devolved administrations to modernization:

1. *collaborative* variant – the devolved administrations embrace the themes of civil service reform and the principles of policy-making they embody (see Cabinet Office 1999b), and use the advisory capacity of UK-level mechanisms to promote them in Scotland and Wales in parallel with England; they are happy to have their achievements advertised as part of a UK-wide project;
2. *neutral* variant – the devolved administrations seek to have a clearly differentiated brand of reform which asserts their own policy objectives and resists any tendency to use the reform processes as a means of constraining their authority, but they are happy to run them alongside similar initiatives at UK level;

3. *conflict* variant – the devolved administrations become suspicious that civil service reform does not recognize the reality of devolution. Ministers see the mechanisms as a reinforcement of devolved officials' traditional links with Whitehall. Links become confined to procedural issues around Civil Service Commissioners' business, and civil service management matters take on a profile previously reserved for policy issues.

The initial post-devolution period has fallen between (1) and (2). The key variable is the political control of the executives, and both officials and commentators are awaiting the prospect of non-Labour administrations that might move relationships in the direction of type (3). If this happened, the Home Civil Service as a concept would probably come to be cast very quickly as a problem rather than a solution.

THE EVIDENCE FROM NORTHERN IRELAND

The best evidence on the effect of freedom from the Home Civil Service comes from Northern Ireland, and suggests that the sociology of the civil service club is just as important as its rule-book. Since devolution, the Head of the Northern Ireland Civil Service (since 2002 Nigel Hamilton) has ceased to be a Second Permanent Secretary at the Northern Ireland Office and a member of the Civil Service Management Board. But he is free to attend the Wednesday meetings of the Permanent Secretaries as in effect an honorary member, and does so from time to time. The same thing happens lower down the line, as with the new pay and appraisal arrangements for the Senior Civil Service; Northern Ireland buys into Whitehall thinking and is within the information net.

Northern Ireland departments have always had a distinct legal personality and their own Permanent Secretaries (Carmichael 2001). Permanent Secretaries work with the ministers that the system has presented to them – in Nigel Hamilton's case, moving in 2001 from a Sinn Féin minister at Education to a Paisleyite one at Regional Development. The departments and agencies have their own personnel divisions which manage and place staff but work under pay and grading frameworks set by the Central Personnel Group using a single Recruitment Service. At the centre, policy coordination is supplied by an increasingly powerful Office of the First Minister and Deputy First Minister (OFMDFM) which has SDLP and Ulster Unionist junior ministers and since 2002 its own Second Permanent Secretary (Will Haire in 2003) and is gaining influence at the expense of the Department of Finance and Personnel.

The Northern Ireland Civil Service (NICS) is protected in part by the procedurally sensitive and often litigious employment culture that has developed since the Fair Employment (Northern Ireland) Act 1989. Recruitment is based on merit with monitoring arrangements in place to profile the community balance within the NICS at all levels. Any departure from this, including any leaning on the system by ministers, would meet with industrial tribunal action. Whitehall's techniques of stretching, aspirational targets might not be feasible in Northern Ireland. The NICS has its own version of the rules in the Civil Service Management Code but it has not yet been possible to finalize a definitive post-devolution version.

The Northern Ireland and Home Civil Services interface in the Northern Ireland Office (NIO). The NIO includes the law and order functions that are eventually set for devolution to the Executive. It uses the Northern Ireland Civil Service (NICS) as its personnel pool for these functions, but its Home Civil Service (HCS) staff do not have access to NICS jobs in return (in a number of individual cases, transfer from the HCS to the NICS has been secured). This is perceived as unfair by the NIO but justified from the NICS side because of what is seen as a legal impossibility of allowing NIO staff but not all other home civil servants to compete for NICS jobs. Nor do NICS staff have access to HCS posts beyond the Northern Ireland Office. Positions are held with some vehemence on this issue, showing how a 'trench' can develop between separate services.

Northern Ireland has not been part of the UK Modernizing Government initiative. It did decide in 1996 to embrace the pay and appraisal mechanisms of the Senior Civil Service, and so gained access to the more market-driven salary levels of the new system, and it has also applied some aspects of the initiative such as business planning and performance management. The NICS's rather old-fashioned procedures on matters like complexity of gradings and the use of departmental seniority are diminishing, but their persistence might be see as the product of a small, conservative service protective of established staff interests. The ability to substitute its own versions of modernizing initiatives from Whitehall on its own time-scale reinforces that impression. It will only be once the new political institutions are fully functioning and in a position to challenge the static patterns of direct rule that the lessons of the separate NICS for Scotland and Wales can be judged.

PRESSURES AND REVIEWS IN THE DEVOLVED SYSTEMS

The Scottish Executive is the devolved system best placed to replicate Whitehall structures and behaviour, because its constitutional pattern is the same. The Scottish Office's long pedigree led to a comfortable assumption of the symbols and processes of a devolved government. The desire to implement the Executive's Programme for Government has produced a centralized administrative structure, with the creation of a Department of Finance and Central Services in June 2001 (but with the Principal Establishment Officer continuing to report directly to the Permanent Secretary). Reinvigoration of senior management, greater innovation in pay and personnel than has been the case in Wales or Northern Ireland, and increasing mutual familiarity with roles and personalities have helped the Scottish civil service to secure its position after a shaky start in relations with its new ministers (Parry and Jones 2000).

In contrast, the National Assembly for Wales has illustrated the problems that arise from a novel constitutional structure. The National Assembly is a single legal entity in which the Assembly clerks are civil servants and where all officials are working for the Assembly, which has delegated its executive functions to an Executive of what are now called ministers (but originally secretaries) who also sit on the appropriate Assembly Committees. What might have been a novel and potentially fruitful constitutional structure has been condemned by most of the actors within the system, and by observers in Whitehall, as an impossible departure from the separation of executive and legislature (Laffin and Thomas 2001). Over time, the clerks' office, the Office of the Presiding Officer, has been separated off and since 2000 has its own budget and staff delegation below Senior Civil Service level; tension over the role of these staff reflects the lack of any pre-devolution precedents or code. In 2002 the executive side was rebranded as the 'Welsh Assembly Government', grasping what in Scotland had become the taboo of the Executive's claiming the 'G word'. If this separation can settle down, the informal aspects of the Welsh system offer potential for new styles of civil service behaviour. In the published words of Martin Evans, a Head of Group who ran devolution planning, 'that the system works owes much to Ministers' commitment to open government. This has created a climate in which officials can speak frankly and constructively without forfeiting Ministers' confidence. It's a more grown-up politics and one we should chalk up as a success to be valued' (National Assembly for Wales 2001, annex).

The first signs of frustration with the Whitehall system have come in Northern Ireland and Wales with ministers' setting up of formal reviews unrelated to Whitehall reforms. In Northern Ireland, a committee under Lord Ouseley was asked to look at ways of making the senior civil service more representative and examine 'the roles of officials and ministers in each stage of the selection process' (DFPNI Press Notice 5 March 2001). Its report was published in June 2002 prior to a consultation exercise (Ouseley 2002). In 2002 a Review of Public Administration was launched to look at the totality of public service delivery in Northern Ireland. In Wales, a review of assembly procedures reported in February 2002 and a Commission on Powers and

Electoral Arrangements is to report by the end of 2003. The statement on the Partnership agreement of October 2001 between Welsh Labour and Liberal Democrats stated that they would 'seek to move towards an increasingly independent and Welsh-based civil service'.

The degree of routine open advertising of appointments has emerged as an important issue. The civil service has traditionally operated through promotion boards that assess suitability for the generic skills of a higher grade and only subsequently allocate successful candidates to a post. The most radical challenge to this approach has come in Wales. The Equality of Opportunity Committee of the Assembly – then chaired by the Minister for Finance, Edwina Hart – commissioned trade union official Roger McKenzie to look at institutional racism and the under-representation of ethnic minorities in Cardiff. He recommended that 'all posts, of whatever grade, should be advertised and open to competition' and that there should be no more recruitment to generic grades (McKenzie 2001).

Reactions of horror in Whitehall to this proposition were not shared by Assembly officials to the extent that might have been expected. Already the Assembly was doing extensive external advertising and had absorbed outside agencies in health and housing without letting them retain any separate personnel functions. The new Staff Deployment and Recruitment Strategy, issued for consultation in January 2002, suggests that, with limited exceptions, posts should first be advertised internally to those at the same grade and 'if no suitable candidate were identified, the slot would then be subject to open recruitment' (National Assembly for Wales 2002a, para. 12). In its comments, the Office of the Civil Service Commissioners expressed 'surprise at the proposal to abandon entirely internal promotion boards in particular the potential impact on staff morale' (National Assembly for Wales 2002b, annex D); although in committee evidence in June 2002 Sir Richard Wilson said 'I do not mind them doing that' (House of Lords Select Committee on the Constitution 2002, p. 367). As well as applying to all grades, the Welsh approach is less kind to tradition is than the Ouseley recommendation in Northern Ireland that 'as a matter of principle, there should be a presumption of all resultant [after level grade transfers] SCS vacancies being filled by open competition. However, it recognizes that there may be occasions for business continuity or practicality reasons when Ministers will wish an alternative approach to be adopted' (Ouseley Report 2002, para. 4.27)

Another issue is that of ministerial involvement in appointments. The Civil Service Management Code offers ground-rules: ministers are entitled to take an interest in some appointments and to know the identities of those being interviewed; 'the Minister may want to meet the lead candidate before deciding to approve the appointment, but he or she cannot pick and choose among the reserve candidates' (p. 21); in the end a minister could veto an appointment and require the process to begin again. But the Code does not specify what the jobs are where a minister can take an interest. The rule seems to be that SASC jobs at least are run past ministers and that, in general, they express satisfaction with the ways that things are being handled. There is no consistent evidence that by virtue of the smaller scale of devolution there is a creep downwards in the range of jobs in which ministers are interested. What is happening is that a process of explanation has to take place in which ministers are reminded that they are subject to what are in effect statutory rules and codes in a reserved area (the civil service). It should also be noted that the civil service rules are quite liberal on temporary secondments of up to one year, and that this provision can be used to draft in additional support and policy advice for ministers. The devolved administrations are not at the leading edge of debates on these matters.

At present the main mechanism for defusing any problems is the external advertising of posts – normal now for permanent secretaries in Northern Ireland, becoming routine for Senior Civil Service posts in Wales, and developing in Scotland in a pattern the closest to that of Whitehall. Initially, as has been the case with most agency chief executive jobs, the appointment procedures confirm the greater strength of internal candidates, but eventually the market begins to move. Scotland, Wales and England have recruited administrative heads for their health departments direct from posts in health service management. In June 2001 London-based Bank of Ireland executive Gerry McGinn was appointed Permanent Secretary of the Northern Ireland Department of Education. In 1999 Aideen McGinley had moved from a local authority chief executive post to the Secretaryship of the Department of Culture, Arts and Leisure. In 2002 the Headship of the Northern Ireland Civil Service was advertised externally. If such appointments become more than exceptional, the effect on the ability of the civil service to steer the careers of its long-term staff would be profound.

CONCLUSION

Civil servants in the United Kingdom have embarked upon a journey in which the stability of their status is not a complete protection against the dynamic political processes of devolution. Their present position can be summarized as follows:

1. The Home Civil Service as such is not a highly salient operational concept; the Northern Ireland Civil Service and the Diplomatic Service have been accommodated inside the tent and it is easy to imagine a federation of UK public services with interchange.

2. But the maintenance of the Home Civil Service in the devolution settlement was a recognition of the fears of civil servants that notions of professionalism and impartiality might be compromised, especially by the introduction of practices similar to local government; therefore the retention of the existing Civil Service Code and Management Code provided a basis of stability and some instruments of leverage for officials on their new ministers – as well as avoiding the enormous job of devising parallel new codes as part of devolution planning.
3. As well as this defensive protection, civil service reform gives an opening to the devolved administrations, because the diversity and business planning aspects of the programme imply innovative forms of personnel management. Local versions of modernizing government are developed, and the UK process is used to gain money and credit from the Whitehall level to which the most senior officials remain strongly orientated.
4. Wales is at the leading edge of problems and opportunities, because its entire political system is being formed as part of the devolution settlement and the Assembly has a stronger handle on civil service personnel matters than in either Scotland or Northern Ireland.
5. The mechanism of change is likely to be the wider external advertising of posts, initially favouring internal applicants, but in time developing a learning process on the kinds of externally-acquired skills that will be suitable for senior positions.
6. The end result could be a unified horizontal leadership group in each nation's public sector, embracing the civil service, the health service and local government, and awaiting the point where different political mandates at the UK and devolved levels lead to political conflict.

This change of orientation would put the devolved administrations ahead of the debate about whether the civil service reform effort since 1998 has been a sufficient response to the demands of ministers, or whether it might be necessary to re-appraise the whole basis of the formation and competences of the permanent government bureaucracy in the UK. It still seems axiomatic to most civil servants throughout the UK that the cultural narrative of the civil service is something to be celebrated and cherished – notably in contrast to that of local government administration. But the survival of the civil service as a career corps of inherited traditions rather than as employer of officials with specific expertise recruited for specific tasks is in question. If it were to fracture, the devolved administrations would feel it first, and might well continue their old tradition of experimenting with change and learning lessons on behalf of the UK as a whole.

ACKNOWLEDGEMENT

This research was undertaken as part of a research project on 'The Home Civil Service as an Integrative Force in the Post-Devolution Polity', supported by the Economic and Social Research Council as part of the Devolution and Constitutional Change Programme, ref L219252034. I am very grateful to Fiona Wager for research assistance. An earlier version was published in *Public Policy and Administration* **16**, 3 (2001), pp. 53–67.

7. Modernization and civil service accountability: the case of Scottish devolution

Iris Kirkpatrick and Robert Pyper

INTRODUCTION

As the Blair Government unveiled its devolution programme for Scotland and Wales, the attention of commentators and analysts tended to focus on the broad political and constitutional implications of the new arrangements for governance. The potential impact of devolution on the functioning of the civil service received considerably less attention, at least in the early phase of the policy's development. Notwithstanding this, it was clear that the advent of new administrations in Edinburgh and Cardiff would bring fresh challenges for officials in the devolved bodies and also in Whitehall. One particular challenge would result from the creation of new regimes of parliamentary accountability. How would the hitherto relatively under-scrutinized elements of the civil service in Scotland and Wales react to the new agents of accountability on their doorsteps?

In this chapter, our interest lies in identifying the initial impact of the Scottish devolution settlement on the civil service. The discussion will be contextualized through an exploration of the linkages between official accountability, devolution and modernization. The chapter represents an interim report on work in progress. The empirical research, which underpins the tentative findings and conclusions, is continuing.

The research is designed to test the extent to which the early phase of the devolution settlement in Scotland has produced significant change in the accountability regime for civil servants in Edinburgh, and to that extent, has contributed to the process of modernization. Our initial work has involved detailed textual analysis of an extensive range of primary documentary sources with the aim of analysing the quality and quantity of the pre- and immediate post-devolution accountability regime for civil servants in Scotland. These sources encompass an array of documents from the Westminster Parliament 1992–99 and the Scottish Parliament 1999–2001. Additionally, the work will include an ongoing programme of elite interviews with selected Members of the Scottish Parliament (MSPs) and Scottish Executive officials. At this stage, we are able to offer a summary of findings from a pre-interview questionnaire distributed to all MSPs.

The control data is from the immediate pre-devolution period (the 1992–97 parliamentary session plus the period preceding the establishment of the Scottish Parliament, 1997–99). This charts the appearances of Scottish Office civil servants before the relevant Westminster parliamentary committees (the Scottish Affairs Committee and the Public Accounts Committee) plus the number and frequency of Parliamentary Commissioner for Administration investigations of civil service actions in this department and its executive agencies. This information will be compared with the emerging data on appearances of officials from the Scottish Executive before committees in the Scottish Parliament between 1999 and 2001 and the number and frequency of the Scottish Parliamentary Commissioner for Administration's investigations of Executive departments and agencies. The views of MSPs on the emerging regime of civil service accountability will be summarized.

The research builds upon Pyper's past work on civil service accountability and the impact of devolution on the civil service in Scotland (see, for example, Pyper 1996 and 1999), and, in time, it will form part of a wider project examining the developing modes of official accountability in both Scotland and Wales.

Before examining the evidence of civil service accountability in the immediate pre- and post-devolution periods, it is appropriate to explore the thematic links between official accountability, devolution and modernization.

MODERNIZATION, DEVOLUTION AND CIVIL SERVICE ACCOUNTABILITY: SOME THEMES

In simple terms, it might be argued that devolution is a feature of modernized government, and, as such, it will have a tendency towards enhancing the accountability of those in positions of power, including civil servants. However, once we probe beneath the surface of such bland generalizations, complexities emerge. Modernization is a rather loose concept, and while it is possible to argue that the type of constitutional change which produced the Scottish devolution settlement is a form of modernized governance at the macro level, we also need to recognize that modernization at the micro level does not necessarily equate with improved official accountability. In any case, although the impact of devolution on the civil service in Scotland is far from clear, as yet, the early indications are that organizational changes have been marginal and incremental, and the regime of official accountability certainly remains rooted in the traditions of the UK polity. Let us examine these points in more detail.

Devolution as a Feature of Modernization

Modernization is a multi-faceted, but curiously imprecise concept. As Toynbee and Walker have noted, the *leitmotiv* of New Labour was:

> never explicitly defined, it shaded into democratization, meaning an effort to breathe new life into participative government by bringing its institutions physically or figuratively closer to the people, making them more accessible, accountable and intelligible. But Blair also wanted to govern effectively. (2001, p. 204)

The extent to which modernization is a continuation and rebranding of the New Public Management (NPM) (in many respects a similarly opaque set of ideas), or represents a significant development in its own right, has been the subject of some debate (see, for example, Falconer, 1999; Hughes and Newman, 1999; Minogue, Polidano and Hulme 1998; Newman, 1999 and 2001). We are not directly concerned with this debate *per se*. Our interest lies in the association between modernization, devolution and official accountability.

Those who comment upon modernization tend to focus on features such as joined-up government, evidence-based policy, information-age government, partnerships, and the management/policy dichotomy. However, as Toynbee and Walker noted, at a wider macro level, modernization, as pursued by the Blair government, has involved elements of structural and constitutional reform. The most significant aspect of this has been devolution. While it might be argued that the link between modernization and devolution is not necessarily causal, and it would be perfectly possible to have a programme for devolved government without explicitly connecting this to a modernization agenda, it has to be recognized that the Blair government eschewed this approach, and instead established (at least in its own terms) a clear connection between modernization at the macro, constitutional level, and devolution. Furthermore, academic analysts perceive clear links between modernized governance and devolution.

It is possible to locate devolution within the framework of modernization in different ways. In his synthesis of the theoretical debates on governance, Rhodes (1997, pp. 46–53) points out that rolling programmes of institutional and constitutional reform, encompassing policies, the political culture and the governing framework, are intrinsic to good governance. It can be argued, by extension, that certain aspects of the process of modernization flow from this approach to governance, and within this, devolution of power can be viewed as a feature of modernization. A similar conclusion is reached by

Newman (2001, pp. 78–82). Her analysis of New Labour's attempts to modernize governance leads her to draw upon a number of conceptual models, one of which, the self governance model, sees devolution as part of a set of initiatives which are designed to develop new policy networks and communities, and sharpen accountability. In brief, therefore, devolution can be viewed as a facet of the Blair government's modernization programme at the macro, constitutional reform level, and one of the explicit assumptions of devolution was that it would enhance accountability. We return to this below.

Modernization and Official Accountability

At the micro level, one product of modernization, and its antecedent NPM, has been a blurring of traditional organizational boundaries, the emergence of new structures for policy-making and delivery of public services. To some extent at least, the creation and implementation of policy via increasingly complex systems and networks of organizations drawn from the public, private and voluntary sectors has effectively resulted in the disaggregation of the conventional structures and processes of public administration. These systems and networks (see Kooiman 1993; Pierre 2000; and Rhodes 1997) can become closely integrated, are resistant to steering by government, and are capable of developing their own policy agendas. Newman summarizes these developments, and stresses the tendency for networks to ' ... cut across organizational boundaries, weave in and out of hierarchies' (2001, pp. 33–7). However, this differentiated polity is distinctly problematic for official (and indeed political) accountability. As Rhodes observes, 'fragmentation erodes accountability because sheer institutional complexity obscures who is accountable to whom and for what' (1997, p. 101). Newman supports this, noting that 'accountability is low ... ' in this context (2001, p. 35). At the level of central government, clear illustrations of this came during the agencification of the civil service (although of itself, this was not the most radical manifestation of the differentiated polity), in the course of which parliamentary modes of accountability struggled to keep pace with the implications of the move from traditional departmental structures to executive agencies.

Although modernization in its various guises clearly has had, and continues to have, significant implications for management in the civil service (including that part of it within the Scottish Executive, which was subject to a tailored version of the Modernizing Government programme produced by Jack McConnell, the first Finance Minister) and across the public sector as a whole, it seems to have little to say about the accountability of the civil service, beyond continuing to stress, *à la* NPM, the importance of managerial forms of accountability (including those based on consumerist and contractual approaches) which tend to focus on outputs rather than policy *per se*. It can be noted in passing that these brands of official accountability (particularly the consumerist forms) coexist rather uneasily with the constitutional norms governing civil service accountability; as we note below, these emphasize the importance of accountability to ministers, to Parliament in only limited circumstances, and to the public not at all!

Devolution and the Civil Service

Given all of this, what can be said about the impact of devolution, as one strain of modernization, on the accountability of the civil service? It is important to stress from the outset that the government's devolution policy contained an unambiguous commitment to the continuity of a unified civil service. Devolution was not to be accompanied by the establishment of constitutionally distinct bureaucracies in Edinburgh and Cardiff. Officially, at least, the civil service itself was to remain unchanged in important respects by devolution.

The manner in which devolution was implemented served to reinforce this policy. Initial analysis of the organizational impact of devolution on the civil service in Scotland (see Parry 1999, 2000; Parry and Jones 2000) emphasized the essential continuity between the former Scottish Office and the new Scottish Executive. This served to prevent any break-up of the existing organizational structure in Edinburgh, and also to secure essential continuity in relations with Whitehall and with established British civil service practices.

> What has emerged is, in many respects, the Scottish Office with the name changed ... it was the best way of resisting any pressures for the fracturing of central functions or the balkanization of the office ... the transition process itself consolidated rather than catalysed ... (Parry 2000, p. 64)

Nonetheless, despite the immediate moves towards consolidation, Pyper (1999) noted the apparent tension between the government's determination to preserve a unified civil service, fundamentally untouched by devolution (the 'concordats' between the Scottish Executive and the Whitehall departments were designed, at least in part, to minimize the prospect of a federated bureaucracy) and devolution's longer term potential to produce changes to the organization and structure of the civil service in Scotland, to the volume, nature and type of work carried out by officials in Edinburgh, and perhaps even to the accountability regime for officialdom north of the border.

FRAMING CIVIL SERVICE ACCOUNTABILITY: THE RULES OF THE GAME

The devolution project was certainly based, in part, on the proposition that the extant 'democratic deficit' produced by the unitary (or Union) state could be overcome through creating a system of enhanced accountability. While this was primarily taken to imply improved accountability of central government to the people of Scotland there was also a somewhat inchoate, but vaguely recognizable aspiration to strengthen the accountability of public servants to the representatives of the people in the Scottish Parliament:

> ... the aim is to make government more accessible, open and accountable ... extend democratic control ... The Scottish Parliament will hold the Executive to account for its actions. Ministers of the Scottish Executive will be answerable to the Scottish Parliament, and that Parliament's committees will be able to scrutinize and report on the effectiveness of the Executive's administrative action and its use of public monies ... (Scottish Office 1997, pp. 2, 3, 13)

Beyond these general aspirations, however, the Scottish devolution settlement's key documents offered virtually no details on the types and forms of accountability to be expected. The Scotland Act (clause 91) merely made provision for the investigation of complaints about actions taken by Scottish Executive ministers or officials, through the Parliamentary Commissioner for Administration scheme, and, in a supplementary schedule to the main body of the Act, indicated that committees of the Scottish Parliament would be set up under standing orders. When it first met, the new Parliament based its operations largely on the recommendations made by the Consultative Steering Group (CSG) chaired by the Scottish Office Minister of State, Henry McLeish. However, the CSG final report (Scottish Office 1998, section 3.4) had also failed to comment upon the types and forms of political and official accountability which might emerge from the work of the Parliament, concentrating instead on a rather dry outline of the procedures and mechanisms (including questions, debates and committees) which might be deployed.

In the event, the aspirations regarding enhanced openness and accountability were apparently to be secured through deployment of a very traditional array of mechanisms and devices, cloned from Westminster, within the existing constitutional norms. Scrutiny of the executive would take place through Parliamentary Questions (in both oral and written answer forms), the ombudsman, debates and committees (although, admittedly, the committees of the Scottish Parliament differed from their Westminster counterparts because they combined the investigatory and legislative functions of select and standing committees).

As the new Parliament set to work, some details emerged concerning the rules governing the accountability of Scottish Executive officials. Essentially, these confirmed and reinforced the Westminster and Whitehall practices. There would be no direct civil service accountability to the Scottish Parliament, but, as at Westminster, official lines of accountability would run via ministers. In this sense, the accountability regime for civil servants in Scotland remained unmodernized to a considerable degree. Effectively, this points to the bounded radicalism of New Labour's constitutional reform. Devolution was accompanied by the continued prevalence of UK civil service norms and Westminster modes of accountability.

A clear illustration of this came in November 2000, when the Scottish Parliament approved a motion on Executive accountability which adhered to the principle that:

> ... officials are accountable to Ministers and Ministers in turn are accountable to the Parliament and it follows that, while officials can provide Committees with factual information, Committees should look to Ministers to account for the policy decisions they have taken. (Scottish Parliament 2000)

This provision of factual information can be seen as equating with the most diluted form of accountability, answerability or explanatory accountability (see Marshall 1986 and Pyper 1996, p. 9), which implies the need to provide answers and information without invoking the stronger elements of accountability, including amendatory actions, redress of grievances or the imposition of sanctions on wrong-doers.

Nonetheless, it might be argued that the significant increase in the numbers of ministers to whom civil servants were accountable by itself brought about enhanced internal accountability of officials to their political masters. The normal size of the ministerial team within the Scottish Office was seven: the Secretary of State, two Ministers of State and four Parliamentary Under Secretaries of State. By contrast, 20 ministers worked in the Scottish Executive (22 if the Law Officers are included), with the First Minister supported by nine full Ministers and ten Deputy Ministers (respectively ten and eleven including the Law Officers). However, this had no impact on official accountability to the Parliament. In that context, the principle of non-accountability, or, perhaps more accurately, mere explanatory accountability, was reiterated and expanded upon in the 'tartanized' version of the Osmotherly Rules (which govern the evidence given by civil servants to select committees) produced by the Scottish Executive in February 2001 (Scottish Executive 2001a). In a similar vein, the civil service guidance on Scottish Parliamentary Questions emphasized the primary accountability of ministers and delineated the role of civil servants in terms which stressed their subsidiarity. 'It is a civil servant's responsibility to help Ministers to fulfil their obligations but ultimately it is the Minister's right and responsibility to decide how to do so.' (Scottish Executive 2000a, para. 33) Notwithstanding this, and given the tendency for changes to take place to the accountability of the civil service *de facto* rather than *de jure* (see the impact of agencification on official accountability to the Westminster Parliament), the impact of the Scottish devolution settlement on the traditional parliamentary accountability of the civil service still merits our attention.

PARLIAMENTARY ACCOUNTABILITY AND THE CIVIL SERVICE: SOME PRE- AND POST-DEVOLUTION TRENDS

For Scottish Office civil servants, the demands of parliamentary accountability were, arguably, less onerous than those faced by officials in other departments of state. This can be explained with reference to their geographical isolation, coupled with the fact that this territorial department generated relatively few investigations by the Public Accounts Committee of the House of Commons, was subjected to oral Parliamentary Questions only once a month and even escaped scrutiny by select committee for an entire Parliament (1987–92) due to the failure to achieve agreement on the composition of the Scottish Affairs Committee (see McConnell and Pyper 1994a, 1994b, 1996). In addition, the very nature of this department of state, as a multifunctional, territorial outpost, meant that specific policy spheres attracted relatively less scrutiny than was the case in the typical single-function Whitehall departments. Finally, the fact that the Scottish Office executive agencies were generally quite far removed from mainstream policy spheres meant that they attracted relatively little scrutiny.

During the period between the implementation of the devolution settlement in Scotland and the end of the 1997–2001 Parliament (effectively two years from the spring of 1999 until the spring of 2001) the Westminster mechanisms of scrutiny and accountability continued to function in relation to Scottish business. Thus, for example, the Select Committee on Scottish Affairs remained, as did the routine of PQs and debates. Naturally, the volume of scrutiny from these mechanisms declined as the focus of attention shifted from the rump Scotland Office in Whitehall to the new Scottish Executive in Edinburgh.

The data set out in Tables 7.1–7.4 reveal a significant increase in the volume or quantity of answerability or explanatory accountability demanded of the civil service in Scotland during the immediate post-devolution period. The most remarkable developments have taken place in the realm of the committees of the Scottish Parliament.

These committees combined the functions of Westminster's select and standing committees: they possessed powers of investigation and scrutiny as well as initiating and processing legislation (see Lynch 2000). To some

Table 7.1 Number of Scottish Office/Scottish Executive civil servants giving oral evidence to the House of Commons Scottish Affairs Committee and Public Accounts Committee for the parliamentary sessions 1992–93 to 2000–01

Departmental origin of civil servants and number of appearances before Scottish Affairs Committee (SAC), and Public Accounts Committee (PAC)

Session	SOAEFD/ SEERAD		SOEID/SEED/ SELLD		SODD/SEDD		SOHD/SEJD		SODH/SEHD		OTHER		Total
	SAC	PAC	SAC	PAC	SAC	PAC	SAC	PAC	SAC	PAC	SAC	PAC	
1992–93	0	0	2	3	1	0	4	0	5	2	3	0	20
1993–94	2	0	6	2	0	0	1	0	6	0	5	4	26
1994–95	4	0	0	0	0	0	0	0	0	0	2	2	8
1995–96	1	0	0	2	5	3	0	0	0	0	3	0	14
1996–97	0	0	0	0	2	0	5	0	0	0	0	0	7
1997–98	0	0	6	2	3	2	0	0	0	2	2	0	17
1998–99	0	0	6	0	3	0	0	0	1	0	0	0	10
1999–00	0	0	0	0	1	0	0	0	0	0	0	0	1
2000–01	0	0	0	0	0	0	0	0	0	0	0	0	0
Total	7	0	20	9	15	5	10	0	12	4	15	6	103

Key: SOAEFD, Scottish Office Agriculture, Environment and Fisheries Department; SEERAD, Scottish Executive Environment and Rural Affairs Department; SOEID, Scottish Office Education and Industry Department; SEED, Scottish Executive Education Department; SEELLD, Scottish Executive Education and Lifelong Learning Department; SODD, Scottish Office Development Department; SEDD, Scottish Executive Development Department; SOHD, Scottish Office Home Department; SEJD, Scottish Executive Justice Department; SODH, Scottish Office Department of Health; SEHD, Scottish Executive Health Department; OTHER, includes Scottish Office Administration, Scottish Office Central Services, Scottish Executive Corporate Services, Scottish Courts Administration, Crown Office, and Registers of Scotland

Notes:
1. Most parliamentary sessions are of a very similar length (November to November each year), although the 1996–97 session was shortened and the 1997–98 lengthened, as a consequence of the General Election in 1997.
2. The new Scottish Executive Departments were created over the period May-July 1999. There is no exact match between the responsibilities of these departments and old Scottish Office departments. They are grouped together here simply on the basis of broad similarities.

Source: Minutes of Evidence, Scottish Affairs Committee and Public Accounts Committee, Sessions 1992–93 to 2000–01.

Table 7.2 Number of civil servants (Scottish Executive Departments) giving oral evidence to committees of the Scottish Parliament 1999–2001

DEPARTMENT AND YEAR

COMMITTEE	SECS			SEDD			SEED			SELLD			FCSD			SEHD			SEJD			SEERAD			OTHER			Total
	99	00	01	99	00	01	99	00	01	99	00	01	99	00	01	99	00	01	99	00	01	99	00	01	99	00	01	
Audit	0	0	0	0	2	0	2	1	0	2	2	0	0	4	0	0	1	6	0	0	0	0	3	0	0	1	2	26
Education Culture and Sport	0	0	0	0	5	4	0	0	0	0	0	0	0	1	4	0	2	0	0	0	0	0	0	0	0	0	0	16
Enterprise and Lifelong Learning	0	0	0	0	4	0	0	0	0	40	11	0	0	7	1	0	0	0	0	0	0	0	0	0	0	0	0	63
Equal Opportunities	0	0	0	0	4	5	3	0	0	0	0	0	0	6	0	0	0	0	0	7	0	0	0	0	0	0	0	25
European	0	0	0	5	0	3	0	1	0	0	1	1	0	0	0	0	0	0	0	0	0	0	3	0	0	0	0	14
Finance	0	0	0	0	3	2	0	1	0	2	2	1	0	10	7	0	2	5	0	0	0	0	0	0	0	0	0	35
Health and Community Care	0	0	0	0	0	0	0	0	0	0	0	0	0	0	1	0	7	7	0	0	0	0	0	3	0	0	0	18
Justice and Home Affairs	0	1	0	0	1	0	0	0	0	0	0	3	0	5	0	0	0	0	6	13	0	1	0	0	0	6	0	36
Justice 1	0	0	0	0	0	0	0	0	0	0	0	0	0	0	6	0	0	0	0	8	0	0	0	0	6	0	0	20
Justice 2	0	0	0	0	0	0	0	0	0	0	0	0	0	0	0	0	0	0	0	3	0	0	0	0	4	0	0	7
Local Government	0	0	0	5	19	5	0	0	0	0	1	0	0	3	0	0	0	1	0	0	0	0	0	0	0	0	0	34
Procedures	0	0	0	0	0	0	0	0	0	0	0	2	0	3	4	0	0	0	0	0	0	0	0	0	0	0	0	9

Public Petitions	0	0	0	0	0	0	0	0	0	0	0	0	0	0	0	0	0	0	0	0	0	0	0
Rural Affairs/ Development	0	0	2	0	0	0	0	0	2	0	1	0	0	0	0	6	33	15	0	0	0	0	59
Social Inclusion, Housing and Voluntary Sector/ Social Justice	0	0	1	11	13	0	0	0	3	1	0	0	0	0	0	0	0	0	0	0	0	0	30
Standards	0	0	0	0	1	0	0	0	0	0	0	0	0	0	0	0	0	0	0	0	0	0	1
Subordinate Legislation	0	0	0	6	0	4	1	0	8	11	0	3	0	5	3	0	2	3	0	0	0	0	47
Transport and Environment	0	0	1	7	7	0	0	0	1	1	0	0	0	0	0	0	7	6	0	0	0	0	31
TOTAL	0	0	15	61	42	5	3	0	2	49	16	7	53	36	8	16	11	7	25	14	10	48	24	1	8	10	471

Key: SECS, Scottish Executive Corporate Services; SEDD, Scottish Executive Development Department; SEED, Scottish Executive Education Department; SELLD, Scottish Executive Education and Lifelong Learning Department; FCSD, Finance and Central Services Department; SEHD, Scottish Executive Health Department; SEJD, Scottish Executive Justice Department; SEERAD, Scottish Executive Environment and Rural Affairs Department. The Category of 'OTHER' comprises the Permanent Secretary, Scottish Court Service, Crown Office and Procurator and Fiscal Service

Notes:

1. The Scottish Parliament was established formally on 1 July 1999 and so figures for this year cover only the remaining six months of that year. Figures for 2000 cover the full calendar year January–December. Figures for 2001 are based on data gathered until the end of July 2001. In effect, therefore, the total figures cover the first two years of the work of the committees in the first two years of the Scottish Parliament.

2. The Justice and Home Affairs Committee existed during the 1999–2000 period. From 2001 onwards, responsibilities transferred to two new committees – Justice 1 and Justice 2. The Rural Affairs Committee existed only during the 1999–2000 period. In 2001, it became the Rural Development Committee. The Social Inclusion, Housing and Voluntary Committee existed only during the 1999–2000 period. In 2001, it became the Social Justice Committee.

3. The General Register Office falls under the remit of the Justice Department.

Source: Official Reports and Minutes of Proceedings.

Table 7.3 *Number of civil servants (Executive Agencies of the Scottish Executive) giving oral evidence to committees of the Scottish Parliament 1999–2001*

EXECUTIVE AGENCY AND YEAR

COMMITTEE	Scottish Prison Service			Historic Scotland			Her Majesty's Inspectorate for Education			Scottish Agricultural Science Agency			Scottish Fisheries Protection Agency			Scottish Courts			Total
	99	00	01	99	00	01	99	00	01	99	00	01	99	00	01	99	00	01	
Education, Culture and Sport	0	0	0	0	0	0	0	7	2	0	0	0	0	0	0	0	0	0	9
Finance	0	0	0	0	0	1	0	0	0	0	0	0	0	0	0	0	0	0	1
Justice and Home Affairs	9	0	0	0	0	0	0	0	0	0	0	0	0	0	0	0	1	0	10
Rural Affairs	0	0	0	0	0	0	0	0	0	0	2	0	0	0	0	0	2	0	2
Total	9	0	0	0	0	1	0	7	2	0	2	0	0	0	0	0	3	0	24

Notes:

1. Figures cited here are only for Executive Agencies whose representatives made appearances before a Scottish Parliamentary committee. Executive agencies where no civil servants gave oral evidence are Scottish Public Pensions Agency, Student Awards Agency Scotland, Fisheries Research Service and National Archives for Scotland.
2. The Scottish Parliament was established formally on 1 July 1999 and so figures for this year cover only the remaining six months of that year. Figures for 2000 cover the full calendar year January-December. Figures for 2001 are based on data gathered until the end of July 2001. In effect, therefore, the total figures cover the first two years of the work of the committees in the first two years of the Scottish Parliament.

Source: Official Reports, Minutes of Proceedings.

extent, this means there can be no direct comparison between the Westminster select committees which were most likely to call civil servants to give evidence (the Scottish Affairs Committee and the Public Accounts Committee) and the new committees of the Scottish Parliament. Indeed, it is possible to draw some misleading conclusions from the raw data. For example, a significant proportion of the civil servants who appeared before the committees of the Scottish Parliament were called by the Justice and Home Affairs Committee (see Table 7.2). However, this committee had an extremely busy legislative agenda, dealing with five bills during the first year, and most of the appearances by civil servants were linked to the processing of bills rather than to administrative scrutiny.

> Such work severely limited the committee's ability to deal with non-legislative matters, and consequently the committee only conducted short inquiries into family law, domestic violence, stalking, vulnerable witnesses, freedom of information and the prison system in 1999–2000, rather than the substantial inquiries conducted by other committees such as Enterprise and Lifelong Learning ... its agenda was predominantly driven by the Executive's legislative programme. (Lynch 2001, p. 75)

The overburdened Justice and Home Affairs Committee was split into two new committees in 2001.

One MSP (a committee chairman) believed that there was a general problem associated with the dual-function system:

> ... predictions of the committees' ability effectively to combine the investigative and scrutiny roles of Westminster's two types of committees were somewhat premature ... the committees are becoming victims of their own success, with several overstretched as a result of the work being allocated to them from various sources. (Watson 2001, p. 164)

Notwithstanding the complications introduced by the fact that the committees combine legislative and scrutiny functions, it is still possible to gauge the impact of the new Parliament on civil service answerability with reference to appearances before committees.

Table 7.1 sets out the numbers of Scottish Office and Scottish Executive officials who gave oral evidence to the Scottish Affairs Committee and the Public Accounts Committee between 1992 and 2001. The total of 103 represents an average of 11.44 per parliamentary session. By contrast, as shown in Tables 7.2 and 7.3, 495 civil servants from departments and executive agencies of the Scottish Executive gave oral evidence to the committees of the Scottish Parliament during its first two years of operation, between 1999 and 2001 (an average of 247.5 per year). Given that the committees took some time to become fully operational following the first elections to the Scottish Parliament, these figures understate the probable future trend. Some MSPs would clearly like to see even greater numbers of civil servants scrutinized in this way. For example, one MSP who participated in the survey we describe below commented that officials are ' ... not brought to Committees enough ... '

It is worth noting that the great majority of the civil servants who appeared as witnesses before the committees of the Scottish Parliament came from the departments of the Scottish Executive. As Table 7.3 shows, only 24 officials from the Next Steps executive agencies appeared before the committees. Admittedly, these agencies are mainly of a fairly peripheral nature, and do not include any to compare in policy importance with the Benefits Agency or the Child Support Agency. However, it might have been expected that the political saliency of the student fees issue would have created a demand from the Parliament for official witnesses from the Student Awards Agency in addition to those from the parent department (Enterprise and Lifelong Learning). On the other hand, perhaps this illustrated the Executive's determination to adhere to the policy/management dichotomy which lies at the heart of the agency concept: the fees issue at that stage was deemed to be primarily a matter of policy and therefore concerned the department rather than the agency.

In relation to committees, there are several other points which are worthy of note. First, there is an imbalance between the committees in terms of the number of evidence sessions involving officials. At one end of the spectrum, there is the Enterprise and Lifelong Learning Committee. During 2000 (and consistent with the point made above), a total of 51 civil servants (mainly senior grades) appeared before this committee, predominantly on legislative matters. These appearances were largely in relation to student loans, student support, and graduate endowments, but also on the inquiry into the governance of the Scottish Qualifications Authority (SQA), following the exams 'fiasco' during that year. At the other end of the spectrum, no officials appeared before the Public Petitions Committee, while the Standards Committee and the Procedures Committee ('housekeeping' committees of the parliament) took evidence from relatively few civil servants. Perhaps more surprising was the fact that a relatively low number of officials (18) gave evidence to the Health and Community Care Committee. The second point to note is that there are some committees whose remit lends itself far more to taking evidence on matters of inquiry, rather than on legislation. This is typified by the Audit Committee whose role is to hold to account officials of bodies and agencies which are charged with spending public money (and not to be explicitly concerned with policy matters). During 1999, the Committee met nine times and produced two reports. In 2000, it met 20 times, produced six reports and by the time the initial research was completed in 2001, this committee had convened 11 times, with two reports published to date. Twenty-six civil servants had appeared as witnesses before this committee. The third and final point to be made with regard to the committees, is that the substantial increase in the numbers of officials giving evidence at Holyrood compared with Westminster seems likely to expand further in future as the committees settle down to their routines of scrutiny and also exploit their powers under the Parliament's Standing Orders (Rule 9.15) to make proposals for bills on matters under their jurisdiction. By June 2001, the only committee to have utilized this power was the Justice (1) Committee, which introduced 'The Protection from Abuse (Scotland) Bill' on 5 June 2001. Once the committees have 'bedded down' it is perfectly possible that this power will be exercised on a routine basis, thus leading to even greater demands on civil servants to give evidence.

Moving beyond committees, early indications were that in other respects the relatively mundane, day-to-day policy management and implementation work of the civil service in Scotland was attracting greater attention in the post devolution period. As Table 7.4 shows, the Parliamentary Commissioner for Administration received fairly small numbers of complaints about the work of the Scottish Office and its associated bodies. A total of 261 cases were handled between 1992 and 2000 – an average of 29 per year. The ombudsman was retained in the immediate wake of devolution, with a marginally restyled Scottish 'arm', the Scottish Parliamentary Commissioner for Administration (Michael Buckley took this post in addition to his roles as PCA, Welsh Administration Ombudsman and Health Service Ombudsman), while a review of the entire public sector ombudsman system in Scotland was initiated (see Scottish Executive 2001b). A new 'one-stop shop' system would be introduced in due course, combining the offices of the Scottish Parliamentary Ombudsman with those of the Health Service and Local Government Ombudsmen in Scotland. In the meantime, the new Scottish Parliamentary Commissioner for Administration noted an immediate increase in his caseload (see Table 7.4) with 53 complaints recorded in the first year of operation.

Although a full analysis of Parliamentary Questions (PQs) relating to the civil service has yet to be completed, the early signs are that there has been a significant increase in volume here too. It could be argued that all PQs for oral and written answer bring about a measure of indirect civil service accountability insofar as they require actions on the part of civil servants (in order to produce the draft answers), and these actions in turn bring about scrutiny of civil service work by their ministerial superiors. However, a relatively small number of PQs have a specific focus on the work of the civil service *per se*. It is this type of questioning which is of particular concern to us. In the course of the period between 1992 and 1999 (covering the last full Parliament before devolution and the immediate pre-devolution phase after the 1997 General Election) the work of the civil service in Scotland attracted

Table 7.4   Ombudsman cases relating to the Scottish Office and the Scottish Executive

Year	SO Caseload	Associated Bodies' Caseload	Total
1992	17	4	21
1993	19	3	22
1994	30 (1)	6	36 (1)
1995	30 (1)	9	39 (1)
1996	32 (2)	7 (1)	39 (3)
1997	26 (2)	6	32 (2)
1997–98	23	5	28
1998–99	22 (2)	7	29 (2)
1999–2000	11(1)	4	15 (1)

Year	SE and Associated Bodies' Caseload	Total
1999–2000	53	53

Key: SO, Scottish Office; SE, Scottish Executive; SPCA, Scottish Parliamentary Commissioner for Administration; PCA Parliamentary Commissioner for Administration.

Notes:
1. Most, but not all of the 'associated bodies' are formally part of the civil service.
2. The figures in parentheses refer to cases of complaint about access to official information.
3. The caseload figures include those carried over from previous years.
4. The PCA reported on residual cases in 1999–2000, but the SPCA's first Annual Report was also published for that session, and this reflected the post-devolution caseload.

Source: Annual Reports of the Parliamentary Commissioner for Administration, 1992–93 to 1999–2000, Annual Report of the Scottish Parliamentary Commissioner for Administration for 1999–2000.

relatively little attention in questions tabled at Westminster. From an early stage, however, it was clear that there would be a reasonable volume of questions in the Scottish Parliament with a specific focus on the civil service. This can be clearly illustrated with reference to the fact that 135 questions about aspects of the civil service in Scotland were tabled at Holyrood between the opening of the new Parliament in May 1999 and the latter part of October that year. The great majority (125) of these questions were tabled for written answer.

Our survey of MSPs, carried out via questionnaire in the early part of 2002, sought to elicit views about civil service accountability to the Scottish Parliament. Fifty-four completed returns were received from 129 MSPs, a

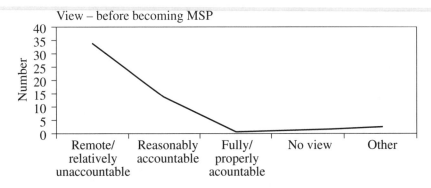

Figure 7.1   MSP views of civil service accountability: pre-election

return rate of 41.9 per cent. As Figure 7.1 shows, at the time of their election, a significant majority held negative perspectives on civil service accountability, with 62.9 per cent of respondents admitting that they believed officials were remote and relatively unaccountable. Before taking up their responsibilities in the Parliament, only 1.9 per cent of our sample believed that civil servants were fully and properly accountable for the work they carried out. Their experience as Scottish parliamentarians resulted in a marked shift towards a more positive view of civil service accountability.

Post-election, 48.1 per cent of our MSP sample rated the accountability of Scottish Executive officials at '3' or above on a scale where '5' represented 'fully accountable' and '1' represented 'unaccountable' (see Figure 7.2).

When asked to rate the mechanisms of scrutiny available to them in terms of effectiveness, MSPs clearly viewed committees most favourably. Figures 7.3 to 7.7 set out the results of our survey. On a scale where '1' represented 'ineffec-

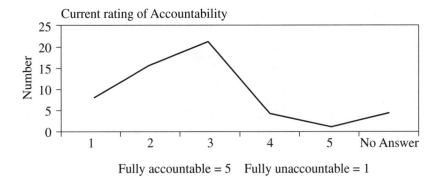

Figure 7.2   MSP views of civil service accountability: post-election

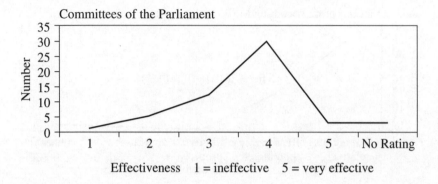

Figure 7.3　MSP rating of committee effectiveness

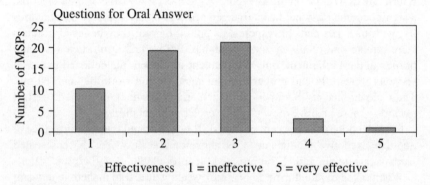

Figure 7.4　MSP rating of oral PQ effectiveness

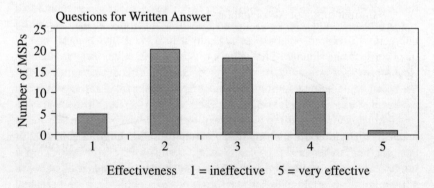

Figure 7.5　MSP rating of written PQ effectiveness

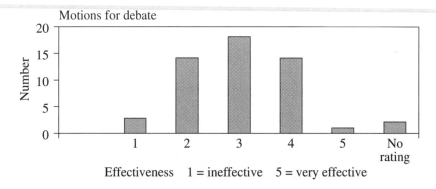

Figure 7.6   MSP rating of debates' effectiveness

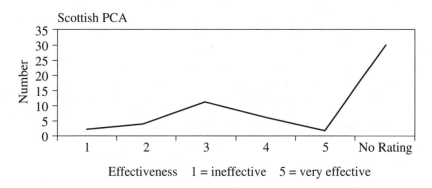

Figure 7.7   MSP rating of ombudsman's effectiveness

tive' and '5' represented 'very effective', 83.3 per cent of our sample rated committees at '3' or above. By contrast, questions for oral answer secured a rating of '3' or above from 46.3 per cent, questions for written answer secured 53.6 per cent, and motions for debate 61.0 per cent. Interestingly, although relatively few MSPs utilized the services of the Scottish Parliamentary Commissioner for Administration in order to subject the work of the Executive to scrutiny (18.5 per cent of respondents), those who did use this mechanism rated it fairly highly (75 per cent of those who offered a rating).

In summary, therefore, it would appear that the day-to-day experience of subjecting the work of the civil service in Scotland to scrutiny, albeit via a fairly traditional, unmodernized set of mechanisms, is having a positive impact on the perceptions of official accountability held by MSPs. Typical comments offered by MSPs in the course of our survey were:

The parliament has sharply increased accountability and will continue to ... in the years ahead.

There is a culture or an attitude which has to be challenged and to change. I believe that process is under way.

CONCLUSION

We have attempted to show that devolution, as an aspect of the Blair government's programme of structural and constitutional reform, can be viewed as a form of macro-level modernization. Beyond this, we have noted the potential for modernization to have a somewhat contradictory and confusing impact on modes of civil service accountability. However, in the context of the Scottish devolution settlement, we have identified the construction of a fundamentally traditionalist regime of parliamentary accountability.

Notwithstanding this, as Lynch has noted, during the early phase of the Scottish devolution settlement, the Executive has 'struggled to cope' with the new regime of parliamentary accountability.

The Scottish Executive as a whole – ministers, departments, civil servants – all face a transition to accommodate the new politics of the Scottish Parliament in all its aspects, such as pre-legislative consultation, committee scrutiny and the demands for more open, accessible government. (Lynch 2001, p. 48)

This chapter has shown that the shift from the former Westminster-Scottish Office regime of accountability to the new Scottish Parliament-Executive axis has brought a substantial increase in the volume of scrutiny. The evidence to date clearly indicates that there has been a significant change in the regime of parliamentary accountability for the civil service in Scotland, and this change has been positively received by MSPs. However, it is apparent that the change has taken place within the overall context of a continued reliance upon traditional mechanisms of parliamentary scrutiny, which by their very nature tend to facilitate the weaker, more anodyne forms of accountability ('answerability' or 'explanatory accountability') rather than leading to enhanced amendatory accountability, redress or sanctions. We should not push this point too far, however, because a full study of Scottish Executive responses to the recommendations contained in committee reports would be required before definitive statements could be made about the amendatory actions taken in response to specific criticisms, and the redress delivered in particular cases. A detailed study of the sanctions element of the accountability equation would also be necessary. There is some evidence that certain officials involved in the SQA debacle of 2000 (when the examination results of large numbers of schoolchildren were inaccurately recorded and/or mislaid) were subject to sanctions, although the precise role played by the Parliament as an agent of accountability in this affair was fairly limited (it was not in session when the crisis was at its height), and the issue of the relative culpability of ministers rather than officials was fudged for political reasons. Technically, the SQA officials are not designated as part of the Scottish Executive departmental or executive agency structure (they inhabit the quangocracy) and for the purposes of our survey do not count as civil servants, but the principles of accountability raised by this affair are worthy of note.

The developing accountability relationship between the civil service in Scotland and the Scottish Parliament will clearly merit further study in the years to come.

8. Implementation of the Human Rights Act 1998 in the Lord Chancellor's department

Amanda Finlay

The following is the text of a talk delivered by the author in September 2001, with an afterword referring to recently published research.

My involvement in human rights implementation dates back to 1997 when the government was elected with a manifesto commitment to introduce legislation to incorporate the European Convention on Human Rights (ECHR) into UK law. The Lord Chancellor chaired the Cabinet Committee charged with overseeing the legislation, which began work straight after that election. He then piloted the Human Rights Bill through the House of Lords between 1997 and 1998. He has therefore always taken a close interest in issues relating to the Act.

I led the Division responsible for advising the Lord Chancellor on the policy issues affecting the Lord Chancellor's Department (LCD) arising from the legislation and for ensuring that the Department and, in particular, the courts and tribunals were fully prepared for its implementation. I continued to have overall responsibility for human rights from July 1999 onwards when my responsibilities expanded to include family and administrative justice. Now that the Whitehall lead on human rights issues has passed from the Home Office to LCD as part of the machinery of government changes following the General Election, they naturally fall within my brief.

I would like to take as my theme today the way in which the programme of work to prepare for implementation of the Human Rights Act within LCD has contributed to and been at the forefront of the Department's wider programme to modernize both itself and the courts and tribunals.

In LCD, our preparations for implementation of the Human Rights Act were two-fold. They covered not just the development of policies, legislation and procedures and staff training, which were common to all Departments, but also, very importantly, preparation to ensure that the courts and tribunals were ready for the new tasks given to them by the Act. This was made more pressing by the fact that the government took a deliberate decision that human rights issues could be raised in all courts and tribunals rather than, say, restricting them to the High Court and Court of Appeal. Therefore, all 3500 full and part-time judges and 30 000 lay magistrates across the country needed to be aware of the Convention and the duties imposed upon them by the Act.

Indeed, courts and tribunals are doubly affected by the Human Rights Act. First, they have to adjudicate in human rights cases and consider the compatibility of legislation. Second, as public authorities under section six of the Act, they have to act compatibly with Convention rights themselves and develop the common law in a way that is compatible with Convention rights.

A PROGRAMME-BASED APPROACH AND STRUCTURE

Once the scope of the legislation was clear, we set up a formal programme structure in the summer of 1998 to pull all this work together. The scope of the programme expanded as LCD's agencies, the Court Service and the Public Trust Office, established related projects to take forward the operational preparations in their own areas.

A Programme Board, chaired at a senior level by the Director-General, Policy, in LCD Headquarters, oversaw the work of the Programme and included all the key players within LCD. In particular, we wanted to ensure that our preparations took full account of the needs of the judiciary at all levels and took on board their knowledge and experience. So, the Board's membership included two Court of Appeal Judges: Lord Justice Brooke and Lord Justice Sedley.

At the time, this was a novel approach but it is now common practice within the Department. Indeed, Lord Justice Brooke has gone on to sit on the Programme Boards overseeing the modernization of the infrastructure of the Crown Court and county courts. It was also indicative of our desire throughout the life of the programme to look outside the Department and draw on the expertise of others. I will expand on this theme shortly.

Below the Programme Board, there was a network of working groups, including a wide range of people involved in every stage of LCD's work from the very start of policy development right through to the day-to-day work of the courts. We considered this cross-fertilization vital if we were to realize the impact on the ground.

IDENTIFYING KEY OUTCOMES

One of the first tasks of the programme was to identify key outcomes for the successful implementation of the Act in the courts and tribunals. Work was then planned and resourced to achieve each of these outcomes. This was in advance of the transition to Resource Accounting and Budgeting that has now taken place within LCD.

We identified a total of 11 key outcomes covering issues such as ensuring:

- that LCD's legislation, policy and procedure was compliant with Convention rights;
- that sufficient numbers of judges, magistrates and their professional advisers and tribunal members were in place to deal with the expected workload;
- that appropriate training took place for judges, magistrates, tribunal members and legal and other staff;
- that staff and the judiciary had speedy access to developing ECHR case law; and
- that rules, practice directions and procedures were in place for handling cases involving Convention rights.

When the Programme Board reviewed the programme at its final meeting, it believed that the key outcomes had stood the test of time and, moreover, lent considerable focus and shape to the programme.

TAPPING EXTERNAL EXPERTISE

One of our greatest challenges lay in trying to develop a picture of what the impact of the Human Rights Act on the courts and tribunals was actually likely to be. This was particularly difficult because human rights experience or knowledge within the Department was limited. We therefore needed to turn to those outside the Department with experience of human rights issues for the benefit of their knowledge.

At the very outset of the programme, we therefore met barristers, solicitors, academics and non-governmental organizations expert in the human rights field in order to produce a picture of what might happen. By doing so, we also developed a network of contacts that we could tap into throughout the life of the programme. We listened to the views expressed at the many seminars run by public interest groups and universities since 1997 and the opinions expressed in articles in legal and other journals. We also looked further afield at Canada and New Zealand to gain pointers from jurisdictions where human rights legislation had recently been introduced, while bearing in mind the unique nature of our legal framework and the human rights legislation itself, which maintains the UK's tradition of parliamentary supremacy.

Training Programmes

This outward-facing approach had other positive spin-offs. For example, a number of our contacts made significant contributions to the training programmes laid on for both LCD staff and the judiciary and magistracy. I believe this was vital given the new ways of thinking required by the Act; for example, in relation to the Strasbourg concept of proportionality.

The training for LCD HQ staff was conducted in conjunction with Justice, one of the leading non-governmental organizations in the human rights field, who were able to lay on top quality seminars from leading practitioners on general ECHR principles in LCD's three major business areas. They were also to emphasize one of the fundamental messages that we wanted to convey through the training. This was the direct relevance of the Convention rights to the service to the public and that the Human Rights Act should not be perceived as merely a technical matter, to be addressed by legal advisers.

External experts also made significant contributions to the training programmes laid on for all full- and part-time members of the judiciary and the lay magistrates. Preparation for the Act was the largest project undertaken by the Judicial Studies Board (JSB) in its history. One particular innovation was a series of evening seminars for the senior judiciary led jointly by a Lord Justice and an academic with three seminars being held each term in the lead up to implementation of the Act on 2 October 2000.

Working Across Departmental Boundaries

Our implementation programme involved not just close liaison with outside contacts but also considerable working across Whitehall boundaries. There was an element of self-preservation at work here resulting from the fact that challenges to the actions and decisions of public authorities would be challenged in the courts and tribunals administered by LCD. We therefore had a vested interest in encouraging steps to be taken to reduce the potential additional workload.

We therefore made it a priority to support the work of the Home Office, which was responsible for preparing public authorities in general for implementation of the Act. An LCD minister sat on the Home Secretary's Human Rights Task Force and LCD ministers made a number of speeches to raise awareness of the Act. We also worked closely with the Home Office and the Crown Prosecution Service to consider the potential impact of the Act on the criminal justice system and to undertake changes to practice and procedure where they were needed.

Furthermore, we took the Whitehall lead in ensuring that tribunals were also prepared for implementation of the Act. Tribunals now decide one million cases per year – more than all of the civil courts' cases put together. There are a large number of tribunals, some large scale and some that sit on an infrequent basis, all sponsored by a variety of departments across Whitehall. Most deal with cases that involve the rights of private citizens against the State. Many handle issues that are central to the fight against social exclusion such as social security, child support, special educational needs and mental health. All this is natural human rights territory.

Using the existing networks of the Cabinet Office, Home Office and Council on Tribunals, we sought to raise awareness, share best practice and encourage take-up of training. The support of the Judicial Studies Board was vital here. For example, it made provision for tribunal members to take part in the seminars it held for the judiciary. It also produced a core training pack based on the Model Rules produced by the Council on Tribunals, which had been revised to ensure they were compatible with Convention rights. It is envisaged that the JSB will build on this wider role in future years following Sir Andrew Leggatt's Review: 'Tribunals for Users'.

NEW METHODS OF POLICY DEVELOPMENT

As with all government departments, LCD needed to be certain that its policy, practice and procedure were compatible with Convention rights. For us, that meant consideration of legislation and procedure in the areas of civil, family and administrative justice.

Brainstorming, training sessions and articles alerted us to possible areas of difficulty, as well as more structured requests for legal advice. But we were also particularly keen that all players in the justice system, not just the courts and ourselves, were able to anticipate the issues that would need to be tackled to give effect to the Act. We therefore ran a programme of hypothetical case-studies between September 1998 and June 2000. We called these events 'walkthroughs' and we believe that they gave considerable impetus to our work. They were a new way of working for LCD and built, once more, on our desire to tap into the expertise of outside contacts and to work across Whitehall boundaries.

The aim of the walkthroughs was to provide the opportunity for everyone involved in a particular type of case to work through the practical implications in a way that would be difficult to achieve otherwise. No one's life, livelihood or liberty was at stake and the events took place under Chatham House rules so a safe environment existed in which to grapple with the completely new arguments raised by the Act. The walkthroughs covered diverse areas of the justice system including the Magistrates' Courts, judicial review, family proceedings, immigration and asylum, discrimination issues and the Youth Court.

One of the great strengths of the walkthroughs was the sheer diversity of the people who attended and whose expertise could be tapped into. These included members of the judiciary at all levels, the magistracy, barristers and solicitors, academics and representatives of a wide range of non-governmental organizations as well as civil servants from a number of departments. The contribution of the senior judiciary was particularly helpful. The (then) Lord Chief Justice, Lord Bingham, and the President of the Family Division each participated in a walkthrough, in addition to six judges from the Court of Appeal and twelve High Court Judges.

We relied heavily on experienced human rights lawyers who gave their time to write a series of case studies to bring out the key issues and then lead the discussion. We were highly indebted to Justice, and Liberty who built on their own contacts for training events to help us to find leading lawyers to perform these roles as well as nominating other participants.

Each walkthrough involved considerable practical preparation and investment of time by the Implementation Team; for example, in securing judicial release and attendance of other useful participants and then writing up reports of the days. We believed, however, that they proved extremely worthwhile, in particular in relation to the energizing process. Sometimes, we found that participants came to the walkthroughs believing that nothing needed to be changed or re-thought. They often went away, however, with a very different view and the walkthroughs therefore helped to provide a general wake-up call.

Modernizing Procedure

As I indicated earlier, the walkthroughs helped us to identify areas of legislation and procedure, which needed to be amended to ensure compliance with the Convention rights. In my experience, these were often areas where change was actually required irrespective of the demands of the Human Rights Act. What the Act did, however, was add momentum to the need for change.

For example, the walkthroughs flagged up the need for the extension of the requirement for magistrates to give reasons for their decisions. In the past, they have only done this in family cases. This was very overdue. It is surely a requirement of a modern justice system that court and tribunal users should be entitled to receive the reasons behind any decision made in their case. Otherwise, they will not have any confidence in the process. There can be nothing worse than receiving an adverse decision in a case and not being told the reasons behind it.

Despite some misgivings about the impact on the throughput of cases, magistrates have generally been very positive about this change, seeing it as a positive step that helps them to make decisions in a much more logical and structured way. In fact, the latest statistics and feedback from magistrates' courts committees suggest that there was a period of adjustment at the beginning of October 2000 but that this is now more than complete. Indeed, in the last quarter, throughput was actually higher than before October 2000.

The Higher Courts

The walkthroughs also flagged up the need for the higher courts to be as prepared as possible for the extra workload that was likely to arise following implementation of the Act. As indicated earlier, courts, as public bodies under Section 6 of the Act, are required to act compatibly with Convention rights. So, among other things, they must develop the common law in a way that is compatible with Convention rights. The courts were therefore likely to come under pressure to revisit common law case law, either to develop it to become compatible with Convention rights or to affirm that it was already compatible.

This impact was always likely to be greatest on the House of Lords, the Court of Appeal and the Administrative Court. Their decisions, dealing with the actions of public bodies, set the standards and precedent to be followed across the public sector. Indeed, this is how events have turned out with the impact of the Act at its most significant so far in the higher courts and relatively few cases raised in the courts of first instance. However, the preparations that we took before the Act came into force – a combination of injecting additional resources at points of most pressure and modernizing procedures – mean that the higher courts have in fact taken the additional workload in their stride and backlogs are actually falling.

The Access to Justice Act 1999 included provisions to help the Civil Division of the Court of Appeal deploy its resources more flexibly and to ensure that appeals are heard at the right level. These changes built on the recommendations of a Review conducted by Sir Jeffery Bowman. The Lord Chancellor then invited Sir Jeffery to conduct a further review of what was, at that time, called the Crown Office List, and is now called the Administrative Court. This was vital given the fact that all our research pointed to the likelihood that the Act would have most impact on judicial review and that use of judicial review was already increasing. As a result of the Bowman

Review, rule changes to the judicial review procedure were introduced from 2 October 2000. These

- simplify procedures,
- encourage early settlement to reduce delays,
- strengthen the capacity of the List to deal expeditiously and fairly with its expanding jurisdiction;
- and allow it to dispose of unmeritorious cases fairly at the earliest possible stage.

The number of judicial review courts was also doubled in the run up to 2 October 2000 to ensure the List was in the best possible state prior to implementation. On top of this, Mr Justice Scott Baker was appointed as the Court's Lead Judge with a brief to oversee the management of the Court's workload and the deployment of its judiciary. This is a further example of how the Human Rights Act has acted as a spur to modernize procedures and improve service in the judicial system.

Use of Technology

The impending implementation of the Human Rights Act also gave added impetus to the work that had already been set in hand to provide the judiciary with information technology (IT). This was necessary because judges were going to need quick access to developing ECHR case law if they were to base their decisions on the most up-to-date information. In particular, they were going to need speedy access to precedent from the higher courts and to decisions from the Strasbourg Court, which the Human Rights Act requires them to take into account.

A detailed survey was therefore undertaken in July 1999 of all full-time members of the judiciary to show how they received information at that time and to identify the best ways of keeping them up to date. The survey received the amazing response rate of 90 per cent. The Court Service used the analysis to determine how information should be provided in the future.

As a result, it accelerated its programme to provide all full time members of the judiciary with laptop computers and to provide them with access to the internet via these laptops. By August 2000, the judges were able to log on to a new 'portal' web page, called LEXicon, provided by the Court Service to give them judiciary speedy links to web-based legal information such as the Human Rights Documentations (HUDOC) database of the European Court of Human Rights. Via LEXicon, judges also receive a customized version of Butterworths Direct, providing them with quick and easy access to the legal reference materials they need. They have on-line access to UK and European cases, commentary and legislation as well as being able to request e-mail updates on key judgments and developments in specific areas of law. This is therefore a step that has helped the work of the judiciary generally, not just in the field of human rights.

In conclusion, I hope that this case study has demonstrated the extent to which the programme to prepare LCD for implementation of the Human Rights Act was at the forefront of the Department's own work to modernize itself and the courts.

- Key outcomes were identified;
- A Programme Board oversaw the work;
- The expertise of the judiciary and outside contacts was brought on board;
- There was considerable work across traditional Whitehall boundaries;
- The walkthroughs represented a new technique for developing policy;
- Procedures were modernized and the potential of IT tapped.

Preparation for the implementation of the Human Rights Act was a complex and significant undertaking for the Department. I believe we rose to the challenge by being receptive to the need for change.

AFTERWORD

On 2 October 2002, LCD published a report entitled *The Impact on the Courts and the Administration of Justice of the Human Rights Act 1998*, by Professor John Raine, of Birmingham University, and Professor Clive Walker, of Leeds University. They conducted research in nine courts located in different parts of the country. The following is from the Executive Summary: 'the study highlights the comparative success with which the courts managed the implementation process and the ways in which they have adapted their practices to accommodate some potentially significant Human Rights issues ... '

Against a background of predictions of chaos and disaster, we can – I think – allow ourselves just a little pleasure in an outcome that was very different.

9. Modernizing policy-making for the twenty-first century: the professional model

Wayne Parsons

MODERNIZING AND PROFESSIONALIZING THE POLICY PROCESS

A key commitment contained in the *Modernizing Government* White Paper of 1999 (Prime Minister 1999) was improving policy-making: better, more professional, policy-making, it argued, would lead to better delivery. This chapter critically examines a defining text of the drive to create a more modern or 'professional' approach to policy-making: 'Professional policy-making for the twenty-first century'. The report is of particular interest to students of the policy process as it is the first time that such a comprehensive internal review has been made of how policy-making takes place in British central government. Its use of case studies and audits of good practice provide a considerable amount of material which provides a unique insight into how policy-making took place in Whitehall at the close of the twentieth century, and the ideas and discourse which framed reform in the Blair governments. Given the ambitions of the modernization agenda it will be many years yet before we can ascertain the actual impact which the report made on the practice of policy-making, much less the extent to which the professional approach has shaped the delivery of public policy. However, at this stage it is possible to examine the significance, strengths and weaknesses of the professional policy-making model as an approach to understanding the policy process and improving policy outcomes.

The White Paper argued that policy-making would aim to be 'forward looking in developing policies to deliver outcomes that matter, not simply reacting to short-term pressures' (Prime Minister 1999). Such was the vision. Chapter two, which specifically addresses policy-making, begins with a very succinct statement about what is meant by the term:

> Policy-making is the process by which governments translate their political vision into programmes and actions to deliver 'outcomes' – desired changes in the real

world. Many of the other issues considered in this White Paper cannot be seen in isolation from the policy-making process. Government cannot succeed in delivering the outcomes people want if the policies and programmes they are implementing are flawed or inadequate. (Prime Minister 1999)

Policy-making in modernizing terms is about translating vision into delivery. Hence, the argument that policy-making cannot succeed (no equivocation here) and outcomes cannot be delivered if the policies and programmes are flawed or inadequate. Perfect implementation is a function of perfect policy design: no flaws, no inadequacies. The modernizing view of policy-making is very much centred on the implementation gap. The White Paper aims to ensure that policy-making and policy implementation are more joined-up, but the approach which is taken is to see the problem of coordination primarily in terms of better design. The concept of policy as distinct from implementation or operationalization in this regard, as in many others, is entirely in line with a classical model of strategic planning (Whittington 1993). Policy failure (that is failure to deliver outcomes) is rooted in poor design. The proposed solution to the eradication of flaws and inadequacies in the process of policy formulation is summed up in the succeeding paragraph.

> Government must be willing constantly to re-evaluate what it is doing so as to produce policies that really deal with problems; that are forward looking and shaped by evidence rather than as a response to short-term pressures; that tackle causes not symptoms; that are measured by results rather than activity; that are flexible and innovative rather than closed and bureaucratic; and that promote compliance rather avoidance and fraud. To meet people's rising expectations, policymaking must be a process of continuous learning and improvement. (Prime Minister 1999)

The paper goes on to set out the key principles which will inform the modernization of the policy process. These comprise:

- designing policy around shared goals and carefully defined result, not around organizational structures or existing functions;
- making sure policies are inclusive;
- avoiding imposing unnecessary burdens;
- involving others in policy-making;
- improving the way risk is managed;
- becoming more forward and outward-looking;
- learning from experience. (Prime Minister 1999)

The modernization of policy-making, the White Paper announced, would build on a variety of initiatives such as the Comprehensive Spending Review and experiments in tackling 'cross-cutting policies' (including the Social

Exclusion Unit, Women's Unit, the Performance and Innovation Unit (PIU), the Drugs Czar and the crime reduction programme). In addition, the paper promised that the government would deliver 'creative, robust and flexible policies, focused on outcomes'; joined-up policy-making; improvements to the legislative process; a more integrated system of impact assessment and appraisal tools; a more corporate approach in the civil service; joint training of ministers and civil servants; peer reviews; more evaluation of policies and programmes; the reduction of unnecessary regulation; and the identification of 'best practice' through the Centre for Management and Policy Studies (CMPS).

THE PROFESSIONALIZATION OF POLICY-MAKING

CMPS was identified as having a major role in taking the White Paper's ideas on policy-making forward. The centre's prime task was defined as being to foster a 'culture of continuous learning and knowledge sharing'. It aimed to help civil servants and ministers 'acquire the skills and tools' to meet the challenge of realizing the 'vision' of the White Paper. To do this the CMPS endeavoured to change 'the way people work, think and connect'. The Policy Studies Division (PSD) within CMPS was established to 'take forward the objective of ensuring that policy-makers across government have access to the best research evidence and international experience; and help government to learn better from existing policies'. The PSD was divided into three divisions: policy evaluation, policy research and policy resources. It was the Policy Research Division (PRD) which was given responsibility for the policy process aspects of modernization. PSD was tasked to 'examine new approaches to policy-making and the policy process' with the aim of identifying, describing, analysing and promoting 'best practice in order to share and encourage good ideas and ways of thinking'. Its work was to be 'focused on identifying what works and on sharing good/innovative ideas around departments'. The PRD aimed to make research and other resources 'more accessible and joined up, in order to support better policy-making' (Cabinet Office 2001).

An important starting point for the work of the PRD was a report by a small 'Strategic Policy-making Team' in the Cabinet Office headed by Alison French in September 1999. The report was the outcome of work that had been done on policy-making at the Cabinet Office following the White Paper on *Modernization*. This document helped to refine and develop the agenda mapped out by the White Paper. In house it became known as the 'French Report', but its full title was *Professional Policy-making for the Twenty-first Century*.

To begin with, the report is somewhat obscure as to what is meant by the concept of 'professional' in the context of policy-making. Coming at the close of a century which had in Britain, as elsewhere, witnessed the so-called 'disabling' of the professions, the title has a certain irony. Given the top-down nature of the exercise, modernizing policy-making appears to involve the enabling professional policy-makers and disabling professional policy deliverers. The report seems to imply that policy-making is professional, as opposed to that which is traditional or amateur, when it adheres to notions of core competencies. Professional policy-making involves the idea that there are specific skills which policy-makers have to acquire in order to be effective. The model identifies these policy-making skills as: understanding the context within which professionals are working; managing complex relationships with many players; well developed presentational skills; a broad understanding of IT; a grounding in economics, statistics and relevant scientific disciplines; an understanding of and familiarity with project management techniques; a willingness to experiment and manage risk; and a willingness to learn new skills (Cabinet Office 1999b, 11.12). Professional policy-making displays a range of characteristics. The professional policy-maker is: forward looking; outward looking; innovative and creative; inclusive; joined up; and involved in ongoing learning, and uses evidence, evaluates and reviews. From which we may deduce that a non-professional policy-maker is: backward looking; inward looking; conservative and uncreative; exclusive; and fragmented or falling apart and does not use evidence; does not evaluate; does not bother to review; and is not interested in learning.

It is another irony that, for a report which looks towards the twenty-first century, the ideas which it contains are so completely embedded in the (somewhat discredited) strategic planning approaches of the 1960 and 1970s such as Planning-Programming-Budgeting Systems (PPBS), which in the immortal words of Aaron Wildavsky, 'failed everywhere and at all times' (Wildavsky 1974, p. 205). Indeed, its usefulness to scholars in the future may be less as a guide to policy-making in the twenty-first century than as a snapshot of what passed for conventional wisdom or ruling opinion in British government in the late twentieth. Perhaps it is an example of Keynes's argument that individuals and institutions tend to get captured by ideas which are invariably out of date by the time they get applied (Parsons, 1983). The kind of 'optimizing precommitment' approach it takes to strategic policy-making is, as Lane and Maxfield note, way past its sell by date in the business world (Lane and Maxfield 1997, p. 70). But, here it is, still on the shelf in Whitehall: rational planning. In broad terms the professional model, like the rational planning model, adopts a mix of so-called design and planning approaches to strategy which were very popular in the 1960s and 1970s and is highly prescriptive (Mintzberg *et al.* 1998, p. 5). One can detect little influence on the authors of those approaches which have emerged in more recent years which question the relevance of rational planning and are more concerned about learning, uncertainty, emergence and complexity than fore-casting, coordination and control (Johnson and Scholes 1999, p. 27).

The peer review of the Cabinet Office reminds us that modernization is not a project so much as an 'ongoing journey' (Cabinet Office 2000b, 2.2). As we journey through the world of the professional policy-maker in the report we encounter little that is new, but a good deal which is very familiar to students of strategic management and planning. In no particular order:

- A preoccupation (if not obsessive preoccupation) with the problem of coordination.
- Policy-making as something which can be systematized and formal-ized.
- Concern for the 'vision'.
- Policy-making driven by data.
- What counts is what we can count.
- Designing control systems.
- Monitoring and planning control.
- Use of action planning.
- Defining objectives.
- Securing commitment.
- Stakeholder planning.
- Institutionalizing planning.
- Audit culture.
- Target setting.
- The belief in forecasting.
- Checklists of core competencies.
- Breaking the policy process into distinct routine steps.
- Analysis as synthesis.
- Top-downness.
- Implementation problems as fundamentally to do with poor policy formulation.
- Linking up analysis, policy-making and the budgetary process.
- Quality schemes.
- Project management.

There are, of course, differences between professional policy-making and strategic planning but they are differences of emphasis or style rather than of content or general methodology or philosophy. Professionalized modern policy-making is working within the box of orthodox strategic planning, not out of it: hence its preference for mechanistic (and militaristic) metaphors such as targets, objectives, leadership, levers, wiring and joining. Its general direction is, for the most part, classical in that it tends to be focused on forecasting, coordination, and the long-term, but it is also something of an eclectic melange of other approaches. In broad terms it operates in the range of the rational planning and logical incrementalist end of the strategic spectrum; that is to say it views policy-making as essentially about how rational decision-makers direct policy and utilize experience and learning. Mixed in with the strategic management is a top-down approach to the problem of implementation, an essentially (rather antique) model of rational decision-making, combined with a fashionable preoccupation with governance in an age of networks.

The professional model is significant in the history of British policy-making, therefore, in that it marks the latest reincarnation or mutation of planning into the language of strategic policy-making. Indeed, if the Thatcher-Major period witnessed the corporate take-over of the physical assets or hardware of the public sector, the report on professional policy-making is all too symptomatic of the way in which the corporate take-over continues apace by re-writing the software of the state. Even though it is hardly cutting edge stuff in management terms, the report is yet another manifestation of the degree to which business and corporate ideas are framing the discourse of modern governance. The title of the report is also of interest in the way in which it abandons the classic Wilsonian distinction as between policy and administration. This is a report about policy-making and policy-makers. By this is meant those civil servants, politicians and others who are involved in the process of 'translating political vision' into action (Cabinet Office 1999a, para. 2.1). Professional policy-making recognizes that policy-making is an activity which cuts across the old policy/administration divide and the differences between politicians and bureaucrats.

SOMEWHERE OVER THE POLICY CYCLE

The Strategic Policy-making Team set out to follow up the white paper by: examining what professional/modernized/strategic policy-making should look like; taking a snapshot of current good practice; and suggesting levers for change. The methodology it chose to deploy was textbook stuff. The team developed a model of what strategic (that is, professionalized) policy-making should look like and then used it to benchmark the policy process and identify core competencies. The project was to focus on the central objective of the White Paper: being 'forward looking in developing policy outcomes that matter, not simply reacting to short-term pressures' (Cabinet Office 1999a, para. 2.1). The case for modernizing policy by making it more professional is stated as being due to the fact that:

- 'The world for which policy-makers have to develop policies is becoming increasingly complex, uncertain and unpredictable'.
- Electorates are better informed and have rising expectations about 'services tailored to their needs'.
- Key policy issues (such as social exclusion and crime reduction) have proved 'resistant to previous attempts to tackle them'.
- The world is increasingly inter-connected and interdependent.
- Policy issues switch from the domestic and the international arena and diverse interests and needs have to be coordinated and harnessed.
- Governments need to be able to respond quickly to events and 'provide the support that people need to adapt to change and that businesses need to prosper'.
- Alongside these 'external pressures' government requires policy-makers to 'focus on solutions that work across organizational boundaries and bringing about change in the real world'. (Cabinet Office 1999b, 2.3)

If public policy is to remain credible and effective, policy-makers have to adapt to this new, fast-moving environment. The modernized model is seen as the way in which credibility and effectiveness can be enhanced in an age of increasing complexity, uncertainty and unpredictability. The main characteristics of the model set out in the White Paper are that policy-making ought to be: strategic; outcome focused; joined up; inclusive; flexible and innovative; and robust. Policy-making needs to change so that it is outcome-focused; inclusive, fair and evidence based; does not place unnecessary burdens on business; involves others; is forward and outward looking; and learns from experience. Taken together these specifications form the basis of the professional model project. The model begins with a rejection of the straw man of the traditional model: the stagist or policy cycle approach (Figure 9.1).

This traditional model corresponds to the idea of seeing policy-making as moving through: problem definition; decision-making; implementation; evaluation; policy change; and redefinition of policy problems. This basic model, however, is taken to be unrealistic as it characterizes the achievement of good results or well thought out and well implemented policies that deliver desired outcomes as dependent on a thorough, competent performance in a sequence of rational stages.

The traditional rational model, apparently, is a 'sequence of closely inter-related and inter-dependent activities which, together, form a cycle geared towards the progressive improvement of outcomes' (Cabinet Office 1999b, 2.6). When the team discussed this model with policy-makers, they discovered that:

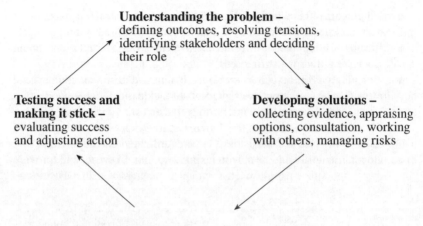

Understanding the problem –
defining outcomes, resolving tensions,
identifying stakeholders and deciding
their role

**Testing success and
making it stick –**
evaluating success
and adjusting action

Developing solutions –
collecting evidence, appraising
options, consultation, working
with others, managing risks

Source: Cabinet Office (1999b), figure 1

Figure 9.1   Traditional stagist model

> Policy-making rarely proceeds as neatly as this model suggests and that no two
> policies will need exactly the same development process. The reasons why policy-
> making gets underway will vary from case to case … as will the existing state of
> the policy, its complexity and range. The policy process is often blown off course
> by pressures or events outside the control of policy-makers … Approaching policy-
> making as a series of sequential steps also tempts policy-makers to leave thinking
> about some stage, such as implementation and evaluation, until late in the process.
> (Cabinet Office 1999b, para. 2.7)

The project quickly abandoned, therefore, the traditional cycle model as a
way of representing the modernized policy process: 'experienced policy-
makers reacted against such a presentation because they felt it did not
accurately reflect the realities of policy-making'. What is defined as effective
policy-making has to have a sense of context (the report's emphasis, para.
2.8). Policy-making takes place in a complex context such that, in addition to
traditional attributes such as knowledge of law and practice, understanding
the views of stakeholders and the ability to design implementation systems
the professional, twenty-first century policy-maker now has to come to grips
with: 'not only the way organizational structures, processes and culture can
influence policy-making, but also understand Minister's priorities … and the
way policies will play in the real world where they will make and impact'
(Cabinet Office 1999b, para. 2.8). The model shows the policy core situated
in the middle of three contextual layers: organizational, political and the
wider public. The diagram (Figure 9.2) aims to show how these different
layers can 'influence different parts of the policy-making process'.

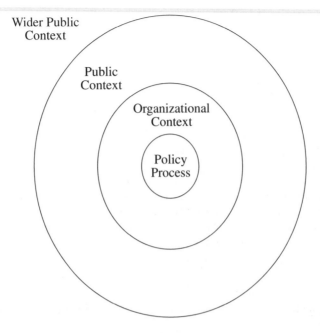

Source: Adapted from Cabinet Office 1999b, figure 3

Figure 9.2   The policy-making process in context

The contextual model developed by the team demonstrates an awareness of the governance narrative and how it fits with a strategic view of the policy process. It shows that policy-making does not take place in a kind of closed system, but involves an increasingly complex process encompassing interaction with and the management of many levels and different actors (Table 9.1).

The 'policy-making process in context' model which is utilized by the report focuses on how the design of policy-making strategies needs to be more attentive to the problems of forecasting, and securing goals, objectives and targets. In truth, a far more accurate description of the contextual model should be 'the policy process in a strategic context', for it is a diagram illustrating the key issues in the development of a strategically orientated approach to the design and implementation of policy. The contextual mapping undertaken by the team is essentially about the mapping and managing of the organizational, political and public environments in order to secure the objectives of the policy core, with a particular (and inevitable) emphasis on identifying stakeholders, strengths, weaknesses, threats and opportunities.

Table 9.1 The policy-making process in context

Organizational context

- How/when should policy effectiveness and contribution to corporate objectives be reviewed?
- Who else within government needs to be involved and how?
- What is the impact of devolution?
- What is the role of the EU?
- How should work be organized?
- How should front line staff be involved?
- What sort of cross-cutting intervention is required (if any)?
- What is the impact on other existing developing policies?
- What are the costs and benefits of different options?
- What evaluation systems and performance targets are needed?
- What are the alternatives to legislation and regulation?
- What training and support for front line staff is needed?
- What IS changes are needed?
- What needs to happen to ensure policy becomes self-sustaining?

Political context

- How can evidence be presented?
- How does the problem/policy fit with government manifesto commitments?
- What policy conflict/priorities need to be resolved?
- Is a cross-cutting approach needed?
- How and when should key political representatives be involved?
- Are ministers signed up?
- What is the strategy for presenting policy?
- Who needs to be told what, when and how?
- How can stakeholders be kept committed and involved?
- What are the quick wins?

Wider public context

- What evidence is needed and/or available to test the 'real world' problem?
- What are the desired policy outcomes?
- Which are the key stakeholders and how should they be involved?
- What are the needs and views of those the policy seeks to influence/affect?
- What evidence is available, relevant and useful?
- What have the experiences of other countries been?
- What are the risks to the policy and how can they be managed?
- What is the impact of possible solutions on equal opportunities, business, women, etc?

Source: Cabinet Office (1999b, Figure 3).

Fuller understanding of the broad context within which policy works should help policy-makers both when thinking about possible approaches to tackling a given problem and when they come to consider putting a particular solution into effect. Whilst organizational and management changes over the past decade have emphasized the separation of policy-making and policy implementation, 'modernized' policy-making demands that they be reintegrated into a single, seamless, flexible process. (Cabinet Office 1999b, XX)

Strategic policy-making thus will facilitate the bridging of the notorious implementation gap. This is a critical claim for the model, which runs throughout the modernization project. But as the representation of the policy-making process in context well illustrates, this is a process of reintegration of policy-making and implementation predicated on a model of improving the capacity of the policy-making core to monitor and regulate the policy network. The problem of the implementation gap thus resolves itself into one of improving design, coordination and control. The result is that for a document concerned with policy-making it has practically nothing to say about politics and the fact that policy-making takes place in a democratic context. And, when it is mentioned, politics appears as something of an irritating obstacle in the way or a problem to be managed and overcome. Hence the report asks: 'How and when should key political representatives be involved?'; 'Are Ministers signed up?'; 'Who needs to be told, what, when and how?' (Cabinet Office 1999b, figure 3). Sadly, ministers are too preoccupied with elections (Cabinet Office 1999b, para. 4.2). However, in lumping together civil servants and ministers into one undifferentiated group of policy-makers the report fails to take account of the very real and significant differences between different kinds of policy-maker. In its urge to abandon the old hierarchical (Weberian) paradigm and embrace the network approach to governance the professional model loses sight of a critical and defining feature of public policy-making in a democratic society: the difference between elected and non-elected policy-makers and between civil servants and policy advisers.

WHAT KIND OF MODEL IS THE 'PROFESSIONAL POLICY-MAKING' MODEL?

Having rejected the policy cycle as being unrealistic for the twenty-first century, the report argues that a 'better way forward was to produce a descriptive model of policy-making'. But this descriptive model (Figure 9.3) does not aim to describe reality or what is, but to describe a model of what ought to be. Despite this, the authors deny that it is prescriptive: it is apparently descriptive of best practice. And yet, if the phrase 'a series of high level features which, if adhered to, should produce fully effective policies' is not

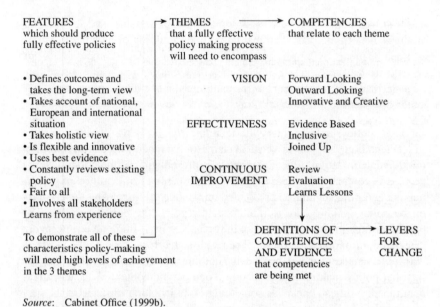

FEATURES   → THEMES   ──────→ COMPETENCIES
which should produce   that a fully effective   that relate to each theme
fully effective policies   policy making process
                            will need to encompass

• Defines outcomes and   VISION   Forward Looking
  takes the long-term view   Outward Looking
• Takes account of national,   Innovative and Creative
  European and international
  situation   EFFECTIVENESS   Evidence Based
• Takes holistic view   Inclusive
• Is flexible and innovative   Joined Up
• Uses best evidence
• Constantly reviews existing   CONTINUOUS   Review
  policy   IMPROVEMENT   Evaluation
• Fair to all   Learns Lessons
• Involves all stakeholders
Learns from experience
                                              DEFINITIONS OF ──────→ LEVERS
To demonstrate all of these   COMPETENCIES   FOR
characteristics policy-making   AND EVIDENCE   CHANGE
will need high levels of achievement   that competencies
in the 3 themes   are being met

Source: Cabinet Office (1999b).

Figure 9.3   The professional model

prescriptive then it is difficult to imagine what would be regarded as a prescriptive statement.

> The model is intended to describe what an ideal policy-making process would look like. It seeks to set the standard of professional, 'modernized' policy-making by defining what professional policy-makers should be able to do. It is intended to guide the policy-making process, not to evaluate the policy which is the outcome of the process, although evaluation of the effectiveness of the policy itself is part of the policy process. We accept that it is possible to produce effective policy without following the policy-making process described here, but would argue that the chances of producing effective policies are greatly improved by doing so. (Cabinet Office 1999b, Annex A, para.3)

There are a number of problems with this argument that following the model will be more likely improve the effectiveness of policy-making. Firstly, what kind of evidence do we have to justify this statement as to the likely outcome of this model? As the professional model lays such an emphasis on evidence and what works, it is somewhat contradictory to be making statements about what works, when we don't know what works. One could just as well say that by following the traditional (stagist) model we can increase the chances of effective policy-making. Secondly, it does not follow that we can show evidentially that this model provides a model of policy effectiveness. It does not follow that rational decision-making or professional policy-making produces better outcomes than that based upon intuition or hunches or whatever can be meant by 'unprofessional policy-making'. Good process does not necessarily lead to effective outcomes. A literature which is relevant to this issue is that concerned with policy failure and so called 'group think'. A major argument against group think theory is that for every policy disaster that one can put down to poor decision-making, one can show examples where concurrence seeking did not lead to failure (see Parsons 1995). And, just as Irving Janis looks for policy failures to demonstrate his arguments for a model which accounts for policy disasters, so the Cabinet Office team went in search of case studies which demonstrate that following the professional model leads to more effective policy-making: a rather dubious methodology, to say the least. A recent volume which deals with the issue of success and failure in a more contextual and methodologically sounder way is: *Success and Failure in Public Governance* (Bovens *et al.* 2001).

Having constructed a descriptive model the team set about collecting case studies of good practice over a three-month period. The cases which they examined were submitted by departments as part of the drafting process leading to the *Modernizing Government* White Paper. Departments were invited to forward examples of good practice and over a hundred were received by the Cabinet Office – although only a few (ten) were actually used. The team sent out a questionnaire based on their model and collected some 50 case studies from a range of government departments. This information was then tested against the competencies contained in the model which was, at this period, still in a developmental phase. The testing was, as the report admits, a subjective process, as the quality of the answers varied and the questionnaire left a lot of room for interpretation. Given this, the authors concluded that their audit provided a useful indication as to the extent to which the modernization agenda had been taken on board. The audit of good practice was also supplemented by interviews with civil servants and policy advisers; the use of focus groups of acting and former civil servants; and a literature review of good practice in policy-making in the UK and elsewhere (especially New Zealand). The team also undertook a training needs analysis which involved responses to a questionnaire completed by 23 ministers and 50 other policy-makers.

The result of their work was not surprising, confirming as it did the analysis of the problem set out in the White Paper: 'policy-makers concentrate their time and effort on policy analysis leading to advice to Ministers, on the design and processing of legislation, on coordination and clearance of policy within central government and developing and appraising policy options' (Cabinet Office 199b, 3.7). Although they discerned a 'recognition' of the importance of joined-upness and inclusiveness, rather less attention appeared to be given to being forward and outward looking and learning lessons from past policies. The main characteristic the team identified was that policy-making tended to be reactive and short term.

> Too often policy-makers react to major problems, formulate solutions, take deci-
> sions, implement them and move on to the next set of problem without being able
> to take the long-term view the White Paper envisages. This is, in part, because
> policy-making is often perceived by policy-makers as a fundamentally reactive
> process and, in part, because of the undoubted pressures under which they gener-
> ally work. (Cabinet Office 1999b, 3.7)

The reality of policy-making was, therefore, a long way removed from the vision of modernized policy-making set out in the White Paper. There were exceptions to this reactive approach to policy-making and the team drew attention to several cases which exemplified some key aspects of the profes-sional model. These included: the Single Work Focused Gateway (One); the New Deal for Lone Parents; the New Deal for Disabled People; and the Regional Strategy Framework developed in Northern Ireland. Such examples of good professional practice had one thing in common: they all utilized project management techniques. This provided them with the tools to 'focus on all aspects of good policy-making simultaneously' (Cabinet Office 1999b: 3.8). Project management is, however, hardly a leading edge twenty-first century idea: it began in the late 1950s. It requires policy-makers to develop a systematic plan; define clear goals and outcomes; deploy stakeholder analy-sis; and use the techniques of risk assessment and management. These techniques help, so the team concluded, to create a 'less risk averse environ-ment in which innovation and creative ideas can come to the fore'. The great advantage of the approach is that:

> Having to specify precise outcomes, products, and milestones early on helps
> policy-makers to build evaluation into the policy-making process from the outset.
> And having in-built mechanisms for monitoring the progress of work helps to
> keep the policy process on track. (Cabinet Office 1999b, 3.8)

Without wishing to challenge the claims for the effectiveness of project management techniques, it would have been more useful for the report to be really contextual: that is, to raise the issue of 'under what kind of conditions, and in what kind of situations does project management work'. The report concludes that project management is an important tool in the professional policy-maker's toolbox. As a tool it does have a track record of doing the job, but given the complexity of policy-making and the pressures of the real world to which the report refers, the central issue here is not whether it works in the case studies cited, but why it might not work in other areas of policy-making.

Toolboxes generally have a variety of tools for a variety of jobs: professionalism is about knowing when to use what tool. The report leaves us none the wiser. It may well be that project management is a special case in policy-making. That is, a tool which is appropriate for cases in which it is possible to have clear, well defined, precise outcomes, outputs, products and milestones; where stakeholders can be identified and involved across institutional boundaries; and in which risk is manageable and in which in-built mechanisms can help to keep the policy process on track. Designing a descriptive model of the policy process in terms of special cases hardly seems to be appropriate in the context of policy-making as being reactive, short-term and subject to uncertainty and rapid change. No less an authority on project management than the Project Management Institute defines the idea of project as:

> a temporary endeavour undertaken to achieve a particular aim. Every project has a definite beginning and a definite end. While projects are similar to operations in that both are performed by people, both are generally constrained by limited resources, and both are planned, executed and controlled, projects differ from operations in that operations are ongoing and repetitive while projects are temporary and unique. (PMI 2000)

It is the temporary and unique aspects of the notion of project that seem to be entirely inappropriate as a way of trying to understand the wider, infinitely more complex tasks of public policy-making as opposed to project management. Policy-making, unlike project management, has no definite beginning and no definite end; and is ongoing rather than about achieving particular aims. This failure (or reluctance) to distinguish between project management and policy-making is a critical weakness in the professional policy model. The focus on those case studies that demonstrated a close fit with the professional model and that also have a remarkable fit with project management techniques avoided the far more important question of what kinds of policy-making have a poor fit with the professional model and for which project management is of little or no benefit. It may well be that the kind of cases that exemplify the key traits of the professional model and that make an effective use of project management techniques, are indeed special cases, which, rather than proving the validity or strengths of the model, actually demonstrate its profound limitations and weaknesses. The 'exemplary' case studies may be 'exemplary as a whole' (Cabinet Office 1999b, 3.8) but what they cannot be is exemplary for the whole policy process. The model needs to be far more concerned with the difference between policies and projects and thus define specific contexts in which it might be predicted that project management will work.

LONG-TERM, FORWARD-LOOKING POLICY-MAKING

At the heart of the White Paper and the professional model is the argument for policy-making to be long-term and forward-looking. It may be possible within the context of certain kinds of projects to be long-term and forward-looking. But, what does being long-term and forward-looking mean for more complex policy domains? The professional policy model aims to get policy-makers thinking about the long term or 'what comes next'. The model intends to bring about an awareness that 'objectives being pursued are long-term but the policies being used to achieve them will need to be adjusted over time as lessons are learned about what works and as the world within which policies take place effect change itself' (Cabinet Office 1999b, 4.1). The definition of what constitutes forward-looking policy-making is unashamedly positivistic and strategic. Long term, for the professional policy means that they:

- clearly define outcomes that the policy is designed to achieve;
- take a long term view predicated (where appropriate) on the best use of statistical trends and informed predictions about society, politics, economics and culture over the next five years. (Cabinet Office 1999b, Annex: 5)

What do we look for as an indicator of professional performance? Professionals will:

- prepare statements of intended outcomes at an early stage in the process;
- engage in contingency planning and scenario planning;
- take account of the government's long term strategy as a whole;
- make use of foresight and futures work;
- take account of and learn from evaluations of previous related policies. (Cabinet Office 1999b, Annex: 5)

The team found that their investigations revealed a policy-making process in which there were 'real obstacles to long-term thinking' (Cabinet Office 1999b, para. 4.2). Ministers, strangely enough, seemed far too preoccupied with the electoral cycle which mitigated against long-term or medium-term thinking. Furthermore, because of uncertainty, policy-makers displayed scepticism about their ability to look more than a few years into the future. However, they concluded that futures work 'has not, as yet, been joined up effectively nor does it feed systematically into mainstream policy-making in the way that it needs to if long-term thinking is to become ingrained in the policy process'. (Cabinet Office 1999b, para. 4.5) The way forward appears to be ensuring more effective coordination in futures work so that a 'collectively agreed analysis of the key challenges that the government will have to face over the next 10 to 15 years' can be developed (Cabinet Office 1999b, para. 4.6). This will ensure that 'assumptions about the future are shared and that those who need to use forward-looking information have it available in standard form' (Cabinet Office 1999b, para. 4.6). However, even assuming that futures work can make a contribution to improving policy-making in the way the White Paper hopes, it does not follow that futures work should be joined up. As proponents of more process and complexity orientated approaches to strategic management (such as Mintzberg (1994) and Stacey (1996)) would argue, given that we cannot possibly know what the future holds, the idea of having a collective agreement about the future or that assumptions should be shared and put into a standard form are positively dangerous.

But again in the spirit of what works, the issue which needs to be addressed is: do these techniques actually work? If so, how, when, and in what situations? The ability to forecast and model the future is absolutely central to the strategic intent of modernized policy-making. It is an open question, nevertheless, as to what the utility of futures work is and whether it is possible that it can be linked up and integrated into the actual policy-making process. Reviewing the literature on this, Mintzberg, for instance, comes to the conclusion that forecasting rarely has much of an impact on the short-term focus of organizations. Forecasting of the kind being advocated in the modernization agenda is more a form of organizational magic which helps to give an illusionary sense of order and control in an entirely unpredictable and turbulent world (Mintzberg 1994, pp. 227–248). Of course, the stress in the report could be said to lay more emphasis on scenarios instead of forecasting: this is very much in line with the general direction of strategic planning. But again, the problem here is what is the evidence about scenario planning actually impacting on policy-making? Having admitted that the world is uncertain, complex and unpredictable, the report makes no acknowledgement that such factors might well mitigate against the kind of strategic policy-making advocated by the White Paper. The existence of scenarios may in practice, for example, do little to alter ways of thinking, as advocates of the technique point out (see Mintzberg 1994, pp. 248–51; de Geus 1999; Schwartz 1998; Van der Heijden 1996). Granted that policy-making has to be forward-looking, the model fails to prompt concern for context. What kind of futures work 'works', in what kind of policy domain, when, how and for whom? In what specific contexts can futures work be integrated into policy-making? What kind of forecasting or foresight is appropriate in complex and turbulent conditions? In this regard, as in many others, the model is asking the wrong questions.

OUTWARD-LOOKING POLICY-MAKING

Outward-looking policy-making involves two issues: learning from the experience of other countries and communicating policy to that big wide world outside Whitehall. There is ample evidence for policy-making being ready to learn from the experience of other countries and the report cites the New Deal for Lone Parents and the Single Work Focused Gateway project as having drawn heavily on the experience of other countries. Indeed, one could argue that British policy has never been slow in learning and imitating other countries: the 1960s and 1970s are replete with examples of Britain copying from other countries in an attempt to revitalize its economy (Smith 1979). In the 1980s the USA provided the benchmark for a raft of Thatcherite reforms to liberalize the British economic and social policy on American lines. Mr Blair's third way was also to be keen to learn from the USA. Britain has been far less enthusiastic about learning from other EU countries. This is noted by the report which argues for greater cooperation between the UK and the EU in crime and other policy areas.

> Our work suggests that there is a need to do more to encourage policy-makers especially in those areas where European work is not already a live, 'bread and butter' issue to build relationships with their counterparts abroad ... In particular, we see value in pursuing moves to encourage departments to ensure that all policy jobs have an explicit reference to Europe in the job description and objectives. (Cabinet Office 1999b, 5.6)

Communicating with the wider world as part of the outward-looking aspect of professional policy-making is more problematic. It seems to be far more to do with controlling the message than communicating, as in listening, to those outside government. And even when communication is about involving others it is expressed in terms of stakeholders. The report suggests four good practice principles for communication policy. To be successful, communication must:

- be planned from the start of the policy process and tackled as an issue throughout;
- be based on the sound awareness of the political and wider context within which the policy is being developed;
- be targeted according to the different audiences and make use of a range of media and formats in order to reach those audiences; and
- involve all those who will have a part to play in presenting policy – Ministers, policy-makers, press officers and service deliverers/implementors. (Cabinet Office 1999b, Figure 9)

The main argument for securing successful communications is, once again, the belief that 'the disciplines of project management seem to provide a mechanism for ensuring that communication does become an integral part of the policy process' (Cabinet Office 1999b, para. 5.8). What is not clear about this aspect of professional policy-making is what successful communications means. Communication does not seem to imply any notion that policy-making is about a dialogue, so much as it involves coordination of what is being said. Communication in professional policy-making is about effective presentation (or spin), rather than effective communication. There is a difference.

INNOVATION AND CREATIVENESS

Having set out a veritable box load of key principles, characteristics and competencies in the preceding chapters, the professional model then asks the would-be professional policy-maker to think out of the box. The White Paper stresses that the modern policy-maker must be 'flexible and innovative, willing to question established ways of dealing with things and to create an environment in which new ideas can emerge and be tested' (Cabinet Office 1999a, Annex 5). The professional must be willing to take risks and bravely go where traditional policy-makers had not gone before. Innovative and creative policy-making is defined as being:

- flexible and innovative in questioning established ways of dealing with things;
- concerned to encourage new and creative ideas;
- making established ways of working better (wherever appropriate);
- open to comments and suggestions of others (wherever possible);
- active in identifying and managing risks;
- keen to encourage experimentation and diversity through the use of trials and experiments. (Cabinet Office 1999b, Annex: 5)

As to the evidence which would demonstrate that this was taking place, the model identifies a number of key indicators.

- The use of unusual ways of working (brainstorming etc);
- The preparedness to take issues back to the beginning;
- Examination of evidence to get a better idea of the problem and why previous attempts failed;
- Definition of success in terms of identified outcomes;
- Effective use of pilots and trials;
- Consciously assessed and managed risk;
- Use of management structures that promote new ideas and effective team working;
- Appropriate use of IT;
- Use of outsiders in policy team. (Cabinet Office 1999b, Annex 5)

In the context of the kind of formulations and checklist approach of the model and the quality mentality in the modernized public sector, this call for creativity and innovation seems somewhat contradictory. As Mintzberg (1994) points out, strategic planning, 'by its very nature defines and preserves categories', whereas creativity 'by its very nature creates categories and rearranges established ones'. Which is why, perhaps, the formalization of professional policy-making – like strategic planning – 'can neither provide creativity nor deal with it when it emerges by other means' (Mintzberg 1994, p. 299). Innovation is difficult to institutionalize. As the Peer Review report of the Cabinet Office noted: 'one cannot "command" innovation or "control" creativity. Neither can one buy "breakthroughs" or "foresight"' (Cabinet Office 2000b, para. 3.5.2). In keeping with the strategic approach to 'innovation and creativity' the professional model also contains a box of eight 'principles of innovation'.

- Organizations need a **mixture of innovation and established systems** – the balance varies according to the organization's particular role and functions
- Equip policy-makers with **techniques to encourage creativity** – these might include De Bono's lateral thinking techniques
- Focus on those areas where innovative solutions are needed most and on **definition of the problems** to be tackled – as much effort needs to go into defining the problem (and signing up those who will have to implement a solution) as into developing the solution itself
- Create a **working environment** that encourages innovative ideas – maybe by getting out of the office or bringing people with different perspectives together or setting ground rules for sessions that outlaw immediate critique of ideas
- Create **momentum** for delivering innovative solutions by setting up projects with tight deadlines (six weeks should be enough to go from a start point to having a range of workable propositions)
- **Make innovative solutions real** by prototyping them, learning from experience and trying them again
- **Challenge assumptions** about innovation by taking them to organizations that are more innovative and by visibly rewarding new ideas
- **Start small** – work to develop a more innovative approach to areas and build from there. (Cabinet Office 1999b, Figure 11)

The aim of such boxes of managerial delight are, of course, to routinize or systematize innovation. And yet, as the report admits at the outset, the best examples of innovation were those which were the outcome of political will, backed by appropriate levels of resources (Cabinet Office 1999b, para. 6.2). In general the team concluded that civil service culture is not particularly welcoming to the challenges of risk, new thinking or change.

There is a general acceptance that fear of failure and the high penalties attached to mistakes are a powerful disincentive to real innovation. Policy-makers do not choose to take risks, in part, because of the way Parliament and other external bodies hold them to account, but also because there is a belief that career progression depends more on being a 'safe pair of hands' than on being innovative. (Cabinet Office 1999b, 6.4)

These substantial barriers to innovation are deep seated and yet the team considered that changing this culture was a relatively simple matter of encouraging major change. Implement the box of principles, bring in outsiders, use secondments and the internet. Above all: experiment. If policy-making is to be more innovative, then it has to be far more prepared to prototype and experiment. Innovative policy-making that seeks creative solutions to complex problems has got to learn all about the management of risk. This was to be considered by the Better Regulation Task Force and the Regulatory Impact Unit. The emphasis on experimentation and creativity is all standard managerialist rhetoric. However, the report seems to be oblivious to the context within which so much of public policy is actually delivered. There is a profound contradiction between the call for, on the one hand, creative and innovative policy-making, and on the other the growth of audit and regulation. Of its very nature the quality audit process, for example, so often mitigates against innovation and fosters playing safe and following guidelines and benchmarks (Seddon 2000, Parsons 2000). How does the call for innovation in education policy work in an OFSTED or QAA regime which is about the enforcement of a given definition of 'quality'? Why should a headteacher or university lecturer take risks and innovate, when it might fail? For the kind of innovation model advanced in the report, the logic leads towards loosely coupled organizational designs, as opposed to the extremely tightly coupled logic of joined up government, 'letting go', rather than command and control (Chapman 2002; Bentley 2002). The professional policy model seems to imply creativity and innovation at the core, but doing what you are told at the street level. Professional policy-makers are, it would seem, the risk taking, innovative and creative officers back at HQ who plan strategy, whilst public service professionals are the poor bloody infantry at the 'front line' whose job it is to obey orders and carry them out – or else.

HOW DO WE KNOW IF 'WHAT WORKS' WORKS?

A critically important aspect of the professional model is the idea that professional policy-making as opposed to unprofessional or amateur policy-making is based on the theory of 'what counts is what works'. The White Paper insists that sound (and in the Prime Minister's terms 'hard' evidence (Cabinet Office 2000f)) is the foundation upon which must rise professional practice.

The definition of what counts as evidence-based policy-making sets out a number of criteria.

- Advice and decisions must be based on the best available evidence from a wide variety of sources;
- Policy-making must involve all stakeholders from the early stage in policy development;
- All evidence must be available in an accessible and meaningful form. (Cabinet Office 1999b, Annex 5)

And we can check if this has happened by seeing if:

- Policy-makers considered existing research and commissioned new research (where appropriate);
- Relevant internal and external experts and consultants were used;
- Policy-makers considered a range of properly costed and appraised options. (Cabinet Office 1999b, Annex 5)

The team found that good practice in evidence-based policy making varied from department to department. It was not to be unexpected; for example, in health and agriculture there was a tradition of scientific testing, whereas in those policy areas (that is, the vast majority) where there was not reliable scientific data, and where issues were more politically contested, the use of evidence-based policy (*aka*, 'what works') was not as widely accepted. Even so, there was hope for the application of 'rigorous scientific method(s)' as witnessed when the team reported on the way in which the DTI dealt with the issue of labelling solvent abuse.

> The DTI commissioned quantitative and qualitative research in which 15 alternative warnings were tested with parents, teachers, young people and others over a period of two years. The then commonly used warning was shown to be largely ineffective ... (and) the new warning 'solvent abuse can kill suddenly' has now been put on millions of products sold in the high street and has been taken up by Health Education Authority's campaign to reduce solvent abuse. The research has been published and has attracted interest world-wide. (Cabinet Office 1999b, Figure 13)

Now there are a number of problems with this case study as an exemplar of the 'what works' mantra. The first is, given this policy initiative what is known about the effects of the intervention? Did this work? Did the use of the warning 'solvent abuse can kill suddenly' actually reduce the number of deaths and injuries caused by solvent abuse? The answer is most probably in the range of 'well yes and no'.

Policy problems and policy solutions are, of their nature highly contextual. What works is about what works, when, where, how and for whom. As advocates of 'realistic evaluation' have argued, government must really stop thinking in terms 'some kind of unitary happening which either does or does not work' (Pawson and Tilley 1997, p. 104). In addition to this, as the team admitted, evidence-based policy-making seems to work in cases which are 'relatively small and well focused'. Using small, well focused, case studies as models of good practice is surely problematic when applied to large, poorly focused, problems? Well no.

> even with larger more complex social problems, evidence can be collected to identify optimum opportunities for intervention, particularly when the nature of the intervention can be targeted very precisely. (Cabinet Office 1999b, para. 7.4)

The example of Sure Start is deployed as an illustration of this argument. But the central issue relates to the point about 'when the nature of the intervention can be targeted very precisely'. Even assuming that, for example, solvent abuse and social exclusion are indeed problems which can be so precisely targeted, there remains the vexed question of 'what about those problems which cannot be so precisely targeted and where there is little agreement about what the problems are, and how best to proceed to find out about them?' Here the team drew a blank.

> Whilst there is plenty of research available in areas such as education, social services and criminal justice, the coverage is patchy and there is little consensus amongst the research community about the appropriateness of particular methodologies or how research evidence should be used to inform policy and practice. These factors perhaps contribute to our finding that, although there are examples of good practice, in some areas of policy the generation and the use of information and research in policy-making is not as strong as it needs to be to support the government's pragmatic approach. (Cabinet Office 1999b, para. 7.5)

Thus the team found little in their interviews to support the idea that policy-making is informed by commissioned research; neither did policy-makers have the skills necessary to interpret research findings. Nor did they find much evidence of policy-makers having good access to those that did have such skills. Research in New Zealand suggested some of the factors which mitigate against the more effective utilization of 'information in policy advice'.

- Time makes the relationship between research and policy-making problematic. Driven as they are by the apparent need for 'quick fixes' policy-makers have little time to wait upon the finding of in-depth research.
- Policy-makers also confront a considerable 'overload' in the information that may well be available.

- There is a lack of skilled people to help interpret and make use of the research.
- Evidence may point in different and contradictory directions.
- The cross-cutting nature of policies requires information and research evidence to be cross-cutting in orientation.

To these we might add other constraints to rational decision-making as set out long ago by Herbert Simon. The team concluded that the task of developing a greater use of evidence in policy-making was to address the capacity of departments to make best use of evidence, and the need to improve the accessibility of evidence to policy-makers. A number of ways forward were advanced.

- Ensuring that departments developed 'single, overarching' research strategies.
- Joining up departmental research strategies.
- Making departments more intelligent customers.
- Addressing the issue of the quality of modelling.
- Improving the accessibility of research.
- The setting up of a centre for evidence-based policy.
- The creation of knowledge pools.
- Developing a policy research role within departments.

It is in the closing paragraph of the report that a measure of the top-down and thoroughly expert/technocratic orientation of the model is revealed.

> There is a tendency to think of evidence as something that is only generated by major pieces of research. In any policy area there is a great deal of critical evidence held in the minds of both front line staff in departments, agencies and local authorities and those to whom policy is directed. Very often they will have a clearer idea than the policy-makers about why a situation is as it is and why previous initiatives have failed. (Cabinet Office 1999b, para. 7.22)

Given this, it is alarming that the report chose to devote just one line to the issue of accessing this critical information, suggesting the use of interviews and surveys to gather up evidence from the 'front line' (Cabinet Office 1999b, para. 7.22).

For the professional model the task is seen as essentially one of the centre 'gathering' evidence from the front lines and feeding that evidence as interview and survey data into the policy core. The centre's role is to collate information from those at the front line and ensure that it is factored in to the core policy-making process, and in turn utilized to redesign policy. The report pays scant attention to the issue of how more implicit or tacit forms of knowledge in the policy process can best be accessed and used. The focus of the professional model is essentially on technical, bureaucratic, scientific and expert knowledge (*epsiteme* and *techne*) rather than on localized, practitioner knowledge or *metis*. Is this so easily accessed and captured by interviews and surveys? Can it so readily be simplified and codified in ways that can be applied outside specific context and locale? Is knowledge of good practice in policy-making as generic as the professional model supposes? In which case identifying, aggregating and disseminating 'best practice' in a field as complex, uncertain and downright messy as public policy may be positively injurious to the task of improving policy-making. Evidence-based policy-making is about scientific or 'explicit' knowledge (Nonaka and Takeuchi 1995, p. 71), whereas so much practical knowledge is tacit and highly embedded in local context. Whereas technical or scientific knowledge can be formalized and expressed in precise form, local knowledge may defy being organized and managed in the way suggested by the disciples of the 'what works' faith. *Metis*, for example, is of its nature difficult to integrate and aggregate into generally applicable (boxed) guidelines or principles. Scott suggests that the difference between *episteme, techne* and *metis* is not unlike the difference between the general knowledge of a captain and the local knowledge of a pilot.

> When a large freighter or passenger liner approaches a major port, the captain typically turns the control of his vessel over to a local pilot, who brings it into the harbour and to its berth. The same procedure is followed when the ship leaves its berth until it is safely out into the sea lanes. This sensible procedure, designed to avoid accidents, reflects the fact that navigation on the open sea (a more 'abstract' space) is the general, while piloting a ship through traffic in a particular port is a highly contextual skill. We might call the art of piloting a 'local and situated knowledge'. What the pilot knows are local tides and currents along the coast and estuaries, the unique features of local wind and wave patterns, shifting sand bars, unmarked reefs, seasonal changes in micro currents, local traffic conditions, the daily vagaries of wind patterns off headlands and long straits, how to pilot in these waters at night, not to mention how to bring many different ships to berth under variable conditions … The pilot's experience is *locally superior* to the general rules of navigation. (Scott 1998, pp. 316–17)

All too often, however, the story of so much public policy in Britain has been one of the Captains of HMS Whitehall and Westminster displaying a considerable reluctance to actually hand over the safe delivery of a policy into the care of local pilots. In the words of Douglas Jay, the man from Whitehall really is supposed to know best and what works. What works, however, is not a question of facts or evidence, so much of values. Evidence-based policy should, from a Lasswellian perspective, be about the process of understanding context and clarifying values: not simply assembling 'hard facts'. This requires a policy process that is open and democratic and which can facilitate a process of deliberation and public learning rather than (strategic) control.

INCLUSIVENESS

The rather narrow managerialistic and technocratic conception of evidence or expert driven policy is situated rather uncomfortably alongside a commitment to inclusiveness in policy-making. The report defines inclusive competencies as encompassing:

- Policy-makers taking account of the impact on and /or meeting the needs of all people directly or indirectly affected by the policy;
- Policy-making which involves key stakeholders directly in the policy process. (Cabinet Office 1999b, Annex: 5)

The kind of evidence which would demonstrate that policy-makers have been inclusive in their approach is specified in terms of:

- Professionals would have consulted all those responsible for service delivery and implementation;
- Competent policy-makers would have consulted with those on the receiving end of policy or those likely to be affected indirectly;
- Inclusive policy-makers would make use of schemes which facilitate consultation (such as Listening to Women and Consulting Older People);
- Policy-makers would make use of impact assessments in decision-making;
- They would have sought feedback on policy from front line deliverers and recipients. (Cabinet Office 1999b, Annex 5)

However, this notion of involving others is framed around a very top-down view, if not corporatist idea of involving. Inclusiveness is not about participation so much as consultation so as to ensure that government 'can develop policies that are deliverable from the start'. (Cabinet Office 1999a, para. 2.6) This idea of inclusiveness has far more in common with 'stakeholding' approaches to strategic (*qua* corporate) planning than facilitating greater deliberativeness and democratization. Consultation, the report notes, 'should be seen by policy-makers as part of the gathering of evidence to underpin policy advice' (Cabinet Office 1999b, para. 8.4). Even so, there are costs and benefits ('pitfalls') to encouraging consultation. The report warns that, as the OECD observed, consultation can enhance the quality and effectiveness of policy-making, yet can also create delay and administrative overload; it can strengthen legitimacy, but also provide a focus of mobilized resistance; and it can increase the responsiveness of citizens, but at the cost of raising expectations and being distorted by unrepresentative interests and lobby groups

(Cabinet Office 1999b, Figure 17). Consultation *qua* involvement is 'essential to find out about how stakeholders perceive policy options' (Cabinet Office 1999b, para. 8.8). It aims to secure from stakeholders and key players sufficient feedback about how policy options are viewed and how possible impacts will be assessed. This is no model for promoting a more participatory policy analysis (as advocated by the likes of Fischer (1995) and de Leon (1997)), but a mechanism for ensuring fairness and a way in which policy-makers can maximize their understanding of how policy will work on the ground and to see its operation from the point of view of the user, thus reducing the likelihood of 'unintended consequences' (Cabinet Office 1999b, para. 8.1). Consultative inclusiveness is thus a way of reducing uncertainty and managing risk, rather than of facilitating a more deliberative exchange of ideas and views. The Captain of HMS Whitehall is still in command of the bridge. Inclusiveness means that he has better policy instrumentation: waters are mapped; challenges are 'flushed out'; possible impacts are identified and marked; and stakeholders are staked out.

OF HOLY GRAILS AND PHILOSOPHERS' STONES

The goal of improving coordination is what has been termed the 'philosophers' stone' (Seidman cited in Bardach 1998, p. v) and the 'Holy Grail' (Rhodes 2001, p. 108) of governmental reform. In keeping with the mechanistic and militaristic tone of the modernization agenda, the task of improving coordination – joined-upness – is viewed as reorganizing and redesigning to facilitate cross-cutting policy-making. Joined-up government requires 'an effective system of incentives and levers'. In order to tackle the 'barriers' the White Paper suggested a number of organizational techniques, including: budgetary arrangements for cross-departmental working; performance indicators and appraisal systems which reward joined-upness. The report defines joined-upness as comprising three main traits:

- Professional policy-makers take a holistic view, looking beyond the institutional boundaries to the government's strategic objectives and seek to establish the ethical, moral and legal base for policy;
- They will consider appropriate management and organizational structures needed to deliver cross-cutting objectives;
- Policy-makers will develop a rewards and incentives system that encourages and maintains cross-cutting working. (Cabinet Office 1999b, Annex A: 5)

What will joined-up policy-making look like in practice?

- It will be a process in which cross-cutting objectives are defined at the outset;
- There will be joint working groups and other arrangements with other departments which will be clearly defined and well understood;
- Barriers to joined up policy-making will have been identified and a strategy will have been developed to overcome them;
- Information will be shared at every stage of the policy-making process – with all those who need to know;
- Implementation is considered part of the policy-making process and there will be evidence of close collaboration with operational staff;
- Policy contained negotiability to enable meaningful discussions with others who may have had competing priorities;
- There will be clear links to PSAs. (Cabinet Office 1999b, Annex A: 5)

The mix of horizontal and vertical coordination strategies was, the report found, 'well understood'. However, policy-makers were still 'feeling their way in how best to achieve it' (Cabinet Office 1999b, para. 9.2). The budgetary process (as was the case with PPBS) is seen as a way of leading the way in ensuring that departments can 'better prioritize their own work to ensure that it contributes to the achievement of long-term goals' (ibid.). The suggested prototypes for overcoming these 'barriers' are innovations such as the PIU, the SEU and the Drugs Czar. But, as the report concedes, the real problem with joined-upness is that, despite all the experimenting going on, there is 'little real experience of what works best in which circumstances' (Cabinet Office 1999b, para. 9.4). This issue, of course, is at the heart of the philosophy of 'what works'. What approaches to joined-upness work in what context? Although the task of joining up is acknowledged to be a 'multi-faceted and long term problem' (Cabinet Office 1999b, para. 9.8) it is surprising that it is so very constrained at the outset. In large part this stems from the 'generative metaphor' (Schön 1979) of joined-up and wired-up government. It implies from the beginning that the governmental machine is out of joint: the parts do not connect or mesh. Government has to be wired up. The problem of coordination and inter agency collaboration is seen almost entirely in terms of fitting the fragmented machinery of modern government together so that it can work effectively. This is to be achieved by results-based policy-making in which goals and objectives, outcomes and performance can be specified and agreed. Hence, one of the benchmark illustrations of joined-upness is that being promulgated by the Home Office, Lord Chancellor's Department, and Crown Prosecution Service on a new criminal justice policy.

When new policy is planned which affects more than one of the three Justice Ministers' responsibilities, the following should be produced, collectively agreed and where necessary revised as the policy is developed:

- A rationale and priority for the policy consistent with the strategic aims and objectives of the CJS;
- A Policy appraisal which specifies objectives and outcomes; identifies options based on evidence; and assesses costs, risks and benefits;
- A Plan and timetable for involving and consulting others;
- A full specification of the policy based on the agreed option which sets out what is to be achieved, by when and how achievement will be measured, at what costs, to whom and how the costs are to be met;
- Plans and timetables for implementing the policy, monitoring progress and evaluating the policy. (Cabinet Office 1999b, figure 21)

This is coordination expressed in mechanistic terms and expressed in the language of strategic planning and results oriented government. What cannot be specified, defined and measured cannot be joined and wired up. One leading scholar of coordination, Eugene Bardach, has drawn attention to the dangers of this kind of approach. Bardach argues that the problem of coordination between different agencies is really about the long-term process of building up Interagency Collaborative Capacity, (ICC). For Bardach, the theory and practice of getting agencies to work together is a matter of behaviour and process, rather than structure. Getting different agencies to work together, however, is less of science of applied mechanics (wiring and joining) than the development of 'managerial craftsmanship'. Building collaborative capacity is not going to happen overnight: it is a very long-term process dependent on the human resources and levels of craft in different agencies over time and space. A major aspect of building ICC, Bardach emphasizes, is creating a 'climate of trust and joint problem solving' – something which may be problematic in a results-focused approach to policymaking (Bardach 1998). Innovation and creativity – two main characteristics of good craftsmanship – are also problematic in a 'what works' culture where a perceived failure may result in experiments being under pressure to perform and deliver. No doubt it is because of this problem of building ICC – through trust and joint problem solving – that coordination has proved in practice such a difficult goal to achieve through pulling levers and improving organizational mechanisms. The evidence on whether joining up works consequently offers little comfort to the erstwhile professional policy-maker (see Wright and Hayward 2000).

POLICY-MAKING AS A LEARNING PROCESS

The White Paper made great play with the idea that policy-making should be a learning process: 'effective policy-making must be a learning process which involves finding out from experience what works and what does not work and making sure that others can learn from it too' (Cabinet Office 1999b, para. 10.1). The evidence that learning is actually taking place specified by the report comprises:

- Information on lessons learned and how good practice was disseminated;
- Accounts of what was done by policy-makers as a result of lessons learned;
- Evidence that a clear distinction between failure of the policy to impact on the problem it was intended to resolve and managerial or operational failures of implementation. (Cabinet Office 1999b, Annex A: 5)

The Cabinet Office team found that policy-makers were well aware of the fact that the policy-making process does not place enough emphasis on the use of evaluation for learning lessons from experience. The use of evaluation varied considerably between government departments, and where such work was conducted it was often 'unsystematic, low profile and had limited impact on Ministerial policy decisions'. The challenge for the team was to investigate possibilities of enhancing the position of evaluation in the policy process, given these deficiencies. Evaluation, defined as 'what works' is seen as the 'principal mechanism for learning purposes' (Cabinet Office 1999b, Annex A: 5). This over investment in evaluation as the critical learning process in policy-making is problematic given the fact that evaluation of the kind advocated by the modernizing agenda is not a very inclusive idea and indeed serves to constrain the role of evaluation within a managerialist and positivistic framework. Professional evaluation appears to be little more than a tool of strategic planning and management, hence its emphasis on the utility of project management techniques.

> The disciplines of project management, which make policy-makers specify from the outset, seem to have been effective in encouraging departments to think about evaluation as an integral part of the policy-making process. They help to counter the pressure on policy-makers to develop, obtain parliamentary approval for and implement policy very fast which leaves little time for them to consider the basic information that will demonstrate whether or not policies and programmes are achieving what they set out to. (Cabinet Office 1999b, 10.4)

Evaluation is consequently viewed primarily as a method of reducing uncertainty (Cabinet Office 1999b, paras 9.8; 10.5; 10.7). However, evaluation, it must be emphasised, has such a poor reputation for impacting upon policy-making because good evaluation rarely, if ever, serves to reduce uncertainty and risk, but invariably tends to increase the complexity faced by policy-makers. Evaluation *qua* 'what works' is therefore less a mechanism for learning, as envisaged in the White Paper, than a mechanism for managing uncertainty and risk in a strategic policy process. Professionalized evaluation is centred on improving the instrumentation of government steering, rather than about improving learning in the sense we find in the works of Schön, Senge, Nonaka and Takeuchi, Stacey and others. The professional approach to evaluation is primarily concerned with learning how to steer with a more sophisticated set of policy guidance systems powered by hard evidence and explicit modes of knowledge. Little reference is made to the world beyond Whitehall, apart from how information can be relayed to, and feedback obtained from, those doing the rowing.

In addition to carrying out formal set-piece evaluations, policy-makers need to set up effective feedback loops to allow those in departments, agencies and local authorities who deliver policy on the ground to inform them about how policy is received and works in practice over time. These mechanisms might include providing regular management information but should allow for softer face-to-face contact between policy-makers and deliverers through workshops or network meetings. These are especially important once a policy is established so that policy-makers can get early warning of any change in circumstances that may affect the outcomes that the policy is designed to deliver. (Cabinet Office 1999b, 10.19)

Evaluation for the model is part of the control and scanning system which can ensure that the policy captains in Whitehall can continue to steer the ship of state in uncertain waters without having to hand over the wheel to local pilots.

CHANGING POLICY-MAKING

The model also sets out an implementation strategy framed around a set of 'levers for change'. These levers comprise an action plan linked to the key features of what a professional (fully effective) policy-making process should look like. These specify actions at the level of departments and actions for the centre (Cabinet Office 1999b, Annex B). The lever metaphor captures the essentially mechanical character of the implementation strategy, as of other aspects of the model: 'change in policy-making will have to be led from the top and the involvement of ministers as well as top managers and policy-making through joint training will be essential to success' (Cabinet Office 1999b, para. 11.14). This is a model of policy implementation in which the people at the top pull levers in order to bring about change in the direction determined at the centre. The report contains little by way of recognizing that change (and strategy) in complex, uncertain and unpredictable contexts may be far more emergent, localized, fragmented and diverse a process to be levered from the top. Given the contingencies of time and space, the idea that the long-term and far-reaching changes envisaged in the model can be levered by the Whitehall machine is yet another illustration of the how the model is overwhelmingly concerned with enhancing the capacity of the centre to regulate and control policy-making and delivery. If policy-making is a learning process, then the issue should be one of how best to create a learning process, rather than how best to enhance the effectiveness of control mechanisms. However, given the outcome and results emphasis in the idea that government must be seen to deliver (and get 'early wins', Cabinet Office 1999b, para. 11.11) there is a real conflict between policy-making as a long-term (decentralized) learning process and policy-making as a (centralized) process by which governments 'translate their political vision into programmes and actions to deliver outcomes' (Cabinet Office 1999a, para. 21). Learning requires, as Schön (1973) argued, periphery-to-periphery interaction, whereas delivering outcomes determined by the centre requires prescription and control to ensure that a given strategy is achieved.

PROFESSIONAL POLICY-MAKING PEER REVIEWED

A key component of the professional model is the use of peer reviews to facilitate the spread of good practice and a learning process. This 'flexible learning tool' is in stark contrast to the inflexible audit weapon inflicted on those involved in policy delivery. These reviews involve teams of six to eight people drawn from other government departments, CMPS and the wider public and private sector. They examine key documents and over a period of a week, interview members of the department as well as policy stakeholders from outside. The recommended tools for this process are, predictably, ISO 9000, EFTQM (The European Foundation for Quality Management Excellence Model), Investors in People and the Charter Mark scheme. The outcome of this process is a report or review intended as a 'learning tool' to improve performance (Cabinet Office 2000e).

The Cabinet Office took a lead in promoting peer review by agreeing to be reviewed itself. The review team was chaired by Jocelyne Bourgon, President of the Canadian Centre for Management Development. The seven other members came from other government departments, the private (corporate) sector, the voluntary sector, local government and academia (Professor Peter Aucoin). Over ten days they interviewed (just in London) ministers, permanent secretaries, and officials at all levels in the cabinet office as well as with stakeholders in and outside government. In respect of policy-making, the team endorsed the approach as 'basically sound' and in line with developments in other countries. However, the team did not feel that they had seen sufficient policy-making in action to come to any judgement about whether modernized policy-making had actually been 'espoused'. Even so, it found these principles well-known and commanded agreement. They found some evidence that there were efforts being made to improve on the lines recommend by the White Paper. (Cabinet Office 2000b, 4.2.1) There were a number of issues, however, which the team thought significant. The first was that although much emphasis was placed on the importance of policy-making taking place in a global and international context, they found scant attention being paid to global issues, international trends or the EU and no evidence of efforts to join up with opposite numbers in Europe (Cabinet Office 2000b, 4.2.2). Second, they raised a number of important points in relation to forward-looking and evidence-based policy-making.

> To ensure that policy work is forward looking requires a clearer distinction between policy research and policy formulation. Policy research should be focused on the mid to long term. It can take years to develop the database and the time series needed to support policy analysis and formulation. Policy formulation operates under different time constraints. Frequently, it responds to emerging crises or to the need to seize opportunities as they occur. It will never be made on the basis of perfect knowledge. The evidence may not provide the policy solutions. In fact, some very successful public policies have come from thinking 'out of the box'. The most important contribution of evidence-based research is to provide a more accurate understanding of the extent of our 'ignorance' allowing us to focus the work needed to close the gap. (Cabinet Office 2000b, 4.2.3; 4.2.4)

This is a pertinent observation to make about the kind of expectations and assumptions which the professional model embodies about the relationship between research and policy-making. The problem about research is that it does operate within a very different context to policy-making: time is one of the important differences. Research and policy-making are, perhaps, fundamentally out of joint and only rarely, if ever, destined to be 'joined up'. For this reason, as for many others, policy-making must always take place in conditions where knowledge is fundamentally imperfect. Hence Lasswell long argued for a relationship in which research (the policy sciences of democracy) helped in the process of clarifying values rather than provided hard facts, or the evidence base for policy, or knowledge about what works. As the review team point out, evidence may not provide solutions. Evidence-based policy is not, nor can it ever be about increasing knowledge, or reducing uncertainty, so much as it can help to illuminate our lack of knowledge and the degree and extent of our ignorance. In which case, the gap which should concern the policy-maker is not the knowledge gap, but what one author has termed the 'ingenuity gap' (Homer-Dixon 2000). The question is, of course, to what extent will the professional model in practice serve to promote creative, innovative 'out of the box' thinking, or will it serve to constrain it. The fact that the model is so rooted in a top down and centralized an approach seems to suggest that the model is ill-designed to facilitate 'out of the box thinking'. There are simply too many boxes.

Finally, on the issue of cross-cutting, inclusive, results-based policy-making the team identified 'much support' from outside government for the way in which policy-making has tried to make more use of external advice and inclusive consultation methods (such as policy action teams). They discerned, however, some scepticism about this aspect of the agenda, but no disagreement with it. The team recommended that the Cabinet ought to play from strength and support the efforts of line departments to link policy more firmly to delivery. In general terms the first peer review of professional policy-making was very positive. It showed that the ideas had gained wide currency in the policy-making network in central government and beyond and that the Cabinet Office was seen as leading the drive to modernize the policy process. Given the fact that the professional model was barely underway at the time, it was difficult to see what more could be said than that the government was on the right track in seeking to bring policy development and delivery closer together. As they admitted, the team saw insufficient examples of the model in practice.

TOWARDS 'BETTER' POLICY-MAKING

The Performance and Innovation Unit (PIU) took forward two core ideas contained in the professional model in their reports *Adding It Up* (Cabinet Office 2000f) and *Wiring It Up* (Cabinet Office 2000g). The former dealt with the issue of improving analysis and modelling, and the latter, the challenge of joining up policy-making. Following the publication of the professional policy-making report the PSD conducted a major survey of senior civil servants throughout the UK. A questionnaire was sent out in November 2000, and responses were submitted by January 2001. The questionnaire was designed to 'capture information on innovation in the policy-making process'. It aimed to find out about ways of developing policy that are 'creative, pioneering and professional' (Cabinet Office 2000c). A guidance note informed respondents that the survey was 'interested in programmes of change (such as the establishment of new units to consider policy-making at a strategic level) as well as initiatives on individual policies (such as new means of consulting and involving people outside Government or different ways of working across organizational boundaries)' (Cabinet Office 2000c). The survey was interested in all kinds of change, 'big or small', 'planned as well as incremental change' (Cabinet Office 2000c: 3). Respondents were asked to list all those areas of policy responsibility in their department which demonstrated 'new, interesting or professional' approaches to policy-making, and to provide details of the approaches by giving three 'striking' examples. The survey also asked questions about what factors drive policy-making initiatives (Cabinet Office 2000c):

- A reaction to a 'crisis' (such as an industrial dispute or epidemic)
- A response to a departmental resource issue (such as reorganization or availability of new resources)
- A reaction to a new issue or problem (such as HIV or the Millennium bug)
- A reaction to a new understanding or way of looking at the issue/problem (such as social exclusion or criminal justice)
- A response to the identification of an emerging area of public opinion (such as fuel processing, gene technology)
- An updating of a policy area that the Department has traditionally owned (such as employee relations, commonhold/leasehold reform)
- Other

Respondents were also asked to identify what features of the professional model is exemplified (forward-looking, outward-looking, innovative, and so on) by their examples of new, interesting or professional approaches to policy-making. The questionnaire probed how the professional model differed from the traditional approach and asked respondents to consider the strengths and weaknesses of the professional model as compared with the traditional approach. It also asked respondents to think about the problems of taking the new approach and who were the main drivers behind adopting the professional model (ministers, special advisers, permanent secretaries, departmental boards, management teams, directors, heads of policy teams and others). An important area covered by the questionnaire was the issue of the resource implications of adopting the professional model: especially staff resources, expenditure and time. The survey also probed whether the professional model actually resulted in a difference to policy outcomes. The questionnaire, it was hoped, would 'facilitate information sharing among policy-makers, and provide an up to date picture of what is going on around Government to modernise the policy-making process'. The results of this study by a team from PSD were published in (November) 2001 as *Better Policy-making* (Cabinet Office 2001). As with the original report, *Better Policy-making*, whatever its strengths and weaknesses, does constitute one of the 'most comprehensive surveys that have ever been undertaken' (Cabinet Office 2001, p. 16) into the policy-making processes of British government. For this much alone it is of considerable value. In keeping with the *Professional Policy-making* report, *Better Policy-making* provides case studies that illustrate aspects of the model in practice. Departments were asked to find examples of policy-making that conformed to the model, and sure enough, they found them.

In addition to *Better Policy-making* the National Audit Office published a report on *Modern Policy-making: Ensuring Policies Deliver Value for Money* (NAO 2001b) to coincide with the PSD's report. The PIU contributed to the discussion on policy-making with a discussion paper on the theme of *Better Policy Delivery and Design* (PIU 2001). Later (in March 2002) a toolkit for *International Comparisons in Policy-making*, was produced by the CMPS's International Public Service Group (IPSG) (Cabinet Office 2002). This toolkit was launched alongside a 'Policy Hub' (an internet-based resource) which aimed to carry: 'examples of successful policy-making and delivery' and support: 'the exchange of information and ideas through innovative "knowledge pools" – designed to break down organizational and geographical barriers and improve collaborative working within and beyond government'.

CONCLUSIONS

As *Better Policy-making* observes, it is evident that, within a comparatively short time, policy-makers were 'assimilating and acting upon the agenda to modernize policy-making' (Cabinet Office 2001, p. 18). In this respect, the success of the report in initiating new thinking about policy-making was clearly demonstrated. However, the professional model, and its subsequent iterations and amplifications, are inadequate as a strategy for improving policy-making for three main reasons. First, it fails in its own terms by setting out to be a model predicated on the philosophy of what works, and yet it is unable in so many ways to demonstrate that what it prescribes works. Although the modernization White Paper places such an emphasis on evidence and the mantra of 'what works' it is curious that it makes the assertion that, 'taken together and if applied consistently, these principles will re-invigorate our policy-making capacity and capabilities' (Cabinet Office 1999a, p. 6). In the spirit of evidence-based policy-making the question arises as to what evidence is advanced, or indeed can be advanced, to support the theory that such principles will reinvigorate policy-making? And, of course, the rider of 'if taken together and if applied consistently' then all will be well begs many questions. Claims are made for the model producing more effective policy-making, but the evidence upon which such claims are made are lacking hard facts. It is also peculiar that a report which is so focused on delivery and what works should have been concerned solely with process, and not outcome. Hence the case studies described in *Better Policy-making* do not demonstrate better delivery, but 'better policy-making'. The question is, does better policy-making lead to better outcomes? And, what does 'delivery' mean? Hitting targets and achieving objectives? The model was designed to 'guide the policy process' towards greater professionalism, 'not to evaluate the policy which is the outcome of the process' (Cabinet Office 1999b, Annexe A, para. 3). Thus the model is concerned solely with whether process has changed, rather than the far more problematic and far more relevant question: does the model actually deliver better outcomes? The case studies in *Better Policy-making*, for example, tell us nothing about whether a policy worked, but only that good systems are in place. They tell us that policy-makers have assimilated the agenda and the strategic discourse, but little about the relationship between process and delivery. As *Better Policy-making* admits, the link between better process and actual outcomes is untested and is the subject of research which is ongoing at the time of writing (Cabinet Office 2001, p. 16). However, given that the whole hypothesis upon which the project is based is untested, it rather undermines the case for the model as a whole. The model seems to break some of its own fundamental protocols. Does better policy-making work? The answer is, apparently, we don't actually know, but we hope it does. Second, the model not only ignores the issue of what works, it also fails to consider the fact that politics and democracy are important dimensions of policy-making. Chapter two of the White Paper begins with a very revealing statement about what is meant by the term policy-making, which largely frames the model: policy-making is about delivery and effective ineffective delivery is the result of 'flawed' or 'inadequate' policy (Cabinet Office 1999a, para. 2.1). Robert Reich, however, reminds us that public policy is also about providing 'the public with alternative visions of what is desirable and possible, and to stimulate deliberation about them, provoke a re-examination of premises and values, and thus broaden the range of potential responses and deepen society's understanding of itself' (Reich 1988, pp. 5–6). As the founding father of the policy sciences, Harold Lasswell argued the policy-making process is also a process of public learning not simply of delivery (see Parsons 1995, 2000). From the outset the modernizing approach to the policy process ignores the political and democratic dimension of the framing and execution of public policy: modernizing appears to be little more than another word for managerializing. This becomes very apparent in the professional model. Policy-making in modernizing terms is narrowly conceptualized as translating vision into delivery. Perfect implementation is a function of perfect policy design. In large part this neglect of politics derives from the way in which the approach which it adopts to strategic policy-making is so utterly grounded in a deeply rationalistic, reductionist, positivistic and mechanistic approach to policy-making *qua* strategic management. This is evident from the policy-making toolkit on international comparisons (Cabinet Office 2002) which provides a workbook for would-be policy-makers structured by a very linear 'vertical axis' comprising agenda setting; objective setting; choosing policy instruments; implementation; and evaluation. For an approach which was about moving away from the traditional stagist model towards new horizons, it has all the hallmarks of being rather *olde worlde* (1960s) policy analysis and is incredibly stagist. Finally, as a piece of modern managerialism it is somewhat deficient. Once again it fails in its own terms: the professional model is an ageing mid-twentieth century model trying to pass itself off as a cutting edge twenty-first century piece of (tool) kit. As *Better Policy-making* reports, a 'significant minority' of policy-makers had doubts about the twenty-first century nature of the professional agenda: it appeared to some respondents that the model had more to do with continuity than a 'significant break with the past' (Cabinet Office 2001, p. 19). The model was thought to be essentially 'business as usual' as opposed to marking a radical departure. The reason for this, it could be argued, is that the model is framed around well-established ideas about strategic planning and management going back to the 1960s. In this sense, it just represents the 'continued development of the techniques and approaches that the civil service has traditionally employed when developing policy' (Cabinet Office 2001, p. 19). For all its modernizing rhetoric, the model badly neglects and ignores the contribution that other recent (if not modern) ideas could make to the formulation of a strategic model that is more attuned to the demands of the early twenty-first century, than the middle of the twentieth, and is more appropriate and relevant to policy-making as opposed to public management (Alford 2001, para. 10, 13). Given that policy-making takes place in conditions of ignorance, unpredictability, uncertainty and complexity (which the report in part acknowledges (Cabinet Office 1999b, 2.3)) a strategic policy model should also aim to incorporate approaches to strategy that are more focused on these factors than is the professional model. And yet, having acknowledged the importance of uncertainty and complexity, the professional model proceeds in a very linear and mechanistic way, making dubious assumptions about the relationship between knowledge and control. This is a point well made by Jake Chapman (Chapman 2002) and Tom Bentley (2002) in their endorsement of (complex) systems thinking and letting go as a way to improve policy-making for the twenty-first century. It is also a criticism of conventional wisdom made by the Director of the PIU himself, Geoff Mulgan, who noted that governments have been reluctant to draw on ideas which are more alive to the issues raised by complexity and non-linearity (Mulgan 2001). Of course, if such approaches had been taken on board by the professional model, they would have gone some way to constrain and subvert the modernizing assumptions about being able to know, predict, join up, command and control.

10. Civil society, virtue, trust: implications for the public service ethos in the age of modernity

Peter Barberis

INTRODUCTION

In recent years there has been a heightening of interest in public service ethics and the public service ethos. A substantial literature abounds (Chapman 1988, 1993, 2000; Lawton 1998, Thomas 1993). From various points on the social and political compass there have been expressions of unease, often predicated upon assumptions of decline or decay. Geras has talked about a 'moral darkness' (1998, p. 57). Selbourne describes a 'moral wasteland' (1998, p. 10) in which there is a 'seeming contempt for the very argument of right and wrong' (p. 46). Sometime Blairite guru and champion of modernity Anthony Giddens acknowledges that civic decline is 'real and visible in many sectors of contemporary societies' and that 'it cannot be dismissed as an invention of conservative politicians'(1998, p. 78).

The implication of any assertion about decline or decay is the existence of some prior age of relative uplift and vigour. With characteristic flourish the late Noel Annan sang the virtues of the 'intellectual aristocrats' of the nineteenth century – those beacons of morality who provided the foundation for much that was good in the British tradition of public service:

> There was a sense of dedication, of living with purpose, or working under the eye, if not of the great Taskmaster, of their own conscience ... They were filled with a sense of mission to improve the shining hour. They felt they had to account for their talents. They held themselves apart from a world given over to vanities which men of integrity rejected. (Annan 1999, p. 14)

Others attest to the notion of the public good upheld by members of the governing classes of the nineteenth and early twentieth centuries – moralists who saw clearly the need for a reinforcement of the social and civic foundations in order that a liberal politico-economic regime could be spared its otherwise potentially wayward tendencies (Watson 1973; Collini 1991). It was, of course, an essentially elitist, 'high' politics with an emphasis upon leadership – the product of a pre-democratic, or early democratic, era. Moreover, when we seek out the past we often find familiar murmurings of disquiet. During the interwar years Walter Lippmann (1929, p. 56) issued one of his famous blasts against the 'acid of modernity' that he believed to be a widely manifest and deeply entrenched western, not solely American, phenomenon.

According to Kernaghan the term public service (or administrative) ethics refers to ' ... principles and standards of right conduct ... not only with distinguishing right from wrong and good from bad but also with the commitment to do what is right or what is good'(1993, p. 16). He goes on to explain that the concept of ethics is based around values – that is 'enduring beliefs that influence the choices we make from among available means and ends' (*ibid.*).

Apart from the obvious matter of what constitutes right (as distinct from wrong), why should people choose that which is right? To this age-old question there are four classic answers. First, we may choose 'right' simply from fear of punishment or in response to incentive. The imperative is a purely external one, the assumption being that in the absence of constraint (or enticement) we are wont to wrong. Second, we may adhere to right because, for good or ill and whether or not it serves our present condition, we have signed up to compliance. It is the classic contract. The 'right' may not touch our hearts. We perhaps reserve our position to renegotiate. But for the time being we feel bound by the agreement that we have made or which has been made on our behalf and which has universal, indeed impersonal, application – the rule of law, loosely stated. It yields an essentially formal, legalistic and, again, instrumental compliance. Third, we may experience mutual advantage: we all gain from upholding 'right' so long as nobody cheats. An obvious flaw here, as Barry (1995, pp. 33–4) points out, is that people may cease to obey if they no longer profit by their compliance or believe that they can 'steal a march' unnoticed. The mainspring is no less instrumental than under the contract regime, though the mechanisms may be social and moral, rather than formal or legalistic. The emphasis then is upon values, conventions and customs – the more widely shared and the more deeply held, the better. This end of the 'instrumental' scale shades off into the fourth classic explanation as to why people uphold 'right' – that is, from a fundamental conviction in its intrinsic worth. Whatsoever may be the source of our belief, we hold fast to that which we consider to be right because, for us, it is right. No other point of reference is necessary. We maintain our position even in the face of adversity – when the prevailing climate is unpropitious and perhaps hostile, or when the temptation of advantage would have us set aside our qualms. It is of course more difficult to sustain a belief when it is not (or no longer) universally shared – where there are competing, indeed conflicting, notions of 'right' or where other considerations supplant their primacy.

Needless to say, it is possible for more than one of these four factors to work in tandem. Moral touchstones sometimes chime in with calculations of mutual advantage (Brittan 1998, p. 35). But the four types of compliance are not coterminous. Explicitly or otherwise, it is the third and fourth of these classic responses to our question that provide the frame of reference for many of the laments. The alleged 'acid of modernity' seems to consist in the fracturing of civil society, the loss of trust as a social lubricant and the absence of a prevailing, indeed perhaps of any, notion of virtue. At the same time, a number of specific factors have been identified as having undermined the traditional public service values as expounded by the likes of Annan (Elcock 1995; Greenaway 1995; Chapman 1997). Such factors include the deification of managerialism, with its emphasis upon audit trails, measurable performance targets and output related pay schemes; the inculcation within public service organizations of a more commercially orientated culture; the tyranny of the short-term expedient, whether in deference to political whim or in satisfaction of public acclaim; the fragmentation of structures and partial retreat both from the ideal and the reality of a distinctive career service; the derogation of professionalism (and professional standards) and self-regulation; and the intrusion of an ever more highly charged media intent upon sensationalism and the 'typification of the sensational'.

What has often brought many of these issues into focus is a perceived decline of probity, integrity and honesty among those entrusted with the conduct of public affairs. Exposures of fraud, deceit, abuse of position and the perversion of convention have, not surprisingly, led to a loss of public confidence. It is to transgressions of such ilk that successive governments have most vigorously and visibly responded. A number of *causes célèbres* have prompted increasing resort to legal or quasi-legal mechanisms, replete with regulatory regimes, explicit codes and other specifications of good practice. The Committee on Standards in Public Life, chaired first by Lord Nolan then by Lord Neill, has become part of the regular landscape. The long-standing Commons' Committee of Parliamentary Privilege is now supplemented by the Committee on Standards and Privileges, and by the work of the Public Administration Select Committee. In addition there is the office of the Parliamentary Commissioner on Standards.

It is important to note that these transgressions and the very visible governmental responses tend to be associated more readily with the first two of the four types of compliance outlined above – that is, with the more formal, contract-orientated approaches that rest essentially upon instrumental, calculative mechanisms. Stronger, more explicit regulations have been formulated to bring transgressors to book and to deter would-be transgressors from perpetrating acts of fraud, dishonesty, dissemblance and so forth. The focus has been upon the outward appearance of propriety and the eschewal of impropriety. It is the argument of this chapter, though, that such responses, understandable and appropriate in themselves, have been accompanied either by a neglect of the other two (that is moral) dimensions or by a misplaced attempt to apply to them the more formalistic, heavy mechanisms devised to deal with a related but different set of problems. For the public service ethos requires more than the outer appearance of propriety. It is about dispositions, inner impulses not only to do what is right but to do it well – to do a good job, to go the extra mile, if necessary applying ingenuity and even courage in order to navigate a tricky passage. If not guaranteed by formal propriety, a public service ethos may be undermined by impropriety, for example where corner-cutting or even mild corruption is countenanced as an agent of effective government. Equally, the tyranny of audit trails, output targets and other appurtenances of the modern management culture can easily displace the public service ethos which may, in time, wither.

The significance of this observation becomes more fully apparent within the context of notions about civil society, virtue and trust. In no sense do these three constitute a 'holy trinity' or an 'iron triangle'. They are separate phenomena, though they often thrive upon one another. Civil society is conducive to the flourishing of trust and virtue; virtue helps to beget trust and is in part sustained by it; while trust, in turn, helps to sustain civil society, though is by no means the only support. It does so to the extent to which it (trust) is commensurate with the freedom, creativity and 'open play' (within an ordered framework) that are characteristic of civil society. Trust is at any rate a much closer bedfellow to civil society than the hidebound rigidities of the heavy procedural regime. It need be no less so in a (post) modernist civil society. Where traditional structures and mores seem less clearly in evidence, some sort of 'social glue' becomes ever more necessary. The relationships involved are complex ones. It will therefore be useful briefly to sketch the character of modernity with reference to contemporary government as a prelude to a discussion, each in turn, of the notions of civil society, virtue and trust. There will then follow an examination of the public service ethos within the age of modernity from which a number of conclusions will be drawn.

THE CHARACTER OF MODERNITY

Post-modernism, post-Fordism, deconstructionism – these and kindred terms that have their own inflections are here subsumed for convenience under the label 'modernity'. That word has no doubt been overworked and overstretched in recent years. Yet it would be foolish to deny substance in some of the observations that have been associated with even the most mystical abstractions. Among the more salient characteristics are disorganization, decomposition, disaggregation, flexibility, variegation and incongruence – whether of structures, systems, processes or values. Fixed parameters, clearly established relationships, ordered hierarchies and many of the old certainties have disappeared or lapsed into recess. Such hallmarks of the old order may never have been quite what they seemed or are now held to have been, but their passing, or diminution, marks a move in broadly such a direction.

Within the polity, no less than in society itself, the fissiparous tendencies of modernism have claimed attention. Structures have become more fragmented, organizations more difficult to classify, procedures more convoluted. The public-private sector distinction is less sharply drawn, both organizationally and culturally, though partial fusion has been accompanied by greater heterogeneity within both the private and the public spheres. There has been much talk about 'hollowing out of the state' (Rhodes 1994); about the 'state under stress' (Foster and Plowden 1996); of de-bureaucratization (Dowding 1995); the end of the civil service as a distinct entity (Chapman 1997); and the possible death of the 'Whitehall paradigm' (Campbell and Wilson 1995). As a concomitant and perhaps partly in consequence of these developments there has emerged what Power (1994, 1997) has variously called the 'audit explosion' and the 'audit society'.

Modernity sustains and feeds upon a culture of exposure. Deeds and misdeeds are more likely to be laid bare before the public gaze. In a sense it is the hallmark of a healthy democracy. It would be a brave, nay foolish, government that ignored or failed to respond vigorously to palpable impropriety or malfunctioning in its midst. The machinations and manoeuvrings of ministers and others over the Scott inquiry into the sale of arms to Iraq brought them no credit whatever.

When things seem more frequently to go wrong, or when exposures become almost part of the routine, then one of two broad types of response may ensue. One is to strengthen the regulatory framework, to tighten the corset, so to speak. In a sense, such response may seem the appropriate one as a counterweight to the fissiparous tendencies of modernism. The other is to go with the grain of modernity, commensurate with the 'open textured', pluralist nature of civil society. The two types of response need not be mutually exclusive. Much depends upon circumstance and context. But the first approach may, if pushed too far or inappropriately, serve to the detriment of civil society, not least because it undermines virtue and trust. It is therefore to the notions of civil society, virtue and trust that we must now turn.

CIVIL SOCIETY, VIRTUE AND TRUST

Civil Society

Interest in the idea of civil society has been rekindled in recent years. For Giddens: 'a democratic order, as well as an effective market economy, depends upon a flourishing civil society. Civil society, in turn, needs to be limited by the other two' (2000, p. 51). The concept of civil society may best be understood by examining three elements: the relationship between state and society; the management of conflict; and the relationship between the private and public realms.

In one sense, civil society draws upon the Tocquevillian notion of intermediary institutions: it is a buffer, a bulwark against excessive statism. According to Gellner: 'civil society is that set of non-governmental institutions which is strong enough to counterbalance the state and, while not preventing the state from fulfilling its role of keeper of the peace and arbitrator between major interests, can nevertheless prevent it from dominating and atomizing the rest of society' (1996, p. 5). Without civil society 'government is subject to no higher authority than itself' (Shils 1997, p. 73). Others believe that to see the relationship between civil associations and the state in adversarial terms is to misunderstand 'the complex politico-economic nature of civil society, its institutions and their relationship to the social division of labour' (Ioannidou 1997, p. 60). Clearly there is a tension between mutuality and counterbalance in the relationship. Whatever the precise mix, civil society implies the existence of non-governmental institutions that have a legitimate political role – perhaps more so than ever in the 'modern' age of 'governing without government' (Rhodes 1996). It is a classic tenet of liberal political theory that the state should manage, if not resolve, conflicts that inevitably arise in a pluralist society. Again, modern (or post-modern) analysis seems to acknowledge and even encourage centrifugal tendencies while limiting the conflict resolution capacities of the state. Giddens says that we need a more 'open public sphere'(2000, p. 85). But if anarchy is not to ensue then this prescription requires a civility that Carter (1998) sees in terms of making multiple sacrifices for the sake of living together. Of course, a completely civil society would cease to be a pluralist society (Shils 1997, p. 350). The connections between the private and the public spheres, between private and public morality, are of central importance.

As Ranson and Stewart point out (1994, p. 60), Athenian civilization rested upon the premise that (among other things) a good person and a good citizen were one and the same. It was the liberal order of the Enlightenment and post-Enlightenment that prised the two worlds asunder. Hence the Scottish moralists of the period such as Adam Smith and Adam Ferguson saw civil society as a bridge between the private and the public (Seligman 1997, p. 147). However closely connected and mutually reinforcing they may be, the assumption is that the private and public realms are distinct, particularly with regard to questions of morality. It then becomes possible to accept some loss in one realm (for example public morality) as an acceptable price to be paid for an enhancement in the other (private) – especially where the precise contours and even the existence of the 'societal' are uncertain. 'Dirty hands' is a notion sometimes mobilized to justify the laying aside of a relatively nebulous public morality in pursuit of more tangible, immediate and measurable benefits, typically private ones. But today's expedient may become tomorrow's prevailing ethic. Moreover, the supposed benefits for which sacrifices have been made are by no means incontestable. Such at any rate are the arguments employed by some of the critics of liberalism who contest the consequentialist premises upon which the private-public distinction rests (Ramsay 2000, pp. 152–3). Slippage here is the unfortunate but acceptable consequence of enhancement there, the sacrifice we are prepared to make. The distinction, though, is by no means an article of faith for all liberals, or even libertarians. Shils believed that civility is simultaneously 'individualistic, parochial and holistic' (1997, p. 335). Such civility he equated with 'public spirit' or 'virtue' (*ibid.* p. 320), a notion that now demands attention.

Virtue

According to Gray modernity implies that government 'practice neutrality, not toleration, in regard to rival contemporary conceptions of the good life ... that it is wrong for government to discriminate in favour of, or against, any form of life animated by a definite conception of good' (1995, p. 19). Here we encounter a Rawlsian notion of proceduralism or contracturalism. It matters little as to what code of morality we subscribe or as to whether different codes of morality are or are not mutually exclusive – only that they coexist within a civilized, regulated order. Such are among the elements of Rawls' idea of justice as fairness. Yet Rawls himself allows the possibility of societal touchstones that go well beyond immediate utilitarian calculus and which may embrace 'higher' systems of morality – provided that they are the product of, and comply with, the canons of procedural justice. The contractarian idea, he says, 'can be extended to the choice of more or less an entire ethical system, that is, a system including principles for all the virtues and not only for justice' (Rawls 1973, p. 17). A procedural liberal can, after all, be a holist (Taylor 1989, p. 176). Some notion of public virtue is by no means incompatible with contemporary revisionist liberalism. It may be possible to sustain a universal ethics within the skein of modernity (Bauman 1993).

What, then, is virtue and why should it be denied in the practice if not by the strict logic of modernity? In discussing the work of Hannah Arendt, Williams draws a distinction between motives and principles. Motives, he says, reside within the self, while principles are 'essentially worldly, the distinctive property of free political action in a sphere we continue to share between us' (1998, pp. 942–3). Thus the good citizen acts for the sake of a principle, the good person 'can only be imputed purity of motive' (*ibid.* p. 944). The latter is a necessary, though not a sufficient, condition for public virtue of which disinterestedness, detachment and conscious reflection are among the hallmarks. At the same time, to quote Lippmann, 'virtue cannot be commanded: it must be willed out of personal conviction and desire' (1929, p. 137). Although social and public in its bearings, it is an interior condition. Of course it may and perhaps must be nourished by external agency – human, societal and even legislative. But the latter in particular will, on its own, bring (at best) what Hunt calls ceremonial observance rather than substantive understanding. As he says, virtue depends upon freedom (Hunt 1997, p. 280), not least the freedom promised by civil society. If so and if, as Ridley (1997, p. 144) claims, virtue is a grace, something almost to be taken for granted, then it is doubtful if government can by fiat construct a public virtue upon which a more vigorous public service ethic could be based.

Alasdair MacIntyre and those who subscribe to his thesis of lost virtue in the modern world would take the argument further. Morality is understood broadly with reference to virtues exhibited by, or intrinsic to, human agents – and in what MacIntyre would call 'practices' rather than rules, regulations or obligations (Miller 1994, p. 245). Moreover, in what he himself describes as a 'disquieting suggestion', MacIntyre insists that 'the language and appearances of morality persist even though the integral substance of morality has to a large degree been fragmented and then in part destroyed' (1985, p. 5). He denies that his diagnosis is one of despair. Yet if his reasoning is sound, it is difficult to see a way forward (or backwards). A possible implication of his argument is that the contemporary nostrums of regulation, codes and exhortation to good conduct may lead us further away from true virtue. They are part of the 'language of morality' mistaken for its real substance.

It is one thing to suggest that the current fashion for rules, regulations and supervision as bulwarks against transgression may serve to deflect attention away from what was described earlier in this chapter as the public service ethos. Thus, as per MacIntyre, we delude ourselves into thinking that by attending to the one phenomenon (fraud, blatant misconduct) we are also serving the other (that is the public service ethos). It is another thing, though, to suggest that the very mechanisms and devices employed to deal with and prevent fraud or indeed to revitalize and sustain the public service ethos are also in part responsible for its demise. Here the argument would be not only about deflection of attention or faulty diagnosis but also that the language and mechanisms are distinctly harmful to the very substance of morality that they are supposed to foster. Among the casualties of this process is the notion of trust.

Trust

For Giddens trust is of central importance to the maintenance of civil society, making possible 'the everyday civility that is crucial to effective public life' (2000, p. 78). In this sense it becomes a piece of 'social capital' (Coleman 1988), a lubricant of the social system. Trust may operate at different levels and within different contexts, for example at the level of personal relationships; the impersonal 'freemasonry' of community or other networks; the relationship between government and citizen; or between government and government. These different dimensions of trust are distinct though they may be interconnected (Dasgupta 1988, p. 50). When personal relationships break down, when networks begin to decay, then citizens may lose faith in their leaders, though not inevitably so. When citizens do lose faith in their political and civic leaders then there may be a loss of respect for the institutions of government and consequent legitimacy crisis for the prevailing regime. Again, these connections are possible though by no means inevitable (Hardin 1999). Whatever the level or precise context, trust is typically characterized by relationships sustained 'not on the basis of explicit rules and regulations but out of a set of ethical habits and reciprocal moral obligations internalized by each of the community's members' (Fukuyama 1995, p. 9). No less significant is Fukuyama's prognostication about the breakdown of trust, when ' ... relations have to be spelled out in detail, unwritten rules codified and third parties brought in to resolve differences. At this point the network ceases to look like a network and begins to resemble ... either a market relationship or an old-fashioned hierarchical corporation' (p. 342).

When trust breaks down, when it is seen no longer to function as a social lubricant but is instead used as a licence to misnomer, then it becomes increasingly tempting to erect formal barriers to contain the latitude for transgression. It requires only a further small step to shift from outlawing, or out-regulating, the bad to codifying the good. But, as Furedi says 'the very attempt to formalize human relations and codify appropriate forms of behaviour actually feeds mistrust' (1999, p. 33). A downward spiral ensues. Trust is not something that can be induced at will. We cannot choose our feelings. But we can behave as if we trusted someone, or some set of people or institutions (Gambetta 1988, pp. 230–32). Trust is not a fixed property: it can be self-reinforcing, gathering strength in the usage. I feel obligated (if nothing else) when someone places their trust in me – unless I am quite bereft of virtue.

There is usually a history, a time scale in which trust can be built up. There is a premium upon reputations and the nurture of reputations.

Not everyone accepts that trust is a value worth nurturing. Tucker (1999, p. 9) asserts baldly that trust has no place in modern politics. He sees it as the antithesis of accountability by which politicians and public servants yield to the empowerment of the citizen. Trust, he says, is symptomatic of a parent-child relationship in which the citizen is the infant partner. Instead he places his faith in the notion of a citizen's contract (pp. 18–26). And while the litigious, culpability-conscious, compensation-seeking culture is a cause for regret to some, it is for others the mark of a vibrant, articulate and well informed citizenry active in defence of its rights (Smith 1997).

It is beyond the purview of this chapter to engage in a disquisition about 'rights', a canvas of many colours. The point is that the 'rights culture' reflects a broader disposition to legality, regulation and general formality. It begets a sharper sensitivity among the citizenry (and its watchdogs) to the behaviour of its public servants. Of course, trust, and its close cousin 'professional honour', cannot be maintained unconditionally (Dunsire 1993). If trust is betrayed and is seen to have been betrayed, then there must be the possibility of what Gambetta (1988, pp. 218–19) calls 'exit'. It cannot be nurtured in a vacuum. It needs reinforcement manifest among those in whom trust is placed (politicians, public servants) and acknowledged among those by whom it is conferred (citizens). The Nolan Committee famously declared both its uncertainty as to whether standards of conduct had declined and its conviction that there existed a widespread belief that they had declined (Nolan 1995, pp. 20–21). More is expected of our public servants; there is greater exposure; there are fewer benefits of the doubt when things go wrong – or, no less significantly, when it is alleged that things may go wrong or might have gone wrong. In such circumstances trust is more difficult to sustain as a matter of practical reality – the more so when its supposed virtues are deliberately derogated. Yet, if trust is a keystone of civil society and if civil society is, as Giddens and others claim, a vital ingredient in (post) modernity then its decline is a matter of some consequence. Modernity has greater need for trust at precisely the same time as its presence is receding (Seligman 1997, p. 97, p. 165). The wider significance of this observation can be established by drawing together the threads of the discussion with reference to the public service ethos in the age of modernity.

THE PUBLIC SERVICE ETHOS IN THE AGE OF MODERNITY

It is worth recounting some of the trends that have characterized modern government in recent years, and some of the governmental responses to new challenges. These trends and responses have taken different forms and have been manifest at different levels. At one level there has been a general drive towards a utilitarian managerialism – by no means a novel phenomenon but one the more corrosive features of which are encouraged by the logic of modernity. League tables, performance targets, outputs (and outcomes), performance-related pay together with mantras such as 'competitive tendering' and 'best value' have been among the watchwords. Common to all these things is a concern for the tangible, the observable, and the measurable. In their proper place and judiciously employed, such techniques are not harmful. But sense of proportion is not an abiding characteristic of the age of modernity. So with the (partial) demise of civil society and weaker notions of public virtue the crude managerialists have enjoyed a relatively open highway. What is of potential benefit becomes self-defeating. Why should the humble clerk, or anyone else, go the extra mile when the meter has stopped ticking? Silent virtue becomes a fool's ransom. And the more elaborate the formal mechanisms for ensuring good practice, the stronger will be the impulse among public servants to ensure that they are seen to be on the right side of the law. They will invest more of their energies in 'covering their backs' than in serving their public. It is better to keep a clean licence than to drive safely.

At another level there has been a growing sensitivity to democracy, accountability and empowerment of the citizen. These objectives are in themselves commendable. Government ministers and other public figures should behave properly, respecting the 'rules of the game'; senior public servants ought to work faithfully to their political masters; through whatever mechanisms, politicians and officials alike must be accountable; the citizen should be protected and feel reassured, perhaps experience some sense of gratification, if not elevation. But these worthy objectives stand to be perverted in the absence of more highly developed civic institutions and a cadre of political leaders and functionaries imbued with a sense of public virtue serving (and supported by) an active and well honed citizenry. If politicians, hence public servants, are consumed by the short-term, hollow clang of popular acclaim and if citizens neither demand nor know any better then the outcome will be a bad one, ultimately, for all concerned. Public figures of today are so consumed with the need to please that they are losing their capacity to serve in any wider sense. The mechanisms of accountability may appear to work smoothly and may indeed be effective within their own terms: but they will be introverted and self-serving unless they are embedded in a vibrant civil society. In the absence of such a society, citizens' charters, administrative audits and the like will not empower, still less enrich, the citizen. Nor will charters, contracts or mission statements make the trains run on time unless all involved have a genuine desire to see that they do. Management techniques may encourage politicians and service providers to engage in more sophisticated manoeuvres to give the appearance of better performance – especially if they fear retribution. So long as they play the game such appearance can be maintained. If they overreach themselves and engage in chicanery then they may, of course, be exposed as deceitful, even fraudulent.

In these circumstances the public service tradition associated with the grandees of the past, the figures revered by Noel Annan, is much more difficult to sustain. But if that tradition was one forged in a pre-democratic or early democratic era, it does not follow that it has no place in the age of modernity. In years and decades gone by, much rested upon the personal qualities of leading public figures. Leadership remains important, but it carries less of a premium – not least because, in the modernist age of 'deconstruction' and 'deconcentration', the activity of government is much more multi-centric. Moreover, followers are far less inclined to follow; citizens are harder to please. Yet their endorsement and compliance, if not their active participation, are ever more necessary. It is no longer possible, if ever it was, to have a healthy public service ethos without the public. It behoves government to pay more attention to the nurture of citizenship.

It is not the intention here to prescribe any particular model of citizenship, or to specify the mechanisms by which it may be fostered. Suffice to say that citizenship is itself a tricky notion: like virtue and trust it is not amenable to executive order. It is something that lies within the hearts and minds of individuals as members of a wider community. But there is much that can be done by way of nurturing citizens in the basic values, principles and institutions by which, in a broad sense, they are governed and in which they have a legitimate role. Such nurture need not preclude critical enquiry born of a healthy scepticism. As, *à la* John Stuart Mill, an educated mass electorate was a precondition for responsible representative government, so perhaps a more finely attuned, sophisticated citizenry is necessary fully to mobilize new governance in the age of modernity.

Renewed citizenship is of a piece with the championing of civil society strengthened by the bonds of virtue and trust. As noted earlier, some would see such a call as the antithesis of accountability. But even in a world of high virtue and perfect trust, certain mechanisms of accountability would remain as checks and balances, part of the pluralistic dispersal of power that is a central feature of liberal regimes. A unified written constitution replete with basic human rights provisions is by no means incompatible with such a world: nor are the formal mechanisms necessary to deal with impropriety. But when checks exceed the immediate reach of institutional pluralism, accountability, human rights and propriety, when they are applied as a surrogate for virtue and trust, then they become dysfunctional. Distrust begets infinite regress. Who checks the checkers?

Illustration may be served by a cricketing analogy – one drawn from the highest levels of the game and confined, for present purposes, to activities on the field of play. At one time, batsmen walked when they knew that they were out; they did not wait for the umpire's signal. Then the imperatives of professionalism determined that the batsman should walk only when so signalled by the umpire. Umpires, though, like all public figures, began to lose their authority; media technology began to expose their occasional misjudgements. It became fashionable for players to remonstrate. So, third umpires and technological aids were brought into play. More rules were introduced as competitors found ways of circumventing existing ones. Sportsmanship gave way to gamesmanship as competitors sought 'clever' advantage. Arguments still abound; no one is satisfied. More time is spent in dispute and adjudication, rather less time playing cricket. Notwithstanding the element of caricature or the inexactness of the analogy it cannot be dismissed as fanciful or out of place in the present discussion. On the contrary, it has many parallels in the day-to-day world of public affairs. Much like the cricketing umpire, Elizabeth Filkin came under heavy pressure from indignant MPs who resented the tenacity with which she scrutinized their affairs in her capacity as Parliamentary Commissioner for Standards. They may or may not have been justified in their complaints. Yet in refusing to 'walk' some of them certainly brought into question not only Filkin's personal authority but also the ground rules governing the office she held. There seems to have been something of a breakdown in the common understanding as to what constitutes right and wrong, or good and bad practice, as well as a lack of agreement as to whether this or that particular case constitutes a transgression even where the boundaries are more clearly drawn. More elaborate codes, more deeply etched 'lines in the sand' will not in themselves provide a solution. It is even possible that solutions may further recede in consequence. Rules, regulations and 'techniques' are a poor surrogate for the anchor of civil society, virtue and trust. Yet as the anchor slips, recourse to formality is an understandable response, especially in cases of flagrant abuse. Thus governments have, as a counterweight to perceived impropriety, invented new machinery as well as having strengthened existing mechanisms, rules and procedures.

The case of the Parliamentary Commissioner for Standards shows that new institutions and heavier procedures do not guarantee plain sailing. A further example of such responses and of some of the wider issues addressed in this chapter is provided by the 'Ministerial Code'. Its origins lie in a directive

issued in August 1945 by Clement Attlee to his ministers following an initiative by cabinet secretary Sir Edward Bridges. Later (1949) codified into the
document *Questions of Procedure for Ministers* (QPM), it continued to evolve
but remained unpublished until 1992 (Baker 2000). John Major determined
that it should be published. The decision was part of his 'open government'
initiative and a response to growing concern about the conduct of ministers
and other public servants. Upon taking office in 1997, Tony Blair reaffirmed
and repackaged the document, now called the *Ministerial Code* (Cabinet
Office 1997). As against the 65 sometimes terse paragraphs of the 1949
document, the present version comprises 135 paragraphs. The Commons'
Public Administration Select Committee (PASC) recently observed: 'Like
Topsy, the Code has just grown' (PASC 2001a, para. 36). More significantly,
there has been a change in its character. The PASC noted (*ibid.* para. 2) that
'what began as notes largely relating to narrowly procedural matters now
encompasses issues of ethics and accountability'. This accretion reflects a
succession of responses to particular episodes and the ensuing outbursts of
indignation. The PASC recognizes that the Code needs to be put into shape,
suggesting the extraction and separate publication of the ethical principles
which it considers to be the most important elements in the existing Code
(*ibid.* para. 34). A year earlier, the Neill Committee (Neill 2000, p. 53) had
considered but rejected a proposal for the creation of an independent ethics
commissioner. But there remains a panoply of codes, rules, regulations, audits
and other investigatory apparatus across the public sector.

   This panoply has gathered not only from a series of responses to transgressions or from heightened trepidation. It arises also from a belief (often
implicit) that it is no longer feasible to rely upon what Peter Hennessy calls
the 'good chap theory of government' (1995, p. 187). Rules and regulations
may not be necessary in heaven, but they are (increasingly) needed on earth.
The point warrants some elaboration.

   Two points arise from the supposed decline of the good chap theory.
First, the seemingly greater propensity to transgress or to be found wanting
begets more finely calibrated corrective measures of the heavy variety. For
their effectiveness, such initiatives require consensus as to what is and what
is not right and proper. Second, then, what if there is no such agreement?
What if values are no longer so widely shared and if virtue has dissolved?
Is not recourse to yet more elaborate rules, codes, audit regimes simply a
rational response? In a sense and within its own terms it is a rational if
ultimately futile and self-defeating response. The less we feel we can rely
upon shared values the more we incline to strengthen the rules – the heavy
approach rather than the light touch, the Justinian Code rather than the Ten
Commandments model (Kernaghan 1993, pp. 20–22). The heavy approach,
though, is not likely to succeed without a supporting morality grounded in a

truly civil society. Without such support, increasing recourse to formal rules and the like may exacerbate the problem. The tighter we try to hold on to the slippery treasure, so to speak, the more it is likely to elude our grasp. Formal arrangements promulgated to compel and sustain good behaviour may sap the very spirit by which it is nourished. Certainly there is little evidence that recourse to a heavier approach has increased levels of trust – rather the reverse.

It is one of the arguments of this chapter, then, that trust is an important ingredient in the public service ethos. Tony Blair evidently thinks so. In issuing the *Ministerial Code* he reaffirmed his 'strong personal commitment to restoring the bond of trust between the British people and their government' (Baker 2000, p. 149). Trust may carry a higher premium if politicians and public servants at all levels possess and are seen to possess a stronger sense of virtue. Leaders must lead: they should of course set a good example. Leadership remains important: but, in the age of modernity, it no longer serves as the talisman. Moreover, as argued earlier, virtue is an interior condition: it is less readily given to the outward manifestation of the measurable. Virtue does not issue from command, though conditions may be more or less propitious to its sustenance, bringing into play the third and fourth types of answer outlined above as to why people should uphold that which is 'right'. Yet if virtue is an interior condition that cannot be commanded then equally it is, in a civil society leavened by trust, a matter of public no less than private morality. The 'privatization of conscience' (Arendt's phrase) is a further defining feature of modernity. John Stuart Mill was right in saying that we need 'good institutions virtuously administered' ([1861] 1910, p. 190). We need good citizens as well as good people.

CONCLUSIONS

It would be easy to conclude with a counsel of despair. The 'acid of modernity' seems to eat away the fibre upon which our hopes hang. The further we fall short of prescribed standards the greater the recourse to the heavy approach that may be superficially attractive but which may ultimately make more difficult the attainment of those standards. To talk about prescribed standards implies the existence of certain broadly acceptable points of reference. Such, as suggested earlier, becomes increasingly difficult but is by no means precluded by the logic of modernity. It may be possible both to maintain a more vigorous ethic and to achieve better service delivery. The PASC has expressed the belief that 'a shared ethical commitment to this [public service] ideal across the public sector continues to provide some of the best underpinnings and guarantees for maintaining and developing good performance and standards' (2001b, para. 12). How, then, can the 'golden goose' be spared? Two broad points may be drawn from this chapter.

First, a distinction was made at the outset between matters of impropriety and the broader, more nebulous notion of a public service ethic or ethos. Many of the more recent initiatives have been addressed, quite appropriately, to transgressions of the former variety. But the nostrums have often been applied indiscriminately, conflating matters of propriety, rights and so forth with detailed supervision, procedural formality and rules for 'good practice' that now threaten to blight the daily lives of public servants. The PASC is wise in proposing a separation of the ethical from the procedural and other elements of the *Ministerial Code*. There may be no harm and perhaps some good in following the Committee's further suggestion that all public servants be given a copy of a public service code incorporating the 'seven principles of public life' set out by the Nolan Committee – selflessness, integrity, objectivity, accountability, openness, honesty and leadership. But that is as far as it should go. Any move towards a catechism culture must be resisted. Virtue needs to 'breathe'; it must not be stifled.

Second, while government can and must play heavy in dealing with impropriety, there is relatively little that it can do directly to guarantee a public service ethos. It can create conditions that are more or less conducive to the promotion of such an ethos. With less effort and perhaps unintentionally it can do – almost certainly has done – a deal of harm. There should be a retreat from the excesses of audit trails and 'management by numbers' that are often self-defeating within their own confines and are at the same time corrosive of the public service ethos. Understandably, the focus of attention is often upon the polity; but there is a vital societal dimension. If public virtue is to carry the day, if civil society is to flourish, then we must have greater regard for the character of the citizenry. The nurture of citizenship may well prove the key to sustaining the civility, virtue and trust upon which a public service ethos depends. In the absence of these conditions there will be a hollow ring to the modernizing agenda of the Blair government and its plans for better public services will have little purchase.

References

Aberbach, Joel D. (1990), *Keeping a Watchful Eye: The Politics of Congressional Oversight*, Washington, DC: Brookings Institution Press.

Aberbach, Joel D. and Bert A. Rockman (2000a), *In the Web of Politics: Three Decades of the US Federal Executive*, Washington, DC: Brookings Institution Press.

Aberbach, Joel D. and Bert A. Rockman (2000b), 'Senior executives in a changing political environment', in James P. Pfiffner and Douglas A. Brook (eds), *The Future of Merit*, Baltimore, MD: Johns Hopkins University Press and Woodrow Wilson Centre Press, pp. 81–99.

Adshead, M. (2002), 'Conceptualizing Europeanization: policy networks and cross-national comparison', *Public Policy and Administration*, **17** (2), 25–42.

Agresta, Robert J. (2001), 'Arbitrary outsourcing', *GovExec.com*, 9 July, http://www.govexec.com/news/.

Alford, J. (2001), 'The implications of "publicness" for strategic management theory', in G. Johnson and K. Scholes (eds), *Exploring Public Sector Strategy*, London: Prentice Hall.

Allison, Graham T. (1999), 'Public and private management: are they fundamentally alike in all unimportant respects?' in Frederick S. Lane (ed.), *Current Issues in Public Administration*, 6th edn, Boston: Bedford/St Martin's, pp. 14–29.

Annan, Noel (1999), *The Dons: Mentors, Eccentrics and Geniuses*, London: Harper Collins.

Aucoin, P. (1990), 'Administrative reform in public management: paradigms, paradoxes and pendulums', *Governance: An International Journal of Policy and Administration*, **3** (2), 115–37.

Baker, Amy (2000), *Prime Ministers and the Rule Book*, London: Politico's.

Ballard, Tanya N. (2002), 'Results Act implementation is limited, straw poll shows', *GovExec.com*, 6 February, http://www.govexec.com/news/.

Bardach, E. (1998), *Getting Agencies to Work Together: The Practice and Theory of Managerial Craftsmanship*, Washington, DC: Brookings Institution Press.

Barr, Stephen (2001), 'Many feel good about government; few want to work for it', 24 October, http://www.washingtonpost.com.

Barry, Brian (1995), *A Treatise on Social Justice – Vol. I: Justice as Impartiality*, Oxford and New York: Oxford University Press.

Barzelay, Michael (2001), *The New Public Management: Improving Research and Policy Dialogue*, Berkeley: University of California Press.

Bauman, Zygmunt (1993), *Postmodern Ethics*, Oxford, UK and Cambridge, US: Blackwell.

Baumgartner, Frank and Bryan D. Jones (1993), *Agendas and Instability in American Politics*, Chicago: University of Chicago Press.

Beer, S. (1982), *Modern British Politics*, London: Faber and Faber.

Bellamy, C. (1999), 'Exploiting information and communications technologies', in S. Horton and D. Farnham (eds), *Public Management in Britain*, London: Macmillan.

Bellamy, C. and J.A. Taylor (1998), *Governing in the Information Age*, Buckingham: Open University Press.

Benefit Fraud Inspectorate (1999a), 'Report on London South Directorate (AD3) Benefits Agency', http://www.dss.gov.uk/hq/pubs/bfi/londons/.

Benefit Fraud Inspectorate (1999b), 'Report on East Devon District Council', http://www.dss.gov.uk/hq/pubs/bfi/devon/.

Benefit Fraud Inspectorate (1999c), 'Report on the Social Security Contributions Agency', http://www.dss.gov.uk/hq/pubs/bfi/devon/.

Benefit Fraud Inspectorate (1999d), 'Annual Report: Securing the System', http://www.dss.gov.uk/hq/pubs/bfi/bfiar/.

Benefits Agency (1999a), *Annual Report and Accounts 1998–99 HC 580*, London: The Stationery Office.

Benefits Agency (1999b), *Supplementary Memorandum Submitted by the DSS Benefits Agency to the Public Accounts Committee, Report on Vote 1 Appropriation Account 1996–97: class XII (Administered Social Security Benefits and Other Payments) HC 419 I, Session 1998–99*, London: The Stationery Office.

Benefits Agency (2001), *Benefits Agency Business Plan* Leeds, Benefits Agency, http://www.dss.gov.uk/publications/dss/2001/babbsubessplan/baplan1.htm.

Bentley, T. (2002), 'Letting go: complexity, individualism and the left', *Renewal*, **10** (1), 9–26.

Bevir, M. (1999), *The Logic of the History of Ideas*, Cambridge: Cambridge University Press.

Bevir, M. and R.A.W. Rhodes (2002), *Interpreting British Governance*, London: Routledge.

Bichard, M. (1999), *Modernizing the Policy Process*, London: Public Management and Policy Association.

Boston, J., J. Martin, J. Pallot and P. Walsh (1996), *Public Management: The New Zealand Model*, Auckland: Oxford University Press.

Bovens, M., P. t'Hart and G. Peters (eds) (2001), *Success and Failure in Public Governance*, Cheltenham: Edward Elgar.

Brittan, Samuel (1998), *Essays Moral, Political and Economic*, Edinburgh: David Hume Institute.

Buller, J. and A. Gamble (2002), 'Conceptualizing Europeanization', *Public Policy and Administration*, **17** (2), 4–24.

Bush, George (2001), 'Memorandum for the heads of executive departments and agencies' (11 July), http://www.whitehouse.gov/news/releases/2001/07/20010711-1.html.

Cabinet Office (1997), *Ministerial Code: A Code of Conduct and Guidance on Procedures for Ministers*, London: Cabinet Office.

Cabinet Office (1999a), *Performance Management: Civil Service Reform*, report to the meeting of permanent heads of departments, Sunningdale 30 Sept.–1 Oct. 1999, London: Cabinet Office.

Cabinet Office (1999b), *Professional Policy-making for the Twenty-first Century*, London: Cabinet Office, www.cabinet-office.gov.uk/moderngov/policy

Cabinet Office (1999c), *Civil Service Reform*, report to the Prime Minister from Sir Richard Wilson, head of the Home Civil Service, London: Cabinet Office.

Cabinet Office (2000a), *E-Government: A Strategic Framework for Public Services in the Information Age*, London: Cabinet Office.

Cabinet Office (2000b), *Peer Review of Cabinet Office*, London: The Cabinet Office.

Cabinet Office (2000c), *Modernizing Policy Development*, London: Centre For Management Studies.

Cabinet Office (2000d), *Civil Service Statistics 1999*, London: Government Statistical Service.

Cabinet Office (2000e), *Peer Review: A Guide to Peer Review*, London: The Cabinet Office.

Cabinet Office (2000f), *Adding it Up: Improving Analysis and Modelling in Central Government*, London: The Cabinet Office.

Cabinet Office. (2000g), *Wiring It Up*, London: The Cabinet Office.

Cabinet Office (2001), *Better Policy-Making*, London, Centre for Management and Policy Studies.

Cabinet Office (2002), *Beyond The Horizon: International Comparisons in Policy-making: Toolkit*, London: Centre for Management and Policy Studies.

Caiden, G. (1990), 'Australia's changing administrative ethos', in A. Kouzmin and N. Scott (eds), *Dynamics in Australian Public Management: Selected Essays*, Melbourne: Macmillan.

Cameron, D. (1998), 'Creating supranational authority in monetary and exchange-rate policy: the sources and effects of EMU', in W. Sandholtz and A. Stone Sweet, *European Integration and Supranational Governance*, Oxford: Oxford University Press, pp. 188–216.

Campbell, Colin (2001), 'Juggling inputs, outputs, and outcomes in the search for policy competence: recent experience in Australia,' *Governance*, **14**(2), pp. 253–82.

Campbell, Colin and Geoffrey K. Wilson (1995), *The End of Whitehall: Death of a Paradigm?*, Oxford, UK and Cambridge, MA: Blackwell.

Caporaso, J. (1998), 'Regional integration theory: understanding our past and anticipating our future' in W. Sandholtz and A. Stone Sweet (1998), *European Integration and Supranational Governance*, Oxford: Oxford University Press, pp. 334–52.

Carmichael, P. (2001), 'The Northern Ireland Civil Service', *Public Money and Management*, **21** (2), 33–8.

Carr, F. (2000), 'The public service ethos: decline and renewal?', *Public Policy and Administration*, **14** (4), 1–16.

Carter, Stephen L. (1998), *Civility*, New York: Basic Books.

Chancellor of the Duchy of Lancaster (1992), *The Next Steps Agencies Review 1992 Cmnd 2111*, London: HMSO.

Chancellor of the Duchy of Lancaster (1993), *Next Steps: Agencies in Government Review 1993 Cmnd 2430*, London: HMSO.

Chancellor of the Duchy of Lancaster (1994), *Next Steps Review 1994 Cmnd 2750*, London: HMSO.

Chancellor of the Duchy of Lancaster (1995), *Next Steps Review 1995 Cmnd 3164*, London: HMSO.

Chancellor of the Duchy of Lancaster (1997), *Next Steps Agencies in Government Review 1996 Cmnd 3579*, London: The Stationery Office.

Chancellor of the Duchy of Lancaster (1998), *Next Steps Report Cmnd 3889*, London: The Stationery Office.

Chancellor of the Exchequer (1987), *The Government's Expenditure Plans 1987–88 to 1989–90, Vol. II, Cmnd 56-II*, London: HMSO.

Chancellor of the Exchequer (1994), *Public Expenditure Statistical Supplement to the Financial Statement and Budget Report 1994–95 Cmnd 2519*, London: HMSO.

Chancellor of the Exchequer (1998), *Public Expenditure Statistical Analyses 1998–99 Cmnd 3901*, London: The Stationery Office.

Chapman, J. (2002), *Systems Failure: Why Government Must Learn to Think Differently*, London: DEMOS.

Chapman, Richard A. (1988), *Ethics in the British Civil Service*, London: Routledge.

Chapman, Richard A. (ed.) (1993), *Ethics in Public Service*, Edinburgh: Edinburgh University Press.

Chapman, Richard A. (1997), 'The end of the civil service', in Peter Barberis (ed.), *The Civil Service in an Era of Change*, Aldershot, UK and Brookfield, US: Dartmouth, pp. 23–37.

Chapman, Richard A. (ed.) (2000), *Ethics in Public Service for the New Millennium*, Aldershot, UK and Burlington, US: Ashgate.

Christensen, T. (1995), 'The Scandinavian state tradition and public administration', paper to the annual meeting of the American Political Science Association, Chicago, 31 August–3 September.

Chryssochoou, D., (1999), 'Eurogovernance and the policy process' in F. Carr and A. Massey, *Public Policy in the New Europe: Eurogovernance in Theory and Practice*, Cheltenham: Edward Elgar.

Chryssochoou, D. (2001), *Theorizing European Integration*, London: Sage.

Coleman, James S. (1988), 'Social capital in the creation of human capital', *American Journal of Sociology*, **94** (S), S.95–S.112.

Collini, Stefan (1991), *Public Moralists: Political Thought and Intellectual Life in Britain 1850–1930*, Oxford, UK and New York, US: Oxford University Press.

Commission of the European Communities (2002), *Action Plan 'Simplifying and Improving the Regulatory Environment*, COM (2002), 278, Brussels: European Commission.

Common, R. (2001), *Public Management and Policy Transfer in Southeast Asia*, Aldershot: Ashgate.

Dahl, Robert A. (1976), *Democracy in the United States Promise and Performance*, Chicago: Rand McNally.

Daniels, M. (2002), 'Planning for the President's fiscal year 2004 budget request', Office of Management and Budget (24 April).

Dasgupta, Partha (1988), 'Trust as a commodity', in Diego Gambetta (ed.), *Trust: Making and Breaking Cooperative Relations*, Oxford: Blackwell, pp. 49–72.

Davis, G. (1998), 'Australian administrative tradition', in J.M. Shafritz (ed.), *International Encyclopaedia of Public Policy and Administration*, Boulder, CO: Westview Press.

Davis, G. and R.A.W. Rhodes, (2000), 'From hierarchy to contracts and back again: reforming the Australian public service', in M. Keating and J. Wanna (eds), *Institutions: the Future of Australian Governance*, Sydney: Allen and Unwin.

Davis, G., P. Weller, E. Craswell and S. Eggins (1999), 'What drives machinery of government changes? Australia, Britain, Canada 1950–1997', *Public Administration*, **77** (1), pp. 7–50.

De Geus, A. (1999), *The Living Company: Growth, Learning and Longevity in Business*, London: Nicholas Brealey.

De Leon, P. (1997), *Democracy and the Policy Sciences*, New York: SUNY Press.

De Montricher, N. (1995), 'Decentralization in France', *Governance*, **8** (3), 405–18.

Department of Work and Pensions (2002), *The Department of Work and Pensions Departmental Report : The Governments Expenditure Plans 2002–02 to 2003–04 Cmnd 5424*, London: The Stationery Office.

Dowding, Keith (1995), *The Civil Service*, London and New York: Routledge.

Drewry, G. and T. Butcher (1991), *The Civil Service Today*, 2nd edn, Oxford: Blackwell.

Dunford, M., H. Louri and M. Rosenstock (2001), 'Competition, competitiveness, and enterprise policies', in R. Hall, A. Smith and L. Tsoukalis, *Competitiveness and Cohesion in EU Policies*, Oxford: Oxford University Press, pp. 109–46.

Dunsire, A. (1973), *Administration: The Word and the Science*, London: Martin Robertson.

Dunsire, Andrew (1993), 'The concept of trust', in Rosamund Thomas (ed.), *Teaching Ethics: Government Ethics*, Cambridge: Centre for Business and Public Sector Ethics, pp. 335–8.

Efficiency Unit (1988), *Improving Management in Government: The Next Steps*, London: HMSO.

Egan, M. (2001), *Constructing a European Market*, Oxford: Oxford University Press.

Ekengren, M. (2002), *The Time of European Governance*, Manchester: Manchester University Press.

Elcock, H. (1995), 'The fallacies of management', *Public Policy and Administration*, **10** (1), 34–48.

Elgie, R. and S. Griggs (2000), *French Politics. Debates and Controversies*, London: Routledge.

Falconer, P.K. (1999), 'The new public management today: an overview', paper presented to ESRC seminar on Recent Developments in the New Public Management, Imperial College, London (May).

Fennig, S. (2000), 'International socialization', *European Journal of International Relations* **6** (1).

Fischer, F. (1995), *Evaluating Public Policy*, Chicago: Nelson Hall.

Foster, Christopher D. and Francis J. Plowden (1996), *The State Under Stress: Can the Hollow State Be Good Government?*, Buckingham, UK and Philadelphia, US: Open University Press.

Frances, J. *et al.* (1991), 'Introduction', in G. Thompson, J. Frances, R. Levacíc and J. Mitchell (eds), *Markets Hierarchies and Networks: The Coordination of Social Life*, London, Sage.

Friel, Brian (2001a), 'OMB chief presses outsourcing, management cuts', *GovExec.com*, 23 February, http://www.govexec.com/news.

Friel, Brian (2001b), 'The Daniels decree', *GovExec.com*, 1 July, http://www.govexec.com/news.

Fukuyama, Francis (1995), *Trust: The Social Virtues and the Creation of Prosperity*, London: Hamish Hamilton.

Furedi, Frank (1999), *Courting Mistrust: The Hidden Growth of a Culture of Litigation in Britain*, London: Centre for Policy Studies.

Gains, F. (2000), 'Understanding department–agency relationships', PhD thesis: University of Sheffield.

Gambetta, Diego (1988), 'Can we trust trust?', in Gambetta (ed.), *Trust: Making and Breaking Cooperative Relations*, Oxford: Blackwell, pp. 213–37.

Gellner, Ernest (1996), *Conditions of Liberty: Civil Society and its Rivals*, Harmondsworth: Penguin.

General Accounting Office (1999), *Managing for Results: Opportunities for Continued Improvements in Agencies' Performance Plans*, GAO/GGD/AIMD-99-215, Washington, DC: USGAO.

General Accounting Office (2001), 'Managing for results: using GPRA to assist oversight and decision-making', statement of J. Christopher Mihm before the Subcommittee on Government Efficiency, Financial Management and Intergovernmental Relations, Committee on Government Reform, House of Representatives, GAO-01-872 T, Washington, DC: USGAO.

Geras, Norman (1998), *The Culture of Mutual Indifference: Political Philosophy After the Holocaust*, London and New York: Verso.

Giddens, Anthony (1998), *The Third Way: The Renewal of Social Democracy*, Cambridge, UK and Malden, US: Polity.

Giddens, Anthony (2000), *The Third Way and its Critics*, Cambridge, UK and Malden, US: Polity.

Goldsworthy, D. (1991), *Setting Up Next Steps*, London: HMSO.

Gore, Albert (1993), *Creating a Government That Works Better and Costs Less: The Report of the National Performance Review*, New York: Plume.

Government Performance and Results Act (1993), Sec. 4; amendment to Chapter 11 of 31 *US Code* sec. 1115, Performance Plans.

Gray, John (1995), *Enlightenment's Wake: Politics and Culture at the Close of the Modern Age*, London and New York: Routledge.

Greenaway, John (1995), 'Having the bun and the halfpenny: can old public service ethics survive in the new Whitehall?', *Public Administration*, **73** (3), 357–74.

Greenleaf, W.H. (1983), *The British Political Tradition, Volume 1, The Rise of Collectivism*, London: Methuen.

Greenwood, J., R. Pyper and D. Wilson (2002), *New Public Administration in Britain*, 3rd edn, London: Routledge.

Gunn, L.A. (1988), 'Public management: a third approach', *Public Money and Management*, **8** (1 and 2), pp. 21–6.

Hall, R., A. Smith and L. Tsoukalis (2001), *Competitiveness and Cohesion in EU Policies*, Oxford: Oxford University Press.

Halligan, J. (1997), 'New public sector models: reform in Australia and New Zealand', in Jan-Erik Lane (ed.), *Public Sector Reform: Rationale, Trends and Problems*, London: Sage, pp. 17–46.

Halligan, J. (2000), 'Public service reform under Howard', in G. Singleton (ed.), *The Howard Government*, Sydney: University of New South Wales Press.

Halligan, J. (2001), 'Comparing public sector reform in the OECD', in B.C. Nolan (ed.), *Public Sector Reform: An International Perspective*, Basingstoke: Palgrave.

Hamilton, Alexander, John Jay and James Madison (1937), *The Federalist Papers*, New York: The Modern Library.

Hansard (2001), answer by Ian McCartney, Minister for the Cabinet Office, to Mr Goggins, 7 March 2001, column 266W session 2000–2001, London: The Stationery Office.

Hardin, Russell (1999), 'Do we want trust in government?', in Mark E. Warren (ed.), *Democracy and Trust*, Cambridge: Cambridge University Press, pp. 22–41.

Harlow, C. (1999), 'Accountability, new public management, and the problems of the Child Support Agency' *Journal of Law and Society* **26** (2), 150–74.

Hennessy, P. (1995), *The Hidden Wiring: Unearthing the British Constitution*, London: Victor Gollancz.

Hennessy, P. (2000), *The Prime Minster: The Office and its Holders since 1945*, London: Allen Lane/The Penguin Press.

Hogwood, B.W. (1997), 'The machinery of government 1979–97', *Political Studies* **45** (4), 704–15.

Homer-Dixon, T. (2000), *The Ingenuity Gap: How Can We Solve the Problems of the Future?*, London: Johnathan Cape.

Hood, C. (1990a), 'De-Sir Humphreyfying the Westminster model of bureaucracy: a new style of governance?', *Governance*, **3** (2), 205–14.

Hood, C. (1990b), 'Beyond the public bureaucracy state? Public administration in the 1990s', London School of Economics and Political Science inaugural lecture, 16 January, London.

Hood, C. (1991), 'A public management for all seasons?', *Public Administration*, **69** (1), 3–19.

Hood, C. (1994), *Explaining Economic Policy Reversals*, Buckingham: Open University Press.

Hood, C. (1995), 'Contemporary public management: a new global paradigm?', *Public Policy and Administration*, **10** (2), 104–17.

Hood, C. (1998), *The Art of the State: Culture, Rhetoric and Public Management*, Oxford: Oxford University Press.

House of Lords Select Committee on the Constitution (2002), *Devolution: Inter-institutional Relations in the United Kingdom: Evidence Complete to 10 July 2002*, HL 147 2001–02, London: The Stationery Office.

Hughes, M. and J. Newman (1999), 'From new public management to New Labour: from "new" to "modern"', paper presented to Third International Symposium on Public Management, March, Aston University.

Hughes, O.E. (1998), *Public Management and Administration: An Introduction*, 2nd edn, London: Macmillan.

Hunt, Lester H. (1997), 'On improving people by political means', in Hugh LaFollette (ed.), *Ethics in Practice: An Anthology*, Malden, US and Oxford, UK: Blackwell, pp. 270–81.

Ingraham, P.W. (1996), 'The reform agenda for national civil service systems: external stress and internal strains', in H.A.G.M. Bekke, J.L. Perry and T.A.J. Toonen (eds), *Civil Service Systems in Comparative Perspective*, Bloomington: Indiana University Press, pp. 247–67.

Ioannidou, Anastasia (1997), 'The politics of the division of labour: Smith and Hegel on civil society', in Robert Fine and Shirin Rai (eds), *Civil Society: Democratic Perspectives*, London and Portland: Frank Cass, pp. 49–62.

James, O. (1995), 'Explaining the next steps in the Department of Social Security: the bureau-shaping model of central state reorganization', *Political Studies*, **43** (4), 614–29.

James, O. (2000), 'Regulation inside government: public interest justifications and regulatory failure', *Public Administration* **78** (2), 327–43.

James, O. (2001a), 'Beyond the "new public management": regulated partnerships in the UK', in A. Byong-Man, J. Halligan and S. Wilks (eds), *Reforming Public and Corporate Governance: Management and the Market in Australia, Britain and Korea*, Cheltenham: Edward Elgar.

James, O. (2001b), 'Business models and the transfer of business-like central government agencies', *Governance* **14** (2), 233–52.

James, O. (2003), *The Executive Agency Revolution in Whitehall: Public Interest Versus Bureau-shaping Perspectives*, Basingstoke: Palgrave-Macmillan.

James, O. (forthcoming), 'Executive agencies and joined-up government', in C. Pollitt and C. Talbot (eds), *Unbundled Government: A Critical Analysis of the Global Trend to Agencies, Quangos and Contractualization*, London: Taylor Francis.

Jensen, L. (1998), 'Interpreting new public management: the case of Denmark', *Australian Journal of Public Administration*, **57** (4), 55–66.

Johnson, G. and K. Scholes (1999), *Exploring Corporate Strategy*, London: Prentice Hall.

Johnson, G. and K. Scholes (eds) (2001), *Exploring Public Sector Strategy*, London: Prentice Hall.

Judge, D., B. Hogwood and M. McVicar (1997), 'The pondlife of executive agencies: parliamentary and informatory accountability', *Public Policy and Administration* **12** (2), 95–115.

Kaufman, Herbert (1977), *Red Tape: Its Origins, Uses, and Abuses*, Washington, DC: Brookings Institution.

Kavanagh, D. and A. Seldon (2000), 'The power behind the Prime Minister: the hidden influence of No. 10', in R.A.W. Rhodes (ed.), *Transforming British Government, Vol. 2, Changing Roles and Relationships*, London: Macmillan.

Keating, M. and J. Wanna (2000), 'Remaking federalism?' in M. Keating and J. Wanna (eds), *Institutions: the Future of Australian Governance*, Sydney: Allen and Unwin.

Kernaghan, Kenneth (1993), 'Promoting public service ethics: the codification option', in R.A. Chapman (ed.), *Ethics in Public Service*, Edinburgh: Edinburgh University Press, pp. 15–30.

Kettl, Donald F. (1997), 'The global revolution in public management: driving themes, missing links', *Journal of Policy Analysis and Management*, **16** (3), 446–62.

Kettl, Donald F. (1998), *Reinventing Government: A Fifth-Year Report Card*, Washington, DC: Brookings Institution.

Kettl, Donald F. (2000a), *The Global Pacific Management Revolution: A Report on the Transformation of Governance*, Washington, DC: Brookings Institution Press.

Kettl, Donald F. (2000b), 'Has government been "reinvented"?', testimony before the Committee on Rules, US House of Representatives, and the Committee on Governmental Affairs, US Senate, 4 May, wwwbrook.edu/views/testimony/Kettl/20000504.htm.

Kickert, J.M. and R.J. Stillman (1999), *The Modern State and its Study: New Administrative Sciences in a Changing Europe and United States*, Cheltenham: Edward Elgar.

Kickert, W.J.M., E.H. Klijn and J.F.M. Koppenjan (eds) (1997), *Managing Complex Networks: Strategies for the Public Sector*, London: Sage.

Kingdon, John W. (1984), *Agendas, Alternatives, and Public Policies*, Boston: Little, Brown.

Kinnock, N. (2001), 'Accountability and Reform of Internal Control in the European Commission', unpublished speech, delivered as UKPAC

Sunningdale Accountability Lecture, Royal Society of Arts, London, 15 October.

Knill, C. (2001), *The Europeanization of National Administrations: Patterns of Institutional Change and Persistence*, Cambridge: Cambridge University Press.

Kooiman, J. (1993), 'Social-political governance: introduction', in J. Kooiman (ed.), *Modern Governance*, London: Sage.

Laffin, M. and Thomas, A. (2001), 'New ways of working: political–official relations in the national assembly for Wales', *Public Money and Management* **21** (2), 45–51.

Lan, Z. and Rosenbloom, D. (1992), 'Editorial', *Public Administration Review*, **52**, 535–7.

Lane, D. and R. Maxfield (1997), 'Foresight. Complexity and strategy', in W.B. Arthur, S.N. Durlauf and D.A. Lane (eds), *The Economy as an Evolving Complex System II*, Reading, MA: Perseus Books.

Lane, J.E. (1997), 'Public sector reform in the Nordic countries', in J.E. Lane (ed.), *Public Sector Reform: Rationale, Trends and Problems*, London: Sage, pp. 188–208.

Lawton, Alan (1998), *Ethical Management for the Public Services*, Buckingham, UK and Philadelphia, US: Open University Press.

Lippmann, Walter (1929), *A Preface to Morals*, London: George Allen and Unwin.

Lodge, M. (2002), 'Varieties of Europeanization and the national regulatory state', *Public Policy and Administration*, **17** (2), 43–67.

Long, Norton (1949), 'Power and administration,' *Public Administration Review*, **9**, 257–64.

Loughlin, J. and B.G. Peters (1997), 'State traditions, administrative reform and regionalization', in M. Keating and J. Loughlin (eds), *The Political Economy of Regionalism*, London: Frank Cass.

Lynch, P. (2000), 'The committee system of the Scottish parliament', in G. Hassan and C. Warhurst (eds), *The New Scottish Politics. The First Year of the Scottish Parliament and Beyond*, Edinburgh: The Stationery Office.

Lynch, P. (2001), *Scottish Government and Politics*, Edinburgh: Edinburgh University Press.

MacIntyre, Alasdair (1985), *After Virtue: A Study in Moral Theory*, 2nd edn, London: Duckworth.

Mairate, A., and R. Hall (2001), 'Structural policies', in R. Hall, A. Smith and L. Tsoukalis, *Competitiveness and Cohesion in EU Policies*, Oxford: Oxford University Press, pp. 315–46.

Marshall, G. (1986), *Constitutional Conventions. The Rules and Forms of Political Accountability*, Oxford: Clarendon.

Massey, A. (1993), *Managing the Public Sector: A Comparative Analysis of the United Kingdom and the United States*, Aldershot: Edward Elgar.

Massey, A. (1995a), *After Next Steps*, London: Cabinet Office.

Massey, A. (1995b), 'Public bodies and Next Steps: an assessment of the application of Next Steps principles to executive non departmental bodies', a report to HM Treasury and the Office of Public Service, London: Cabinet Office.

Massey, A. (1997), 'In search of the state: markets, myths and paradigms', in A. Massey (ed.), *Globalization and Marketization of Government Services: Comparing Contemporary Public Sector Developments*, London: Macmillan, pp. 1–15.

Massey, A. (1999), 'The Joint European Torus: an historical case study in European public policy', *Public Policy and Administration*, **14** (4).

Massey, A. (2001), 'Policy, management and implementation', in S. Savage and R. Atkinson, *Public Policy Under Blair*, Basingstoke: Palgrave.

McConnell, A. and R. Pyper (1994a), 'A committee again: the first year of the revived Select Committee on Scottish Affairs', *Scottish Affairs*, **7**, Spring.

McConnell, A. and R. Pyper (1994b), 'The revived Select Committee on Scottish affairs: a case study of parliamentary contradictions', *Strathclyde Papers on Government and Politics 98*.

McConnell, A. and R. Pyper (1996), 'The Select Committee on Scottish Affairs: emerging themes and issues', *Scottish Affairs*, **15**, Spring.

McKenzie, R. (2001), 'Lifting every voice: a report and action programme to address institutional racism at the National Assembly of Wales', Cardiff: National Assembly for Wales EOC-03-01, www.wales.gov.uk.

McRae, H. (1997), 'It is hard to play by the rules when there are none left', *The Independent*, 19 March, p. 19.

Mill, J.S. (1861), *Considerations on Representative Government* (introduction by A.D. Lindsay, 1910), London: Dent.

Miller, David (1994), 'Virtues, practices and justice', in John Horton and Susan Mendus (eds), *After MacIntyre: Critical Perspectives on the Work of Alasdair MacIntyre*, Cambridge: Polity, pp. 245–64.

Miller, Gary and Andrew B. Whitford (2001), 'Trust and incentives in principal–agent negotiations: the "insurance/incentive trade-off"', paper presented at the 59th Annual Meeting of the Midwest Political Science Association, Chicago, IL, 19–22 April.

Minister for the Cabinet Office (1999), *Next Steps Report 1998 Cmnd 4273*, London: The Stationery Office.

Minister for the Cabinet Office (2000), *Executive Agencies 1999 Report Cmnd 4658*, London: The Stationery Office.

Minogue, M., C. Polidano and D. Hulme (1998), *Beyond the New Public Management: Changing Ideas and Practices in Governance*, Cheltenham, UK and Lyme, US: Edward Elgar.

Mintzberg, H. (1994), *The Rise and Fall of Strategic Planning*, London: Prentice Hall.

Mintzberg, H., B. Ahlstrand and J. Lampel (1998), *Strategy Safari: A Guided Tour Through the Wilds of Strategic Management*, London: Prentice Hall.

Mulgan, G. (2001), 'Systems thinking and the practice of government', *Systemist*, **23**, 22–9.

National Assembly for Wales (2001), 'Assembly review of procedures: analysis of staff responses' Cardiff: National Assembly for Wales, ARP 01-02, www.wales.gov.uk.

National Assembly for Wales (2002a), 'Lifting every voice: progress on action plan', Cardiff: National Assembly for Wales EOC-01-02, 30 January, www.wales.gov.uk/equalityofopportunitycommittee.

National Assembly for Wales (2002b), 'Lifting every voice: progress on action plan', Cardiff: National Assembly for Wales EOC-05-02, 26 June, www.wales.gov.uk/equalityofopportunitycommittee.

National Audit Office (1988), *Department of Health and Social Security: Quality of Service to the Public at Local Offices HC 451, Session 1987–88*, London: HMSO.

National Audit Office (1996a), *Management of Telephones in the Benefits Agency HC 126 Session 1995–96*, London: HMSO.

National Audit Office (1996b), *General Report of the Comptroller and Auditor General for 1994–95 on Appropriation and Other Accounts 15-XIII*, London: The Stationery Office.

National Audit Office (1997), *Financial Auditing and Reporting 1995–96 General Report of the Comptroller and Auditor General 11-XII*, London: The Stationery Office.

National Audit Office (1998a), *Underpayments to Public Service Pensioners on Invalidity Benefit HC 681, Session 1997–98*, London: The Stationery Office.

National Audit Office (1998b), *Benefits Agency: Performance Measurement HC 952, Session 1997–98*, London: The Stationery Office.

National Audit Office (1998c), *Department of Social Security: Progress on Measures to Combat Housing Benefit Fraud HC 31, Session 1998–99*, London: The Stationery Office.

National Audit Office (1998d), *Financial Auditing and Reporting 1996–97 General Report of the Comptroller and Auditor General 251-XIX*, London: The Stationery Office.

National Audit Office (1999a), *Department of Social Security: Progress on*

Measures to Combat Housing Benefit Fraud HC 319, Session 1998–99, London: The Stationery Office.

National Audit Office (1999b), *Financial Auditing and Reporting 1997–98 General Report of the Comptroller and Auditor General 251-XIX*, London: The Stationery Office.

National Audit Office (1999c), *Fire Service College Accounts 1996–97 and 1997–98*, London: National Audit Office.

National Audit Office (1999d), *The Passport Delays of Summer 1999 HC 812, Session 1998–9*, London: The Stationery Office.

National Audit Office (2000a), *State Earnings-related Pension Scheme: The Failure to Inform the Public of Reduced Pension Rights for Widows and Widowers HC 320, Session 1999–2000*, London: The Stationery Office.

National Audit Office (2000b), *Financial Auditing and Reporting 1998–99 General Report of the Comptroller and Auditor General 11-XIX*, London: The Stationery Office.

National Audit Office (2000c), *Good Practice in Performance Measurement and Reporting in Executive Agencies and Non-departmental Public Bodies*, London: The Stationery Office.

National Audit Office (2001a), *Measuring the Performance of Government Departments HC 301, Session 2000–01*, London: National Audit Office.

National Audit Office, (2001b), *Modern Policy-making: Ensuring Policies Deliver Value for Money, Report by the Comptroller and Auditor General, HC 289, Session 2001–2002: November 2001*, London: National Audit Office.

Neill, Lord (2000), *Sixth Report of the Committee on Standards in Public Life: Reinforcing Standards, Vol. 1, Cmnd 4557-I*, London: Stationery Office.

Neustadt, Richard E. (1990), *Presidential Power and the Modern Presidents*, New York: The Free Press.

Newman, J. (1999), 'The new public management, modernization and organizational change: disruptions, disjunctures and dilemmas', paper presented to ESRC seminar on Recent Developments in the New Public Management, Aston University, November.

Newman, J. (2001), *Modernizing Governance. New Labour, Policy and Society*, London: Sage.

Nolan, B. (2001), 'Conclusion: themes and future directions for public service reform', in B.C. Nolan (ed.), *Public Sector Reform: An International Perspective*, Basingstoke: Palgrave, pp. 185–96.

Nolan, Lord (1995), *First Report of the Committee on Standards in Public Life, Vol. 1, Cmnd 2850-I*, London: HMSO.

Nonaka, I. and H. Takeuchi (1995), *The Knowledge-creating Company: How*

Japanese Companies Create the Dynamics of Innovation, New York: Oxford University Press.

Nunberg, B. (1995), 'Managing the civil service: reform lessons from advanced industrial countries', World Bank discussion paper 204, Washington DC: World Bank.

Office of Management and Budget (2001), 'Improving Government Performance,' *The Budget for Fiscal Year 2002*, http://www.whitehouse.gov/omb/budget/fy2002/bud01.htm.

Olsen, J.P. (1983), *Organized Democracy. Political Institutions in a Welfare State – The Case of Norway*, Oslo: Universitetsforlaget.

Organisation for Economic Co-operation and Development (1990), *Public Management Developments: Survey 1990*, Paris: OECD.

Organisation for Economic Co-operation and Development (1992), *Public Management Developments: Update 1992*, Paris: OECD.

Organisation for Economic Co-operation and Development (1993), *Public Management Developments: Survey 1993*, Paris: OECD.

Organisation for Economic Co-operation and Development (1995), *Governance in Transition: Public Management Reforms in OECD Countries*, Paris: OECD.

Organisation for Economic Co-operation and Development (1998), *Council Recommendation on Improving Ethical Conduct in the Public Service*, Paris: OECD.

Organisation for Economic Co-operation and Development (2000), 'Building public trust: ethics measures in OECD countries', PUMA policy brief no. 7, Paris: OECD.

Organisation for Economic Co-operation and Development (2001), *Issues and Developments in Public Management: New Zealand – 2000*, Paris: OECD.

Osborne, D. and T. Gaebler (1992), *Reinventing Government: How the Entrepreneurial Spirit is Transforming the Public Sector*, Reading MA: Addison-Wesley.

O'Toole, B. (1997), 'The concept of public duty', in P. Barberis (ed.), *The Civil Service in an Era of Change*, Aldershot: Dartmouth, pp. 82–94.

Ouseley Report (2002), *Review of the Appointment and Promotion Procedures for the Senior Civil Service of the Northern Ireland Civil Service*, Belfast: Northern Ireland Executive, www.nics.gov.uk/scsreview.

Painter, M. (2000), 'Contracting, the enterprise culture and public sector ethics', in R.A. Chapman (ed.), *Ethics in Public Service for the New Millennium*, Aldershot: Ashgate, pp. 165–83.

Parry, R. (1999), 'The Scottish Civil Service' in G. Hassan (ed.), *A Guide to the Scottish Parliament. The Shape of Things to Come*, Edinburgh: The Stationery Office.

Parry, R. (2000), 'The Civil Service and the Scottish Executive's structure and style', in G. Hassan and C. Warhurst (eds), *The New Scottish Politics. The First Year of the Scottish Parliament and Beyond*, Edinburgh: The Stationery Office.

Parry, R. and A. Jones (2000), 'The transition from the Scottish Office to the Scottish Executive', *Public Policy and Administration* **15** (2), 53–66.

Parsons, W. (1983), 'Keynes and the politics of ideas', *History of Political Thought*, **4** (2), 367–92.

Parsons, W. (1995), *Public Policy: An Introduction to the Theory and Practice of Policy Analysis*, Cheltenham: Edward Elgar Publishing.

Parsons, W. (2000), 'Public policy as public learning', inaugural lecture, Queen Mary University of London.

Pawson, R. and N. Tilley (1997), *Realistic Evaluation*, London: Sage.

Peckenpaugh, Jason (2001), 'Bush administration blasts proposed freeze on contracts', *GovExec.com*, 29 June, http://www.govexec.com/news/.

Peckenpaugh, Jason (2002a), 'In a first, Bush links funding to programme performance', *GovExec.com*, 4 February, http://www/govexec.com/news/.

Peckenpaugh, Jason (2002b), 'House Democrats plan "in-sourcing" amendment for defence bill', *GovExec.com*, 30 April, http://www/govexec.com/news/.

Pendlebury, M., R. Jones and S. Yarbhari (1992), 'Accounting for executive agencies in the UK government', *Financial Accountability and Management* **8** (1), 35–48.

Perez-Diaz, V.M. (1993), *The Return of Civil Society*, Cambridge, MA: Harvard University Press.

Performance and Innovation Unit (2000), *Wiring It Up: Whitehall's Management of Cross-cutting Policies and Services*, London: The Stationery Office.

Performance and Innovation Unit (2001), *Better Policy Delivery and Design: A Discussion Paper*, London: PIU.

Peters, B.G. and D. Savoie (1994), 'Civil service reform: misdiagnosing the patient', *Public Administration Review*, **54** (5), 418–25.

Peters, B.G. and Vincent Wright (1996), 'Public policy and administration, old and new', in Robert E. Goodin and Hans-Dieter Klingemann (eds), *A New Handbook of Political Science*, New York: Oxford University Press, pp. 628–39.

Pierre, J. (2000), *Debating Governance: Authority, Steering and Democracy*, Oxford: Oxford University Press.

Polidano, C. (1999), 'The bureaucrat who fell under a bus: ministerial responsibility, executive agencies and the Derek Lewis affair', *Governance* **12** (2), 201–29.

Pollitt, C. (1993), *Managerialism and the Public Services: Cuts or Cultural Change in the 1990s?*, 2nd edn, Oxford: Blackwell.

Pollitt, C. (1995), 'Justifications by works or faith? Evaluating the new public management', *Evaluation* **1** (2), 133–54.

Pollitt, C., K. Bathgate, A. Smullen and C. Talbot (2000), 'Agencies: a test case for convergence?', paper presented to the Fourth International Symposium on Public Management, Erasmus University Rotterdam, April.

Pollitt, C. and G. Bouckaert (2000), *Public Management Reform: A Comparative Analysis*, Oxford: Oxford University Press.

Pollitt, C. and H. Summa (1997), 'Trajectories of reform: public management change in four countries', *Public Money and Management*, **17** (1), 7–18.

Power, Michael (1994), *The Audit Explosion*, London: Demos.

Power, Michael (1997), *The Audit Society: Rituals of Verification*, Oxford and New York: Oxford University Press.

Pratchett, L. (2000), 'The inherently unethical nature of public service ethics', in R.A. Chapman (ed.), *Ethics in Public Service for the New Millennium*, Aldershot: Ashgate, pp. 111–25.

Price, D.K. (1983), *America's Unwritten Constitution*, Baton Rouge: Louisiana State University Press.

Prime Minister (1999), *Modernizing Government Cmnd 4310*, London: The Stationery Office.

Prime Minister, Chancellor of the Exchequer and Chancellor of the Duchy of Lancaster (1994), *The Civil Service: Continuity and Change Cmnd 2627*, London: HMSO.

Prime Minister, Minister for the Civil Service and the Minister of State, Privy Council Office (1990), *Improving Management in Government – The Next Steps Agencies Review 1990 Cmnd 1261*, London: HMSO.

Prime Minister, Minister for the Civil Service and the Minister of State, Privy Council Office (1991), *Improving Management in Government – The Next Steps Agencies Review 1991 Cmnd 1760*, London: HMSO.

Project Management Institute (2000), *A Guide to the Project Management Body of Knowledge*, Newtown Square, PA: Project Management Institute, http://www.pmi.org/projectmanagement/success.htm.

Public Accounts Committee (1999), *Minutes of Evidence Wednesday 28 April 1999 HC 419 I, Session 1998–99*, London: The Stationery Office.

Public Accounts Committee (2000), *Appropriation Accounts 1997–98, Class XII, Vote 1 (Central Government Administered Social Security Benefits and Other Payments) HC 103, Session 1999–2000*, London: The Stationery Office.

Public Administration Select Committee (2001a), *Third Report, The Ministerial Code: Improving the Rule Book HC 235, Session 2000/2001*, London: The Stationery Office.

Public Administration Select Committee (2001b), *Seventh Report, Making*

Government Work: The Emerging Issues HC 94, Session 2000/2001, London: The Stationery Office.

Public Administration Select Committee (2002), *Seventh Report, The Public Service Ethos HC 263-1, Session 2001–02*, London: The Stationery Office.

Pusey, M. (1991), *Economic Rationalism in Canberra: A Nation Building State Changes Its Mind*, Sydney: Cambridge University Press.

Pyper, R. (1996), 'The parameters of accountability' in R. Pyper (ed.), *Aspects of Accountability in the British System of Government*, Eastham: Tudor.

Pyper, R. (1999), 'The Civil Service: a neglected dimension of devolution', *Public Money and Management*, **19** (2).

Ramsay, Maureen (2000), 'Are Machiavellian tactics still appropriate or defensible in politics?', in Phil Harris, Andrew Lock and Patricia Rees (eds), *Machiavelli, Marketing and Management*, London and New York: Routledge, pp. 148–62.

Ranson, Stewart and John Stewart (1994), *Management for the Public Domain: Enabling the Learning Society*, Basingstoke: Macmillan.

Rawls, John (1973), *A Theory of Justice*, Oxford and New York: Oxford University Press.

Reich, R. (1998), *The Power of Public Ideas*, Cambridge, MA: Ballinger.

Rhodes, R.A.W. (1994), 'The hollowing out of the state', *Political Quarterly*, **65** (2), 138–51.

Rhodes, R.A.W. (1996), 'The new governance: governing without government', *Political Studies*, **44** (4), 652–67.

Rhodes, R.A.W. (1997), *Understanding Governance. Policy Networks, Governance, Reflexivity and Accountability*, Buckingham: Open University Press.

Rhodes, R.A.W. (1998), 'Different roads to unfamiliar places: UK experience in comparative perspective', *Australian Journal of Public Administration*, **57** (4), 19–31.

Rhodes, R.A.W. (1999), 'Traditions and public sector reform; comparing Britain and Denmark', *Scandinavian Political Studies* **22** (4), 341–70.

Rhodes, R.A.W. (ed.) (2000), *Transforming British Government, Vol. 2, Changing Roles and Relationships*, London: Macmillan.

Rhodes, R.A.W. (2001), 'The Civil Service', in A. Seldon (ed.), *The Blair Effect*, London: Little Brown and Company.

Rhodes, R.A.W. and P. Weller (eds) (2001a), *The Changing World of Top Officials. Mandarins or Valets?*, Buckingham: Open University Press.

Rhodes, R.A.W. and P. Weller (2001b), 'Conclusions: "Antipodean exceptionalism, European traditionalism"', in R.A.W. Rhodes and P. Weller (eds), *The Changing World of Top Officials: Mandarins or Valets?*, Buckingham: Open University Press.

Rhodes, R.A.W., P. Carmichael, J. McMillan and A. Massey (2003), *Decen-*

tralizing the Civil Service: From Unitary State to Differentiated Polity in the United Kingdom, Buckingham: Open University Press.

Richards, D. (1996), 'Appointments to the highest grades in the Civil Service – drawing the curtain open', *Public Administration* **74** (4), 657–77.

Richards, D. and M. Smith (2002), *Governance and Public Policy in the UK*, Oxford: Oxford University Press.

Ridley, Matt (1997), *The Origins of Virtue*, Harmondsworth: Penguin.

Royal Commission on Australian Government Administration (1976), *Report*, Canberra: AGPS.

Sabatier, P. (1988), 'The advocacy coalition framework: revisions and relevance for Europe', *Journal of European Public Policy*, **3** (1), 98–130.

Samuels, M. (1997), *Benchmarking Next Steps Executive Agencies*, London: Cabinet Office.

Sandholtz, W. and A. Stone Sweet (1998), *European Integration and Supranational Governance*, Oxford: Oxford University Press.

Schick, Allen (1996), 'The spirit of reform: managing the New Zealand state sector in a time of change', a report prepared for the State Services Commission and the Treasury, New Zealand, Wellington: State Services Commission.

Schön, D.A. (1973), *Beyond the Stable State: Public and Private Learning in a Changing Society*, Harmondsworth: Penguin Books.

Schön, D.A. (1979), 'Generative metaphor: a perspective on problem-setting in social policy', in A. Ortony (ed.), *Metaphor and Thought*, Cambridge: Cambridge University Press.

Schwartz, P. (1998), *The Art of the Long View: Planning for the Future in an Uncertain World*, London: Wiley.

Scott, J.C. (1998), *Seeing Like a State: How Certain Schemes to Improve the Human Condition Have Failed*, New Haven: Yale University Press.

Scottish Executive (2000a), *Guidance on Scottish Parliamentary Questions*, Edinburgh: Executive Secretariat.

Scottish Executive (2000b), *Final Protocol Between Committee Clerks and the Scottish Executive*, Edinburgh: Scottish Executive.

Scottish Executive (2001a), *Scottish Executive Evidence and Responses to Committees of the Scottish Parliament*, Edinburgh: Executive Secretariat.

Scottish Executive (2001b), *A Modern Complaints System. Consultation on Proposals for Public Sector Ombudsmen in Scotland*, Edinburgh: The Stationery Office.

Scottish Office (1997), *Scotland's Parliament Cmnd 3658*, Edinburgh: The Stationery Office.

Scottish Office (1998), *Shaping Scotland's Parliament. Report of the Consultative Steering Group on the Scottish Parliament*, Edinburgh: The Stationery Office.

Scottish Parliament (2000), *Official Report*, vol. 8, No. 14, 1 November, columns 1197–1247, Edinburgh: The Stationery Office.

Seddon, J. (2000), *The Case Against ISO 9000*, Dublin: Oak Tree Press.

Selbourne, David (1998), *Moral Evasion*, London: Centre for Policy Studies.

Seldon A. (ed.) (2001), *The Blair Effect: The Blair Government, 1997–2001*, London: Little Brown and Company.

Seldon, A. and D. Kavanagh (1999), *The Powers behind the Prime Minister*, London: HarperCollins.

Seligman, Adam B. (1997), *The Problem of Trust*, Princeton: Princeton University Press.

Senge, P.M. (1990), *The Fifth Discipline: The Art and Practice of the Learning Organization*, London: Century Business Books.

Shils, Edward (1997), *The Virtue of Civility: Selected Essays on Liberalism, Tradition and Civil Society*, Indianapolis: Liberty Fund.

Skowronet, S. (1997), *The Politics Presidents Make: Leadership from John Adams to Bill Clinton*, Cambridge, MA: Belknap.

Smith, Roger (1997), *Justice: Redressing the Balance*, London: Legal Action Group.

Smith, T.A. (1979), *The Politics of The Corporate Economy*, Oxford: Martin Robinson.

Social Security Committee (1998), *Social Security Committee: Minutes of Evidence, Thursday 21 May 1998 HC 587iii, Session 1997–98*, London: The Stationery Office.

Spragia, A. (1998), 'Institution-building from below and above: The European Community in global environmental politics', in W. Sandholtz and A. Stone Sweet, *European Integration and Supranational Governance*, Oxford: Oxford University Press.

Stacey, R.D. (1996), *Strategic Management and Organizational Dynamics*, London: Pitman.

Stevenson, R.W. (2002), 'Bush budget links dollars to deeds with new ratings', 3 February, http://www.nytimes.com/2002.

Stewart, J. and G. Stoker (1989), 'The "free local government" experiments and the programme of public service reform in Scandinavia', in C. Crouch and D. Marquand (eds), *The New Centralism: Britain Out of Step in Europe?*, Oxford: Blackwell, pp. 125–42.

Stillman, R. (1999), 'Conclusion: American versus European public administration', in J.M. Kickert and R. Stillman, *The Modern State and its Study: New Administrative Sciences in a Changing Europe and United States*, Cheltenham: Edward Elgar.

Stone Sweet, A. (2000), *Governing With Judges: Constitutional Politics in Europe*, Oxford: Oxford University Press.

Stone Sweet, A., and W. Sandholtz (1998), 'Integration, supranational governance, and the institutionalization of the European polity', in W. Sandholtz and A. Stone Smith (1998), *European Integration and Supranational Governance*, Oxford, Oxford University Press.

Talbot, C. (1996), 'Ministers and agencies: responsibilities and performance', in The Public Service Committee, *Second Report Ministerial Accountability and Responsibility, Vol. 2, Minutes of Evidence HC 313, Session 1995–96*, London: HMSO, pp. 39–55.

Talbot, C. (forthcoming), 'Small step or giant leap? Evaluating ten years of the "Next Steps" agencies in the UK (1988–98)', *Public Money and Management*.

Tarditi, S., and G. Zanaias (2001), 'Common agricultural policy', in R. Hall, A. Smith and L. Tsoukalis, *Competitiveness and Cohesion in EU Policies*, Oxford: Oxford University Press, pp. 179–216.

Taylor, Charles (1989), 'Cross-purposes: the liberal-communitarian debate', in Nancy Rosenblum (ed.), *Liberalism in the Moral Life*, Cambridge, MA: Harvard University Press, pp. 159–82.

Thomas, Rosamund (ed.) (1993), *Teaching Ethics: Government Ethics*, Cambridge: Centre for Business and Public Sector Ethics.

Tiersky, R. (2000), *François Mitterand*, New York: St Martins Press.

Toynbee, P. and D. Walker (2001), *Did Things get Better? An Audit of Labour's Successes and Failures*, Harmondsworth: Penguin.

Treasury and Civil Service Committee (1990), *Eighth Report, Progress in the Next Steps Initiative Session*, HC 481 session 1989–90, London: HMSO.

Treasury and Civil Service Committee (1993), fifth report, *The Role of the Civil Service Volume II Minutes of Evidence*, HC 27-I, session 1993–94, London: HMSO.

Trosa, S. (1994), *Next Steps: Moving On*, London: Office of Public Service.

Tucker, Andrew (1999), *Why Trust Has No Part in Modern Politics*, London: Centre for Reform.

Van der Heijden, K. (1996), *Scenarios: The Art of Strategic Conversation*, London: Wiley.

Vogel, D. (1997), *Trading Up: Consumer and Environmental Regulation in a Global Economy*, Cambridge, MA: Harvard University Press.

Volcker Commission (1989), *Leadership for America: Rebuilding the Public Service*, Lexington: D.C. Heath and Company.

Waldo, D. (1999), 'Foreword: modern public administration as model and portent', in W. Kickert and R. Stillman, *The Modern State and its Study: New Administrative Sciences in a Changing Europe and United States*, Cheltenham: Edward Elgar.

Watson, George (1973), *The English Ideology: Studies in the Language of Victorian Politics*, London: Allen Lane.

Watson, M. (2001), *Year Zero. An Inside View of the Scottish Parliament*, Edinburgh: Polygo.

Weller, P. (2001), *Australia's Mandarins: The Frank and the Fearless?*, Crows Nest, NSW: Allen and Unwin.

Wettenhall, R. (1990), 'Australia's daring experiment with public enterprise', in A. Kouzmin and N. Scott (eds), *Dynamics in Australian Public Management: Selected Essays*, Melbourne: Macmillan.

Whittington, R. (1993), *What is Strategy and Does it Matter?*, London: Routledge.

Wildavsky, A. (1974), *The Politics of the Budgetary Process*, 2nd edn, Boston: Little Brown.

Wildavsky, A, (1995), *But is it True? A Citizen's Guide to Environmental Health and Safety Issues*, Cambridge, MA: Harvard University Press.

Williams, Garrath (1998), 'Love and responsibility: a political ethic for Hannah Arendt', *Political Studies*, **46** (5), 937–50.

Wilson, James Q. (1975), 'The rise of the bureaucratic state', *Public Interest*, **41**, 77–103.

Wilson, Sir Richard (1998), 'Modernizing government: the role of the senior civil service', speech to Senior Civil Service Conference, October.

World Bank (1992), *Governance and Development*, Washington, DC: World Bank.

Wright, V. and J.E.S. Hayward (2000), 'Governing from the centre: policy coordination in six European core executives', in R.A.W. Rhodes (ed.), *Transforming British Government, Vol. 2, Changing Roles and Relationships*, Basingstoke: Macmillan, pp. 27–46.

Zifcak, S. (1994), *New Managerialism: Administrative Reform in Whitehall and Canberra*, Buckingham: Open University Press.

Index

Nolan Committee 11, 194, 200, 214
Nolan, B.C. 214
Nonaka, I. 171, 177, 214
non-governmental organizations 140,
    141, 143, 190
Northern Ireland
    Child Support Agency 83
    Civil Service (NICS) 8, 100, 109–110
    Court Service 100
    Department of Education 113
    devolution 67, 99–115, 160
    Office 110
Norway, public and private sectors 9
nuclear fusion technology, civil 65
Nunberg, B. 1, 2, 215

Office of the Civil Service Commission-
    ers 112
Office of Management and Budget 52,
    215
oil crisis, early 1970s 2
Olsen, J.P. 29, 215
Ombudsman 121, 132, 135
openness 198, 200
Organisation for Economic Co-opera-
    tion and Development 11, 17, 22,
    215
Osborne, D. 2, 12, 215
Osmotherly Rules 122
O'Toole, B. 10, 215
Ouseley Report (2002) 111, 112, 215
outsourcing 53

Painter, M. 11, 15, 215
Parliament 34, 72
    single house, New Zealand 31
    UK, and European law 69
parliamentary
    accountability 123–36
    sovereignty 69
Parliamentary Commission for Adminis-
    tration 92, 117
Parliamentary Commissioner on
    Standards 187, 197
Parliamentary Questions (PQs) 131
Parry, Richard 13, 99–115, 120, 215,
    216
Parsons, Wayne 14, 62, 147–84, 216
partnership agreement 74, 112
party political affairs 19, 20, 21

Passport Agency 82
payment system, DSS 54, 89
Peckenpaugh, Jason 44, 53, 216
peer reviews 66, 72, 149, 178
Pendlebury, M. 78, 216
pensions, state 89
Perez-Diaz, V.M. 26, 216
performance
    agreement 41
    indicators 6, 7, 23, 173
    information, US 55
    management, UK 107
    monetary incentives for 49, 50, 53,
        62, 195
    targets 84, 91–5, 187, 195
    versus profits 54–6
Performance and Innovation Unit 74–5,
    106, 149, 180, 216
Performance and Reward Division 104
personnel policy 43, 49, 114
    in US 49
Peters, B.G. 4, 9, 26, 41, 216
Pierre, J. 119, 216
pilots, use of 165
planning 151
Planning-Programming-Budgeting
    Systems 150
pluralism 26, 190, 197
police forces 81
policy making 64, 142, 147–84
Policy Research Division (PRD) 149
    Studies Division (PSD) 149
Polidano, C. 78, 118, 216
political
    context 156
    control, Netherlands 25, 31
    interactions, Europe 65
    rationality, US 40
politicization 19–22, 33
Pollitt, C. 3, 4, 9, 26, 78, 217
postal service in US 38, 47
post-modernism 188
Power, Michael 217
power, partition of, in US 37, 38
Pratchett, L. 10, 217
Price, D.K. 217
Prime Minister 75, 147–8, 217
Prison Service 97
private
    sector 5, 6, 41, 43, 46, 47